England, Ireland, Scotla
Tour Guidebook 2u24

With Maps, Pictures, And Detailed Up-to-date Info for First-timers & Seasoned Tourists, Travelers, & Adventurists. With Bucket List + Itinerary.

Table of Content:

Introduction

This guide is like a treasure trove, uncovering the incredible experiences waiting for you across England, Ireland, and Scotland. It's not just a book; it's a crafted journey into the heart and soul of these amazing lands.

Why We're Here:
Dive Right In: Picture yourself stepping into these countries - feeling their vibes, tasting their foods, and embracing their stories. That's what we're aiming for - a real, immersive experience.

All the Scoop: Whether you're a first-time traveler or a seasoned globetrotter, this guide spills the beans on everything - the must-sees, secret gems, delicious local eats, historic spots, and a bunch of activities you just can't miss.

Safety Matters: Alongside the fun, safety is a big deal. We've got your back with tips, advice, and guidance to make sure your journey is not just enjoyable, but also secure.

What We Cover:
Let's Explore: From cities to countryside, we're taking you through it all - famous landmarks, hidden treasures, and those spots where the magic truly happens.

Culture Dive: We'll dive deep into the culture, showing you the celebrations, traditions, and habits that make these places tick.

Helpful Stuff: Need to know how to get around or the best places to stay? We've got the practical side covered too.

This guide is your invite to an adventure that'll change the way you see these incredible countries. It's all about embracing their unique heritage and the cool stuff happening there right now.

Highlights You Can't Miss:
Get Around: We've laid out routes for every kind of traveler - whether you're into scenic drives, historic tours, or hiking adventures.

Local Wisdom: It's not just about the touristy stuff. We're sharing tips from the locals, so you get the real deal.

Food Journey: Taste your way through traditional dishes, unique to each place. You won't want to miss these culinary delights!

History Alive: Walk in the footsteps of ancient times, royal histories, and the events that made these countries what they are today.

Interactive Fun: We've got cool maps, itineraries, and even QR codes for more cool info and experiences.

Why This Guide Rocks:
Insider Intel: Experts and local guides share their knowledge, giving you a well-rounded view.

Stay Safe: Exploring's fun, but we're all about keeping it safe. You'll find advice to keep your adventure worry-free.

Eco-Travel: We're big on responsible tourism - showcasing sustainable ways to enjoy your trip.

Easy Peasy: No fuss! Our guide is super easy to navigate and find what you're looking for.

The Bottom Line:
This guide isn't just about travel; it's about diving headfirst into culture. It's your sidekick, your storyteller, and your ticket to really understanding these amazing places. Whether you're an explorer, adventurer, or culture buff, get ready - this guide's going to be your best travel buddy!

Chapter 1: Planning a Journey to England, Ireland, and Scotland

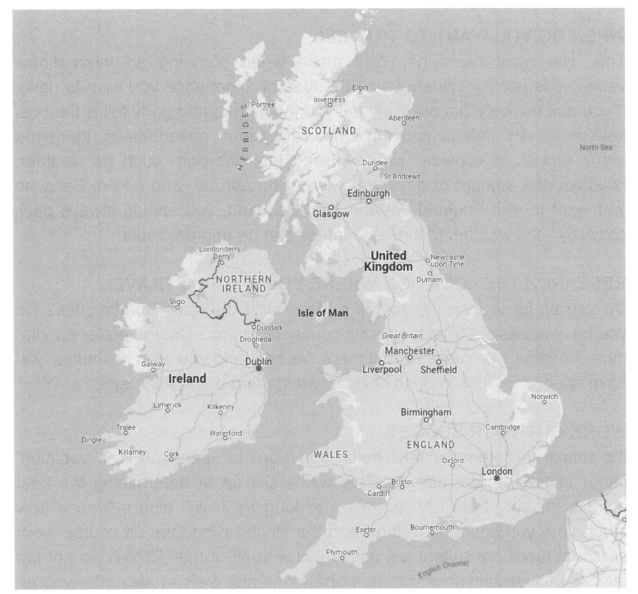

The British Isles are made up of five countries: Ireland, Northern Ireland, England, Scotland, and Wales. Any of these destinations would be on any traveler's bucket list, but why stop there? If you're thinking about visiting England, Ireland, or Scotland, you might want to think about extending your vacation to include extra sights and experiences.

When planning a holiday to Ireland or the United Kingdom, there are numerous factors to consider, and it can be difficult to know what to expect. If you don't already know the answers to the following questions, our travel experts will go over your alternatives with you to help you plan the perfect multi-country vacation!

WHEN DO YOU WANT TO TRAVEL?

This, like most decisions you'll make when planning an international vacation, is heavily influenced by the type of experience you wish to have. If you ask us, we will most likely tell you that late spring/early fall is the best season to visit Ireland and the United Kingdom; nevertheless, there are many factors to consider when making this decision, such as weather, holidays, the amount of days you wish to be abroad, and so on. Because you want to visit England, Ireland, and Scotland, you should always pack correctly - the weather in these countries can be unpredictable!

RESEARCH THE LOCATION WHERE YOU WISH TO TRAVEL.

Do you prefer to take the scenic route or visit the major tourist sites? Do you have ancestors from a specific county or region? Do you prefer popular movie locations or castle attractions? We can help you plan it whether you have specific regions in mind or merely a starting point of thoughts.

WORK OUT YOUR BUDGET.

It's critical to determine how much you want to spend on your vacation, either in total or per person. This will assist us in determining the best options for you, from transportation to lodging. It will also influence how much time you spend in Ireland and the United Kingdom. Of course, your personal travel consultant will assist you with all of this! Before we get too far into customizing your vacation arrangements, we can also offer you an approximate idea of how much items will cost.

PLAN AHEAD AND BOOK YOUR ATTRACTIONS.

There will be a lot of things you want to see and do on a multi-country holiday. We can assist you choose the best sights and attractions within your time constraints and book them for you! The best part about traveling with Tenon trips is that you'll have access to all of your trip data via our mobile app, allowing you to update and schedule trips while on the move.

Of course, planning ahead is usually preferable, but some of our tourists like to be more flexible.

Chapter 2: Scottish Visa Procedures and Immigration Requirements

Currently, decisions on visas and immigration are made by the UK Government, so keep this in mind as you explore your alternatives.

Scotland has a well-deserved reputation for extending an extremely warm and open welcome to anyone who wishes to visit. In fact, the welcome is so warm that some people never want to leave, and we can't blame them.

It is sometimes feasible to travel without a visa if you are visiting for tourist or a brief business trip. Anyone who is neither British or Irish, however, will normally require a visa for longer visits to Scotland, including coming for employment or study.

CITIZENS OF THE EU

Scotland, as part of the United Kingdom, formally exited the European Union on January 1, 2021. While the partnership is evolving, EU nationals are still as welcome as they have always been.

If you are an EU, EEA, or Swiss citizen, or a family member of an EU, EEA, or Swiss citizen, and you lived in Scotland before the end of December 2020, you can apply for settled status through the EU settlement system.

BRITISH NATIONALS IN HONG KONG (OVERSEAS)

The Hong Kong British National (Overseas) visa route was launched on January 31, 2021, and allows British National (Overseas) citizens normally resident in Hong Kong, as well as their immediate family members, to study or work in the UK without meeting any additional requirements. The Scotland Welcome Pack for British Nationals (Overseas) from Hong Kong contains more information about this immigration route. We hope this guidance is useful in establishing a new life for you and your family in Scotland. This book offers helpful information for obtaining that assistance, such as assistance in locating housing, jobs, and a school for your children.

The Scottish Hong Kong Welcome Hub is an online resource for Hong Kong residents who are visiting Scotland. This website's material will assist you in settling in Scotland and feeling at home in your new community. The portal, which is available in both English and Traditional Chinese characters, covers everything from housing to school, jobs, healthcare, and more.

UKRAINIANS

Scotland will do everything in its power to make you feel welcome. People who normally live in Ukraine will be allowed to use NHS services for free, just as those who live in Scotland. People who have fled Ukraine can now receive free maternity care, mental health treatments, and treatment for particular ailments while they are still in the country.

Furthermore, JustRight Scotland, a human rights law organization, provides free, private legal advice to Ukrainians and their family members seeking refuge in Scotland. You can use the service in one of two ways:

Phone number: 0800 995 6045

Tuesday, 2 p.m. to 5 p.m. (UK time)

Thursday, 10 a.m. to 1 p.m. (UK time).

Send an email to ukraine@justrightscotland.org.uk.

MOVE FROM OUTSIDE THE UK AND IRELAND TO SCOTLAND

Every day, individuals from all over the world visit Scotland, from America and Canada to China, Australia, and everywhere in between. The good news is that you can come and join them if you have the proper visa!

The sort of visa you require will be determined by a number of variables, and there are numerous types of visas available to you. Remember to apply for your documentation before traveling to Scotland, as you may be denied entry if you do not have the necessary documents.

TRAVELING TO SCOTLAND

From crumbling castles to pristine beaches, breathtaking scenery to vibrant city centers, a trip to Scotland will never leave you bored. With so many options, it's critical to ensure you have your paperwork in order so you can get started right away.

Chapter 3: Ireland International Travel Information

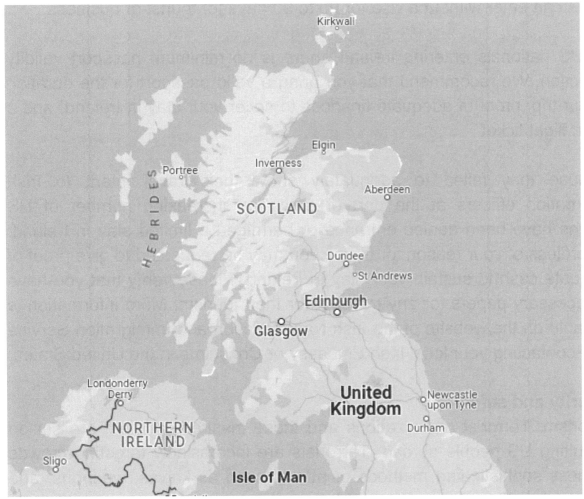

PASSPORT VALIDITY: Your passport must be valid for the entire duration of your stay in Ireland.

PASSPORT PAGES: At least one page must be blank.

NO TOURIST VISA IS REQUIRED.

CURRENCY LIMITS FOR ENTRY: 10,000 EUR or equivalent

EXIT CURRENCY LIMITATIONS: 10,000 Euros or equivalent

Requirements for Entry, Exit, and Visas

To enter Ireland, you must have a valid passport. Citizens of the United States can enter without a visa for up to 90 days for tourist or business.

For US nationals entering Ireland, there is no minimum passport validity restriction. We recommend that you bring a valid passport for the duration of your trip, proof of adequate finances to cover your stay in Ireland, and a return flight ticket.

Because they failed to adequately show their travel intent to Irish immigration officers at the port of entry, an increasing number of US citizens have been denied entrance or permitted a limited stay in Ireland. Regardless of your reason for travel, you may be requested to give proof of adequate cash to sustain your stay in Ireland. Please verify that you have all necessary papers for any travel other than tourism. More information is available on the website of the Irish Naturalization and Immigration Service or by contacting your local Irish Embassy or Consulate in the United States.

Security and safety
Terrorism: Terrorist organizations and those inspired by them are set on assaulting US people abroad. Terrorists are increasingly targeting crowds with less sophisticated methods of attack, such as knives, weapons, and automobiles. They frequently target unprotected or vulnerable targets, such as:
- High-profile public events (sporting competitions, political rallies, marches, holiday celebrations, etc.)
- Tourist-friendly hotels, clubs, and eateries
- Worship areas
- Parks and Schools
- Markets and shopping malls
- Subways, buses, trains, and scheduled commercial flights are examples of public transportation networks.

Crime: Although Ireland has a low rate of violent crime, when traveling, you should always use common sense personal security practices and be alert of your surroundings.

Theft and petty crime have increased in recent years, and criminals frequently target tourists. In rare instances, these offenses entail physical attack or violence, which occurs more frequently in Dublin's city center and famous tourist locations.

Rental cars are often targeted. They are easily identified by the rental business labels on the vehicle's rear window. Remove these stickers if feasible, and always secure your car when leaving it unattended. Do not leave valuables in automobiles unattended. When visiting city centers, park your car in a safe lot and keep the parking ticket with you.

While driving, keep the automobile doors locked. Leave no visible luggage or valuables inside a parked car, and never leave luggage on a roof rack. When returning your rental car, never leave the keys in the ignition while loading or unloading luggage.

When using ATMs, keep your PIN safe at all times and inspect ATMs for signs of tampering before using them. Criminals may employ small electronic devices called "skimmers" mounted to the outside of ATMs to obtain ATM or credit card data.

In congested places, robbers use ATM distraction techniques such as waiting until the PIN is entered before pointing to money on the ground or asking for loose change. Another person will swiftly withdraw cash and go while the ATM customer is distracted. If you become sidetracked in any way, immediately cancel the transaction.

When paying with a credit card at a restaurant, bring a portable card reader with you. Restaurant employees should not take your card to another location to process a charge.

Victims of Crime: Contact the local police at 999 or 112, and the US Embassy at +(353) (1) 668-8777.

Victims of sexual assault in the United States are encouraged to seek aid from the US Embassy.

Keep in mind that local authorities are in charge of investigating and prosecuting offenses.

Tourism: The tourism business is generally regulated, and restrictions are enforced on a regular basis. Hazardous areas/activities are marked with proper signage, and professional assistance is usually present to assist with scheduled activities. In the event of an injury, adequate medical care is generally available across the country. Outside of a major urban area, first responders and medical experts may take longer to stabilize a patient and deliver life-saving aid. Citizens of the United States are encouraged to acquire medical evacuation insurance.

Local Laws and Extenuating Circumstances

You are subject to local laws in terms of criminal penalties. You may be expelled, arrested, or imprisoned if you violate local laws, even if you do it unknowingly. Individuals practicing a profession that necessitates additional permissions or licensing should get information from the appropriate local authorities before beginning work.

Furthermore, regardless of local legislation, some laws are punishable throughout the United States.

Arrest Notification: If you are arrested or detained, ask police or jail officials to promptly alert the US Embassy.

Special Circumstances: Most Irish banks will not accept $100 bills from the United States. Traveler's checks are no longer accepted or cashed by several Irish financial institutions. Although ATMs are generally available, some, particularly in remote locations, may not accept debit cards issued by US banks.

Travelers Requiring Accessibility Assistance: Individuals with impairments may encounter accessibility and accommodations that varies significantly from what is available in the United States.

Government Buildings: Access to government buildings for people with disabilities is required by Irish law, and this requirement is strictly enforced. According to Irish legislation, public service providers must make their services accessible to those who have mobility, sensory, and/or cognitive disabilities.

Parking: There are usually a set number of accessible places available in on-street parking, public building parking lots, and internal parking lots. A permission is necessary to use these places, and information on applying for one can be obtained on the website of the Disabled Drivers Association of Ireland. Local governments and commercial establishments, such as shopping malls, are not required by law to provide outdoor disabled parking for their customers.

Buses and trains: The majority of buses and trains in Ireland's major cities are now accessible to persons with restricted mobility, vision, or hearing impairments, while some train stations and paths may not be as easily accessible.
Special moveable ramps allow boarding from platforms to carriages on mainline and suburban trains. These ramps are available at all terminals, significant crossroads, and stations where staff is present. They can also be found on some trains. It is recommended that travelers contact Irish Rail in advance to ensure that such services are available. Dublin Bus's website has information on its travel assistance program. Bus Eireann operates regional and intercity bus services.

Private Businesses: Accessibility varies greatly in private businesses like as hotels, bed and breakfasts, stores, and restaurants. Before making bookings, travelers should inquire about accessibility difficulties with companies.

Disability Allowance: People who live in Ireland and meet the medical criteria for a disability allowance may apply for free travel tickets; those who qualify may also get a blind/invalidity pension from the Irish Department of Social Protection.

Health

Patients who do not receive benefits from Ireland's Department of Social Protection must pay all fees at the time of treatment and then request for reimbursement from their insurance provider later.

- Ireland has modern medical facilities and highly skilled medical practitioners.
- Expect long lines to see medical professionals and hospital admissions for non-life-threatening medical illnesses. It is not uncommon for emergency rooms to be overcrowded, or for post-treatment admissions to require a lengthy (often overnight) wait on a gurney in a hallway.
- We recommend keeping your medical history, as well as a thorough record of any medications you are currently taking (with dosage and brand name), in your wallet, handbag, or luggage.
- Most over-the-counter drugs are available, however many American brands are not. Some over-the-counter drugs accessible in the United States may require a prescription in Ireland.
- Irish pharmacists may be unable to dispense medication prescribed by U.S. physicians and may direct you to an Irish doctor.
- The Irish College of General Practitioners website has a list of Irish general practitioners in each region of Ireland.
- There are numerous ambulance services accessible.
- Dial 112 or 999 for emergency services in Ireland.

Be advised that US Medicare/Medicaid does not apply outside of the United States. Most hospitals and doctors in other countries do not accept American health insurance.

Medical Insurance: Confirm that your health insurance plan covers you abroad. Most international caregivers only take monetary payments. More information about insurance providers for foreign coverage can be found on our website. More information on the sort of insurance you should consider before traveling abroad may be found on the website of the Centers for Disease Control and Prevention in the United States.

We strongly advise you to purchase additional insurance to cover medical evacuation.

Carry your prescription medication in its original container, together with your doctor's prescription, at all times. Check with the Irish government to check that the medication is legal in Ireland.

Transportation and Travel
Road Conditions and Safety: Cars in Ireland drive on the left side of the road. If you are unfamiliar with driving on the left, you should proceed with caution, as visitors driving on the wrong side of the road cause several serious accidents each year.

The roads are normally in decent shape, but after you leave the major highways, the roads are likely to be tiny, uneven, and winding. Summer and vacation weekends are particularly hazardous on the roads. Drivers should be cautious of cyclists and pedestrians, especially in congested areas.

Most crossroads in Ireland employ circular "roundabouts" rather than traffic lights, thus drivers must pay strict attention to signage and surrender the right of way to those already in the roundabout.

Most rental automobiles in Ireland have manual transmissions; automatic transmission rental cars can be difficult to find.

Traffic laws: Police set up roadblocks on a regular basis to check for drunk drivers. Driving under the influence has serious consequences.

Turning on a red light at a stoplight is unlawful; you must wait for a full green (any direction turn permitted) or directional green light (straight, left, or right) before proceeding with caution.

You may use your existing United States driver's license in Ireland for a brief stay of up to one year. Some insurance companies and car rental companies may need you to have an International Driving Permit in addition to your regular driver's license. Please contact the American Automobile Association to apply for an International Driving Permit. If you become a resident of Ireland, you must apply for an Irish driver's license.

Travelers wishing to drive to Northern Ireland must follow UK driving laws while there. Traffic signs in Northern Ireland may differ from those in the Republic of Ireland. For additional information on traffic rules in Northern Ireland, visit the United Kingdom Country Information page.

Taxi fares vary depending on the time of day and location. If you want to go out during less busy periods, ask your hotel for the number of a call-dispatched taxi service.

In general, intercity bus and train services are excellent.
Local bus service in cities is generally adequate, albeit many buses are crowded, frequently late, and routes do not always connect readily. Pay particular attention to bus stop locations in both directions, as drop-off and pick-up points may be several blocks apart.

Aviation Safety Oversight: The United States Federal Aviation Administration (FAA) has determined that the government of Ireland's Civil Aviation Authority meets International Civil Aviation Organization (ICAO) aviation safety criteria for oversight of Ireland's air carrier operations. More information is available on the FAA's safety evaluation page.

Maritime Travel: Mariners contemplating a trip to Ireland should also check for maritime advisories and alerts from the United States. The US Coast

Guard homeport website and the NGA broadcast warnings website may also be updated with information.

Chapter 4: Visa-Free Access to the UK for Nationals of 111 Countries

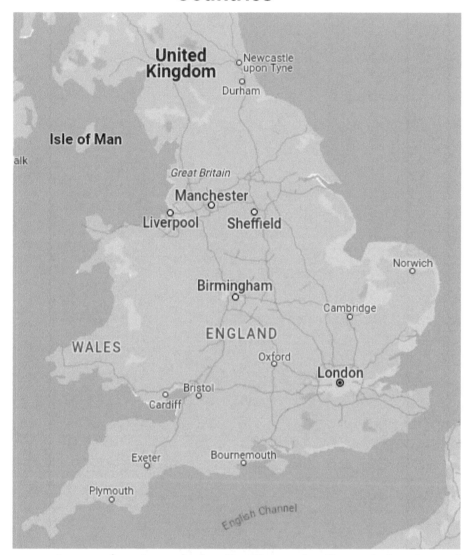

One of the most popular travel destinations in the globe has been the United Kingdom! There are many things that ambitious travelers have always wanted to experience, including visiting the stunning Scottish Highlands, tasting real Irish coffee, and experiencing the fast-paced, bustling city life of London. Most people need a tourist visa in order to realize their travel fantasies of taking a trip to this island nation. But there are numerous nations whose people don't even require a visa! Learn about the list of nations that can visit the UK without a visa.

The UK is open to visitors from over 111 countries without the need for a tourist visa! Travelers from the US, Israel, Germany, Aruba, Australia, and other countries are exempt from applying for any kind of travel document because of the visa restrictions established by the British government. All they need to get started is a passport!

Citizens of these nations do not need a tourist visa in order to visit the UK.

Austria	Anguilla	Antigua and Barbuda	Argentina	Aruba
Australia	Bermuda	Bahamas	Barbados	Belgium
Belize	British Virgin Islands	Bonaire, Sint Eustatius, Saba	Bosnia and Herzegovina	Namibia
Brazil	Cayman Islands	British Overseas Territories	Brunei	Bulgaria
Canada	Curacao	Chile	Colombia	Costa Rica
Croatia	Falkland Islands	Cyprus	Denmark	Czech Republic
Estonia	Grenada	Finland	France	Germany
Greece	Ireland	Guatemala	Guinea	Hong Kong, China
Iceland	Latvia	Israel	Italy	Japan
Kiribati	Maldives	Liechtenstein	Lithuania	Luxembourg
Macao, Malaysia	Micronesia	Malta	Marshall Islands	Mauritius
Mexico	New Zealand	Monaco	Montserrat	Nauru
Netherlands	Peru	Norway	Palau	Panama
Papua New Guinea	Saint Barts	Pitcairn Island	Poland	Portugal
Romania	Slovakia	Samoa	San Marino	Seychelles
Singapore	Spain	Slovenia	Solomon Islands	South Georgia and the South Sandwich Islands
South Korea	Sweden	Ascension Island, Saint Helena, Tristan da Cunha	Saint Vincent and the Grenadines	Saint Lucia
Saint Martin, Sint Maarten	Trinidad and Tobago	Switzerland	Taiwan	Togo
Tonga	Turks and Caicos Islands	USA	Tuvalu	Uruguay

The UK grants visa-free entry to nationals of these 105 nations for a maximum of six months. They must, however, adhere to the conditions outlined for the Standard Visitor Visa, which include leaving the UK after the trip, having sufficient money to support oneself while there, and not intending to stay or establish permanent residence there. The only need for entry into the UK for citizens of these countries is a valid passport; no other documentation is needed.

Nonetheless, a number of changes to the British government's visa regulations will alter the current framework for visa-free travel to the UK. The United Kingdom has implemented the Electronic Travel Authorization (ETA) program, which is akin to the United States' Electronic System for Travel Authorization (ETSA). Citizens of the aforementioned nations will soon need to apply for an ETA in order to enter the UK.

What is a Electronical Travel Authorization?
With the impending implementation of ETA, visitors entering the UK who do not need a visa will need to obtain authorization from the government in advance. This document essentially serves as the UK Visas and Immigration Department's pre-approval for crossing the border. Permission to travel will be granted through the electronic linkage of the ETA to the passport. The price is GBP 10 (around USD 12).

The ETA will be in effect for Qatar starting on November 15, 2023. When traveling on or after February 22, 2024, citizens of Bahrain, Jordan, Kuwait, Oman, Saudi Arabia, and the United Arab Emirates will also require the ETA. Beginning in 2025, citizens of the US, France, Germany, Switzerland, and other nations with visa-free travel will need to apply for an ETA.

Applications can be submitted via the UK ETA app or the official GOV.UK website. Three working days is the projected period for a decision; however, if more checkers are required, this time may extend. The decision will be sent via email because it is connected to the passport; printing that paper out is not required. The ETA is valid for two years and allows for multiple entries.

Who won't require an ETA?

Those possessing passports from the UK and Ireland, as well as those with visas allowing them to travel, reside, work, or study there, will not require an ETA. Additionally, legitimate Irish citizens visiting the UK without a visa from Ireland, Guernsey, Jersey, or the Isle of Man will not require an ETA.

The current Electronic Visa Waiver (EVW) scheme will continue to operate for a number of countries to enable easy, visa-free travel to the UK prior to the start of the ETA. You may read more about EVW and the nations that must apply for it below.

What is a Electronical Visa Waiver?

Known as EVW, this initiative was launched by the British government in 2014 and is presently available to citizens of specific nations. It permits them to travel to the UK for up to six months without a visa.

Those who qualify for this waiver of a visa must apply three months to 48 hours prior to departure. People must present the EVW, which is issued by email, together with their passport. One does not need to carry a printout because it is provided digitally and may be viewed on an electronic device like a smartphone.

The details of a valid passport, the address in the UK where the applicant intends to remain, travel information, and other pertinent details must be provided, together with any information specified in the application. The EVW only allows one admission, so each time a visitor plans to come, they will require a new one. Applying will set you back GBP 30 (USD 36).

Countries that are EVW-eligible:
Bahrain
Kuwait, Oman
Qatar
Saudi Arabia
United Arab Emirates

How much time is it possible to enter the UK without a visa?
Visitors from nations that have visa-free entry into the UK are permitted a maximum stay of six months.

What paperwork is required for me to enter the UK without a visa?
To enter the UK, inhabitants of the 111 nations mentioned above only need to present a valid passport. An electronic visa waiver is required for visitors from Bahrain, Kuwait, Oman, Saudi Arabia, and the United Arab Emirates. An ETA will be necessary for citizens of Qatar starting in November 2023; eventually, this will also apply to EVW nations and the 159 nations that do not require a visa.

Can I enter the UK through England without a visa and then travel to other regions of the country, such as Scotland and Wales?
Visas are not required for entry into England, Scotland, Wales, or Northern Ireland by citizens of nations exempt from visa requirements.

If I'm traveling to another nation, is it possible for me to pass through the UK without a visa?
If the UK serves as a hub for travel to another nation, citizens of visa-exempt nations are not required to obtain one.

Chapter 5: Exploring the UK: Navigating Britain's Landscape

You'll find everything you need on the various ways to get about Britain, whether it's lush green countryside, stunning coasts, beautiful villages, or bustling metropolis.

England's capital, London, is the busiest, most populous, and diversified metropolis in the country. While many of the central districts are walkable, you will almost certainly require transportation throughout your trip. If you know where you want to go, you may use Transport for London's (TfL) simple journey planner to determine the shortest routes for your journeys in and around London.

Exploring other British towns and cities

Taking public transportation is an easy and inexpensive method to get around Britain's cities and villages, and it's a terrific way to get a feel for the local culture.

Train travel in the United Kingdom

Train travel is a green, picturesque, and peaceful way to explore Britain. The rail network here spans large swaths of the country, with over 2,000 stations covering England, Scotland, and Wales. It's a quick and easy way to get about, with several train companies serving different areas. You may plan your travel using the National Rail travel Planner, and you could be in Brighton, Scotland, or almost anyplace else before you know it. Journey times aren't too long either; jump on a train in London and you'll be in Scotland in four hours.

It is also simple to travel between regions and towns. Plan your trip and purchase tickets from major travel agencies, internet ticket providers, and all railway stations.

Purchasing your ticket in advance can save you money, and it's sometimes even cheaper to buy two distinct singles than one return, so check this before booking. A BritRail card, which is only available to tourists, provides unlimited journeys and numerous savings, allowing you to travel at your own leisure.

Driving throughout the United Kingdom

Driving around Britain allows you to experience the country's different landscapes, cities, villages, and secret coastal corners whenever you choose. Furthermore, the wide network of highways facilitates mobility.

Coach travel in the United Kingdom

Traveling by coach is a terrific way to save money compared to using the train or driving, but journey durations may be longer.

If you know where you want to go, plan ahead of time and book your coach from a major operator like National Express or Megabus. You can also take a coach trip to areas of interest, which can run anywhere from a few hours to a few weeks. Choose from beach resorts and chocolate-box villages, historic places and bustling cities. Booking coach excursions or longer coach journeys before you arrive is a good idea.

Air travel in the United Kingdom
If you're pressed for time, large cities and some towns are adequately served by airports. This is an expensive alternative that, when you take in travel time to and from airports, is not necessarily the most time effective.

Domestic flights from large cities such as London to Glasgow, Edinburgh, and Aberdeen take about 1 hour and 30 minutes.

Boating around the United Kingdom
Britain boasts thousands of miles of inland waterways and hundreds of islands dispersed around its coastline, many of which can be explored by canal boat or ferry.

You can rent canal and narrowboats or go on a boat tour. Visit the Canal & River Trust website for more information about Britain's canals, rivers, and lakes.

Ferries in Scotland travel to a variety of destinations, including the Western Isles' Isle of Skye, Stornaway, and Lochboisdale. Most ferry operators provide a number of ticket options, including island-hop passes.

River ferries offer a fascinating alternative to more traditional modes of transportation, such as the ferry that runs between Liverpool and Birkenhead on the Mersey River and the London river boats that sail from Westminster to Greenwich and beyond. Visit local destination websites to learn more about ferry routes and schedules.

How to Get Around in the United Kingdom
You'll be able to travel to most destinations in the UK fast and see a lot during your stay here, whether you live in the city, the countryside, or

anywhere in between. The Eurostar, international coaches, and excellent flight connections put the rest of Europe right on your doorstep.

Trains The United Kingdom has a substantial train network that connects cities and towns throughout the country; for example, it takes slightly more than two hours to travel by train from London to Cardiff and slightly more than four hours to get from London to Edinburgh.

Anyone between the ages of 16 and 25, as well as full-time students of any age, can apply for a 16-25 railcard, which allows you to save one-third on train travel within the UK. There is also a railcard for people aged 26 to 30 that provides the similar benefits.

You can also obtain significant discounts on train tickets if you buy ahead of time or with a group or season ticket.

Metro and Underground networks
Underground rail networks are available in London, Glasgow, Liverpool, and Tyne & Wear.

Travelers on the London Underground (also known as the 'Tube') can save money by topping up their Oyster cards. Add pay-as-you-go credit as needed, or purchase a weekly, monthly, or annual travel card. You can also purchase a Student Oyster card and combine it with a 16-25 Railcard or a 26-30 Railcard to gain further discounts, including a third-off all off-peak travel inside the network. To avail these reductions, ask a member of staff at your local Underground station to manually'merge' your Oyster card and railcard. Top-up, pay-as-you-go, and student cards are also available in other cities.

Eurostar
Eurostar's high-speed train services between the UK and Paris, Lille, Calais, Brussels, and Amsterdam run frequently, allowing you to travel from London to the continent in just over two hours every day of the week.

Buses are available in the majority of UK towns and cities. You can buy a ticket from the driver when you board, use a travel card or Oyster card, or, in some situations, a debit or credit card. To save money on frequent trips, consider purchasing a season ticket.

Coaches

Hundreds of UK towns, cities, and airports can be reached by coach (a bus that travels longer distances than local buses). If you are between the ages of 16 and 26 and a full-time student, you can save up to 30% by purchasing a Coachcard from National Express.

Citylink is the main coach service provider in Scotland, and Translink is the main coach service provider in Northern Ireland. If you wish to travel further afield, Eurolines, Flix Bus, and National Express are usually inexpensive and convenient ways to get around mainland Europe.

Flights With 24 international airports in the UK and a wide range of low-cost flights available, it's simple to travel between UK cities and beyond. Fly from London to Manchester in one hour, or from the UK to over ten European destinations in less than two.

Taxis and automobiles

Taxis are readily available in all major cities and towns. As in any other country, check sure the taxi you use is safe. Consider using a cab service recommended by your university or college.

Depending on where you live in the UK, booking a trip through an app like Uber or Bolt is also becoming more prevalent and often more cost effective.

If you want to drive a car in the UK, you'll need a valid driver's license and insurance. In addition, the vehicle must be registered and taxed. If your car is more than three years old, it must be checked annually for roadworthiness with a MOT.

Cycling is quite popular in the UK and is a fantastic way to travel around town, save money, and stay fit. Many universities feature bicycle clubs or buddy programs, as well as workshops on bike safety and maintenance.

City cycle hire schemes are available in some UK cities, including London, Liverpool, and Belfast. These let you to pick up a bike from a docking station for a modest fee and return it to another docking station within 24 hours. Before utilizing the bikes, make sure to read the details of each cycle hire plan.

UK nations

The United Kingdom (UK) is a union of four nations: England, Northern Ireland, Scotland, and Wales, each has parallels and peculiarities that make studying in each distinct.

Language English is widely spoken throughout the United Kingdom, but it is not the only native official language. It is claimed that over 300 languages may be heard in London alone.

Holidays Immerse yourself in the UK's rich history and present culture by attending world-renowned events, local celebrations, and public holidays.

Weather

The weather in the United Kingdom can be erratic. But, with the correct gear and attitude, you can enjoy the UK regardless of the weather.

Religion

The United Kingdom is a multi-faith community in which all religions are largely accepted.

Food

Enjoy the vast array of food available in the United Kingdom. Here are our top eight university buying, cooking, and eating out tips.

Chapter 6: Seven Hotel Alternatives Redefining Travel Accommodation

Finding a place to stay when you're away from home may be an exciting and stressful experience. On the one hand, there's the concept of staying somewhere new and taking a break, whether for work or pleasure; on the other, there's the stress of finding somewhere good that's also affordable.

While hotels have been the standard option for decades, they may be costly. Fortunately, there are lots of accommodation options for everyone, from families to lone business travelers. Here are our seven favorite hotel selections for both long and short visits.

Consider your preferred location (urban or rural?). reasonable budget (serviced apartments for luxury, hostels for low-cost stays) and accommodation size (do you require a complete house or just a room?)

1. Serviced Residences

Look no further than a serviced apartment for real luxury and superb service. Serviced flats, a mid- to long-term alternative to hotels, offer five-star hotel-like service and amenities to both single travelers and groups.

While serviced apartments are on the more expensive side of the budget, the comfort, security, and relaxing elegance are unparalleled. Serviced apartments, sometimes known as aparthotels as a portmanteau of an apartment and a hotel, are large, private places that provide a true home-away-from-home for your stay.

A serviced apartment, with various rooms, including a fully equipped kitchen and separate living area, is ideal for stays that last more than a few days. Living at a hotel for more than a few nights might be fairly oppressive for many people.

Despite the convenience of a hotel room, the smaller size and lack of a kitchen can make visitors long for their own houses. A serviced apartment, on the other hand, gives a larger area that can comfortably accommodate guests, allows for personal meal preparation, and provides the type of calm comfort that relaxes the mind.

Serviced apartments, like hotels, cater to the specific demands of their customers. Many include concierge and security services for convenience and protection, and all have modern amenities and are cleaned to a high quality on a regular basis with regular housekeeping services.

Ideal for: Business travelers searching for long-term lodging.
Guests seeking a luxurious experience
Families spending precious time in London
Looking for a Serviced Apartment?

2. Holiday Rentals

Vacation rentals, with the development of Airbnb and VRBO, now provide a wide range of possibilities for travelers. Individual landlords offer their property for short-term rental through one of the service sites, and this is how vacation rentals work. While Airbnb allows hosts to list any property, including flat shares and spare rooms in their own houses, VRBO operates on an entire premises basis, thus only complete properties are available on their platform.

Vacation rentals can be a fantastic budget alternative to hotels in cities and across the country, but there are no assurances of quality and care must be given to thoroughly research and read reviews.

Because each vacation rental is unique, special attention must be taken to guarantee that the booking is satisfying. Before making a decision, check the parking, wifi, provided bedding, surrounding services, and other considerations.

Excellent for: A wide range of alternatives and locations
Budget-conscious travelers would like this option.

3. Bed and breakfast establishments

Bed and breakfasts, often known as guesthouses, are family-run businesses in which a bigger home has been transformed to give private bedrooms as an alternative to hotels. B&Bs are often tiny and cosy, with less than ten beds available, but offer little in terms of luxury.

Modern bed & breakfasts may include en-suite bathrooms, but older establishments usually have common bathrooms. Breakfast is included, as the name implies, with a full English (as well as raw fare like cereal and yoghurts) available in the breakfast room each morning.

Though less expensive than higher-quality hotels, B&Bs are priced on par with chain hotels such as Travelodge or Premier Inn. Their settings are usually pretty nice, with city guesthouses nearby.

B&Bs are often fairly versatile, offering both short- and long-term stays, due to their modest family-business mentality.

Ideal for: Budget-conscious business travelers
Short stays in suitable areas
Weekend escapes

4. Hostels

Hostels, another low-cost option, offer a low-cost, no-frills bed for the night in a variety of places, including city centers. Hostels in London are plentiful and reasonably priced alternatives to hotels.

Although some hostels provide private bedrooms and even en-suite bathrooms, the most affordable alternative is usually dorm-style accommodations in which guests share space with others. While useful for young adults looking to meet new people, hostels are often unglamorous and lack privacy.

Good for: Budget-conscious young folks who want to meet new people and socialize
Short-term city stays at a low cost

5. Caravans and Camping

Camping is traditionally associated with "roughing it," but with the expansion of the glamping (glamorous camping) sector in recent years, as well as a selection of wonderful budget caravan alternatives, camping now offers a solid alternative to hotels that may even be rather luxurious.

Your camping options are undoubtedly broad, with accommodation that can accommodate larger parties and families and often a wide range of services that can include swimming pools and on-site bars.

At the low end, presuming you own your own tent and don't mind trudging over the grass to the toilet block, there are lots of campsites across the UK that will allow you stay for as little as £10 per night.

Caravan parks frequently offer off-season savings that are comparable in price for couples and smaller families while providing a significantly more comfortable stay. Glamping lodges with warm wood fireplaces and wool carpets are ideal for a romantic trip on a tight budget.

Camping and glamping alternatives suffer from being very seasonal, with many places (quite understandably) closing throughout the winter, and it's quite difficult to find nice sites strategically located in cities, but if your journey is during the sunny months, camping may be a fantastic cheap option.

Ideal for: Budget travelers Families
People looking for rural and beach settings

6. House Share
Not all hotel solutions are suitable for short-term stays. If you need long-term temporary housing, one option for prolonged stay alternative lodging is to acquire a flat or house share.

SpareRoom is a website dedicated to locating mid- to long-term shared housing accommodation; excellent for students, single professionals, or couples looking for housing in a competitive market.

While not appropriate for short-term lodging or families, SpareRoom provides an effective service for city stays in London and throughout the UK, with a wide range of budget and facility options.

Ideal for: Students looking for college or university housing.
Professionals who require extended stays
Weekday contractors who work away from home

7. Home Exchange

Stay in a house instead of a hotel! Sites like Home Exchange and Family Home Swaps provide a viable alternative to hotels for families looking for the ultimate low-budget choice.

The concept is straightforward: you register your family's home on the site and arrange a mutually beneficial swap with another family somewhere else. You get to stay in a fully-equipped (often down to the toys) family home while they do the same, visiting your home for their own thrilling break.

Home swapping can be free depending on the site. There is a registration cost and insurance choices for some, but the entire experience is free for others. Of course, there are some restrictions: you must normally own your own home (landlords typically frown on the notion), and you must be comfortable with the thought of a family of strangers enjoying your home while you are not around. If that is not an issue, home swapping provides a unique option for short and mid-term visits anywhere over the world.

Home exchange does need some work, and travel must be planned well in advance; also, unlike holiday rentals, there are no certainties regarding your destination. It is critical to conduct research and communicate effectively.

Good for: Adventure-seeking families
Homeowners who are confident
Worldwide vacations on a shoestring budget

What Should You Do If You Don't Own a Hotel?
The walk-in nature of a hotel is often superior to the majority of the alternatives. If you find yourself suddenly in a city overnight with no plans, hotels will give you with a safe room for the night. Alternatives, while potentially less expensive or a better long-term choice, generally necessitate previous booking.

Consider bed & breakfasts as a hotel alternative that is equally willing to welcome last-minute customers. Similarly, hostels can be beneficial to backpackers and other single travelers. If you have the time, go on sites like Airbnb to see if there are any nearby short-term possibilities that may be hired for that night.

Choosing the Most Appropriate Hotel Alternative
Location, money, and size are all important considerations. These three criteria have the greatest influence on hotel reservations. Take the time to explore the possibilities that meet those three criteria, and you will locate a suitable hotel alternative. We certainly hope that this list has provided some further ideas for a unique holiday concept in the future.

Chapter 7: Diverse Accommodation Choices

Do you want to know what kinds of accommodations are available? From B&Bs to elegant country hotels, glamping at gorgeous locations to staying in unconventional venues such as lighthouses, train carriages, or tree huts, Britain has something for everyone and any budget. More information on hotel alternatives in individual locations across the United Kingdom can be found below.

Pubs and coaching inns: From the bar to the bed

Everyone enjoys a genuine British pub, and staying in one is much better. These drinking (and often eating) establishments are something of a British institution. Many scenic ones also feature accommodations, so your journey from bar to bed will never be long! Stay in a Pub can help you find pubs offering rooms all throughout the UK.

Inns differ from pubs in that, in the past, travelers from all across Britain would stop at them to relax on lengthy travels. These are often well preserved old buildings dating back hundreds of years and are referred to as coaching inns.

Bed and Breakfast

Staying in a Bed & Breakfast is another excellent way to meet locals, fellow travelers, and British staycationers. B&Bs are found all over the country, ranging from luxurious city-centre properties to storybook-style cottages.

Bed & Breakfast lodging provides a room for the night as well as breakfast the next morning, as the name implies. The decor spans from opulent escapist to no-frills options, with new luxury and boutique homes opening all the time.

Hotels

There are numerous hotels in Britain, ranging from stunning Georgian piles in rural villages to stylish hotels with sea views or staying in the midst of a bustling city packed with skyscrapers. There's the low-key, the commercial, the weird, and the magnificent. Those with a large budget can have anything from roof-top bars with swimming pools to golf courses and Michelin-starred restaurants.

Hostels

There are many of options accessible all around Britain for those on a tight budget who want to meet other like-minded travelers, such as backpackers. While they are typically intended at younger persons of student age, they are also used by travelers of all ages and families.

Dormitory-style rooms (shared rooms with four to ten beds - commonly bunk-beds) are common in hostels, however individual rooms are available for a little more money. Depending on the size of the hostel, rooms may be organized by gender and have shared facilities such as restrooms, kitchens, and living areas.

The Youth Hostel Association (YHA) operates approximately 150 hostels in England and Wales, several of which are in stunning locations. Hostelworld also offers a selection of independent and boutique hostels for booking.

Caravaning and camping

Camping is a cheap, fun way to enjoy the great British outdoors, and there are sites all throughout the country. You can bring your own tent or hire one that has already been put up. Some also provide a more deluxe accommodation, such as glamping or tipis. There will be shared bathroom facilities at a bare minimum, however some campgrounds will offer on-site shops, cafes, playgrounds, and swimming pools.

If you don't like sleeping in a tent, another choice is to rent a motorhome, which gives you more flexibility to explore and can also be parked for the night in most campsites' caravan parks, giving you access to the site's services.

Visit Pitchup, Hipcamp, The Camping and Caravanning Club, or campsites.co.uk for a list of campsites and caravan sites in the United Kingdom.

Britain also has a number of static caravan parks, many of which are located in seaside resorts. These can be more big and modern than camp-sites, with kitchens and bathrooms, and additional on-site amenities, such as clubhouses with bars that provide nighttime entertainment, as well as a swimming pool and restaurants. These are all very family-friendly locations to stay.

Self-catering Accommodation
Self-catering accommodations may be preferable if you are traveling in a group or with family. These can be cottages or cabins, vast countryside houses, or private flats, but they all have one thing in common: you can come and go as you like, cook and eat, sleep and wake up whenever you choose. Some contain a games room, a pool, or a hot tub in addition to a private kitchen. AirBnB, Holiday Cottages, and the National Trust all offer a wide range of the strange, amazing, and everything in between.

Glamping and unique lodging
Thinking about staying somewhere a little different? There are so many unique places to stay in Britain and Northern Ireland, from eco-friendly treehouses to converted windmills and water towers, shepherd's huts to age-old castles.

This type of accommodation is typically more expensive than regular options, but many include luxurious details such as Swedish hot tubs, cozy fire pits, and welcome baskets. Some of these inventive locations can be found on websites such as Canopy and Stars and Cool Stays.

Chapter 8: Exploring the UK's Top Five Iconic Landmarks

Whether you're a student who has just started studying in the UK or a lifelong visitor, the UK is full of fantastic places to explore and must-see landmarks. Take a step into Britain's bright future by visiting these iconic landmarks that define each region.

The Angel of the North

The Angel of the North is one of the most recognizable landmarks in the United Kingdom. Gordon Young designed the 137-meter-high steel sculpture, which is located in Gateshead, Northumberland.

The Angel of the North is also known as the "Angel of the Tyne" since it guards the River Tyne. The statue was unveiled on July 4, 1998, and has since become a symbol of British culture.

The Angel of the North is a landmark that people from all across the UK may admire. It is also a famous tourist spot, with visitors coming from all across the country to see it.

Buckingham Palace

Buckingham Palace is one of the most recognizable landmarks in the United Kingdom. It is the official residence of the British Royal Family and one of the country's most popular tourist attractions.

Buckingham Palace was erected in the 17th century as a vacation residence for King Charles II. It has evolved into one of the most well-known and popular tourist sites in the United Kingdom. Buckingham Palace gardens, the State Apartments, and Holyroodhouse are among the many unique sights at the palace.

Buckingham Palace also houses one of the most famous residences in the world, Buckingham Palace. Sir Christopher Wren designed and built this magnificent structure in the 17th century. It is a spectacular example of Baroque architecture and has been dubbed "the most iconic landmark in England."

If you plan to study in London, make sure to visit Buckingham Palace! It is one of the most famous landmarks in the United Kingdom and is likely to captivate you. Many of our London partners are within walking distance.

London Eye

The London Eye is one of the country's most recognizable monuments. It is a bronze observation wheel located on London's River Thames. The attraction first opened to the public in 2000 and has since grown to become a popular international tourist destination.

The London Eye is 179 meters tall and 394 meters in circumference. Cycling around the wheel takes roughly 20 minutes. As you ride around, you will get panoramic views of London.

Trip Advisor has given the London Eye five stars, indicating that it is one of the top attractions in the world. It is also one of just six attractions worldwide to have received five stars from both the UK Travel Association and Lonely Planet.

Stonehenge

Stonehenge is one of the most well-known landmarks in the United Kingdom. It is a megalithic structure composed of massive standing stones dating back over 4000 years.

Stonehenge is one of the world's oldest and most well-known megalithic monuments. It was built approximately 3000 BC and has been standing for thousands of years.

The round layout of Stonehenge is one of its most remarkable aspects. The stones were arranged in a circle, with each stone placed in a certain location to be read as a symbol or message.

Stonehenge is still utilized for religious worship today. People come from all over the world to see it, and it has become one of the most recognizable sites in the United Kingdom.

The Windsor Castle

Windsor Castle is the most recognizable landmark in the United Kingdom, recognized for its gorgeous architecture and grounds. Henry II erected the castle in 1085 as a mansion for himself and his wife, Eleanor of Aquitaine. The castle has been destroyed and rebuilt several times over the years, but it has remained one of the most famous and well-known landmarks in the UK.

Windsor Castle is indeed a magnificent structure and it is one of the most famous tourist destinations in England. It is also home to many famous paintings and sculptures, including a statue of Queen Victoria. Windsor Castle is surely an iconic monument that everyone should see at least once in their lifetime.

Chapter 9: Delving into London's Top Ten Must-Try English Dishes

London is home to some of the world's most iconic cuisines, and no visit to this powerhouse of a city would be complete unless you sample the greatest local fare. Many of these foods, such as fish and chips and beef Wellington, have gone over the world, but there's something special about eating them in their hometown.

In the city, you'll find a variety of meals representing the finest of British cuisine in both fine-dining and casual settings, while some are exclusive to one or the other. Discover the best native English dishes in London.

Steak and Kidney Pie

Steak and kidney pie, as the name implies, is a popular dish in taverns and bars that includes diced beef and kidney. The kidney component of the pie is usually beef, although it can also be lamb or pork.

Along with the namesake components, this pie frequently includes brown gravy and fried onion, as well as black pepper and Worcestershire sauce. It's available in almost every pub in London, as well as several decent sit-down restaurants.

Breakfast in the English style

Despite having numerous delectable components, the typical English meal, often known as a full breakfast, is presented as a single dish. Bacon is served alongside fried, poached, or scrambled eggs. In addition, toast, sausages, and black pudding are common breakfast items.

This dish is so popular that it can be found in almost every cafe in London. Most bars also serve it, so you won't have to travel far to try it all out for yourself. However, you'll notice that many restaurants prepare it somewhat differently.

Sunday roast with Yorkshire pudding

Sunday roast with Yorkshire pudding is a classic dinner that is frequently, but not always, eaten on Sundays and consists of roasted beef with potatoes, stuffing, and dessert. The roast itself can vary greatly, with common meats including chicken, lamb, beef, and hog. Duck, turkey, and gammon are seasonal variations.

The pudding portion of this dish is prepared with eggs, flour, and milk, however it can be produced in a variety of ways depending on the cook. This meal is accessible in almost every cafe in London, as well as local eateries.

Fried fish and fries

Fish and chips is one of the world's most popular British dishes, and London allows you to experience this informal and uncomplicated cuisine taken to the next level. This meal has been a staple of England for nearly two centuries, and you can get it in a variety of versions all around London.

There are various casual fish and chips shacks throughout town, but several local restaurants offer a more sophisticated version. It may even be available at select fine-dining establishments that specialize in British cuisine.

Afternoon Tea

Afternoon tea is more of a meal than a drink because it effectively serves as a catch-all word for all kinds of mid-afternoon meals. This mealtime can include a variety of dishes, but the most common are sweet pastries and breads.

As you may expect, tea plays a significant role in this lunch, hence the name. During the dinner, you can drink whatever tea you choose, although most people choose a tea that compliments the biscuits they're eating. This is available in almost every cafe and restaurant in London.

Bangers and mashed potatoes

Bangers and mash is a sausage and mashed potato meal that comes in a variety of flavors and is often served with onion gravy. Sausages can be produced with a variety of meats, including pork, lamb, and beef.

For the most part, this cuisine is regarded as pub fare. This is due to the fact that it is simple to construct and can be produced in huge quantities at a low cost. It is expected to be available at nearly every pub in London.

Beef Wellington

Beef Wellington is a hallmark of British fine dining, with a substantial fillet encased in puff pastry for an outstanding taste. This is an upscale dish that demands a skilled chef to execute perfectly, so expect to pay a premium when ordering it in one of London's fine-dining places.

While the beef version is the most common, there are numerous varieties that use proteins other than beef, such as sausage and salmon. Vegetarian variants with beets and mushrooms, among other ingredients, are also available. This item is often found in more upscale establishments.

Ploughman Lunch

Ploughman's lunch is a popular meal that consists of bread, cheese, and onions, with a few other things sprinkled in. The components are all modeled on what a rural English person would have used centuries ago, albeit preparation has evolved with the times.

This dish is frequently served with beer, making it particularly popular in London's pubs and inns. It's generally considered a lunchtime meal, however most pubs serve it for far longer than that.

Beef Stew

Beef stew is a popular dish practically everywhere, but London provides a distinctive beef stew made with London broil, a lean and rough meat. Beef stew in London is typically made using marinated pieces of steak that are cooked medium-rare and thinly sliced.

When you combine London broil with other components in a stew, such as substantial potatoes and veggies, you may have a rich flavor that will make you feel like you're at a fine dining establishment without the posh setting. This stew may be found all throughout town in restaurants both cheap and expensive.

Sticky Toffee Pudding

Sticky toffee pudding is a traditional North West England delicacy that consists of chopped dates in a moist sponge cake covered with toffee sauce. It's usually accompanied by custard or ice cream, with vanilla being the most popular flavor.

Because this is the classic British dessert, it can be found at almost any restaurant in London that serves dessert. It's also popular with children, so if you're traveling with the whole family, you won't want to miss it.

Chapter 10: London's 14 Must-Try Foods in 2024

London is a fascinating and ancient city, but when compared to other more recognized worldwide culinary hubs, you might not instantly recognize it as the home of superb cuisine. However, you'll be pleasantly pleased by the exquisite foods available in our capital, including both national favorites and must-try specialties that even some Londoners have yet to discover. Here is my list of the top foods to try in London for your consideration.

The Best Foods and Drinks in London
English cuisine is distinct from other European cuisines such as Mediterranean or Nordic, but it is no less wonderful. Hopefully, this list will provide you with a thorough introduction to our country's favorite meals while also highlighting London's best snacks.

14. Jelly Eels
This dish first appeared in the 18th century in London's East End. It was a nourishing and economical lunch for the poorer working-class populations. They might even catch the eels themselves because they were abundant in London's most famous river, the Thames.

Eel is now considered a cockney (East End) delicacy, owing to the scarcity of jellied eel stores. It's chopped and served in a spicy fish stock that serves as the jelly base. While vinegar is the traditional and favored condiment, chile vinegar has become popular in recent years.

F Cooke Hoxton in Hoxton, East London is where to get it.

13. Fish & Chips

Although the traditional chip store (or "chippie") is disappearing, fast-food restaurants and even fine-dining establishments continue to provide this national favorite. The name says it all: the fish is usually cod fried in a thick golden batter and served with fried potato chips. Other white fish, such as haddock and pollock, are also popular.

Traditional British fish and chips can be found in tourist hotspots such as Leicester Square and Tower Hill. Local chip businesses outside of these areas sell larger fish at a lower price and take pride in their generous size.

Where to get it: Tower Hill's Great British Fish & Chips.

12. Beef Wellington

According to legend, this dish was named after British military commander and prime minister Arthur Wellesley, the Duke of Wellington. His signature dish is an entire fillet steak coated in pâté with mushrooms or duxelles - a mushroom, onion, and shallot combination. The combination is cooked into a shortcrust pastry, which pairs well with the tender cut of beef.

Celebrity chef Gordon Ramsay popularized it by promoting its culinary merits and incorporating it into his dishes. Furthermore, many customers believe it is his best meal!

Gordon Ramsay Bar And Grill in Mayfair is where to get it.

11. Frog In The Hole

This batter pudding dish has an unusual name, but it contains no amphibians, frogs or toads. It was invented in the 18th century in the United Kingdom, but no one knows how it received its name. What we do know is that it's a tasty and hearty combination of sausages in a Yorkshire pudding batter (Yorkshire pudding is another traditional British meal).

Toad in the hole, like many medieval English meals, was a helpful way to stretch food in lower working-class areas. It's still a popular snack, with well-preserved serving rituals like soaking the crispy batter in onion sauce. It's more popular in the north of England, where the Yorkshire pudding basis came from. The batter in the south is typically softer and more buttery.

Where to get it: Lambeth's Bistro Union.

10. Bubble and Squeak
According to some London historians, the unusual moniker bubble and squeak comes from the noises made while frying the ingredients. It's essentially a vegetable cake comprised of mashed potatoes, cabbage, Brussels sprouts, and kale fried in a frying pan. This meal is made with vegetable leftovers by Londoners.

The mix of healthful veggies and waste reduction appeals to the environmentally concerned, but all diners owe it to themselves to try this traditional British vegetable cake. It's frequently found on breakfast and lunch menus due to its smaller size and easy-to-digest ingredients.

Where to buy it: Dartford's Bubble And Squeak Cafe.

9. Bread & Butter Pudding
You'll be pleased to learn that this baked delicacy is actually made of buttery bread, since Britain has a long heritage of unique titles for their favorite dishes. Slices of buttered bread are topped with raisins and egg custard, then baked with vanilla, nutmeg, or cinnamon.

This treat is comparable to French toast in that it has an amazing custard center. Surprisingly, stale bread, bread crusts, and tough bread rolls can all be used as the bread base.

Sweet Boulangerie & Patisserie in Clerkenwell is where to get it.

8. Shepherd's Pie

Shepherd's pie is a favorite among Londoners, with its wonderful layers of minced lamb or mutton, mashed potatoes, vegetable mixture, and cheese topping. Many famous English recipes from the 17th and 18th centuries were created by families attempting to make the best of their leftovers, and this dish is no exception. Its creamy, cheesy covering and stuffing of mince and vegetables established it as a solid favorite rather than a cheap dish.

Its appearance in Harry Potter has caused a stir among book and film enthusiasts. There are multiple references, but the most important one occurs in Chapter 7, as Harry's school detention with Gilderoy Lockhart approaches. And don't confuse it with a similar English dish, cottage pie, which has a beef filling rather than lamb or mutton.

Where to acquire it: Mayfair's Windmill.

7. Eton Mess

This luxury dessert is supposed to have originated at Eton College, where it was sold in the tuck shops (snack stores). It is still served at the annual cricket match between Eton and Harrow, two of the premier schools in the United Kingdom. However, its high-class origins do not always translate to its appearance. It is a "mess" both in name and in nature.

However, it's a delectable concoction of strawberries, raspberries, cherries, whipped cream, and meringue. Modern ones are more visually appealing. While this dish is more difficult to find than others, it's worth the effort to see what all the hype is about and to compare the sculptured and more messy varieties.

Aviary in Moorgate is where to obtain it.

6. Banoffee Pie

An English dish with condensed milk as a key ingredient sounds fascinating. Its crushed digestive biscuit base (or a pastry base replacement) is very intriguing. Banoffee pie is a delectable blend of cream, bananas, caramel sauce, and, of course, condensed milk.

Nigel Mackenzie, a restaurateur, is credited with developing this dessert in 1971. Banoffee pie is so quintessentially English that it was featured prominently in the "quintessentially English" love film Love Actually.

Where to get it: Bloomsbury's Savoir Faire.

5. Scotchtails

Although the name suggests Scottish origins, this food is most usually associated with Yorkshire, England. Even yet, the original origins of the Scotch egg - a boiled egg baked in a breadcrumb layer of sausage meat – are unknown.

Innovative food sellers in Shoreditch and Borough Market have created their own artisanal versions that are moister and more flavorful than the original. However, due to their popularity, the originals are easier to find and can be found in most London supermarkets.

Scotchtails can be found at Borough Market.

4. Sticky Toffee Pudding

This delectable treat consists of a black sponge cake baked with chopped dates. The name entices the palate to expect an opulent pleasure, and it delivers. It's moist and sweet, practically melting in your mouth. Furthermore, no plate would be complete without the toffee sauce topping.

Sticky toffee pudding is traditionally served with vanilla or caramel ice cream, whipped cream, or custard. Kate Middleton, the Duchess of

Cambridge, is one of its celebrity devotees, claiming it is her favorite dessert.

Where to get it: Kensington's The Abingdon.

3. Sunday Roast

This family supper, traditionally served on Sunday, holds a special place in the hearts of the British. There are variants, but the basic dish consists of roasted pork, Yorkshire pudding, and vegetables such as roasted potatoes, parsnips, carrots, boiled broccoli, Brussels sprouts, and peas.

Those experiencing it for the first time may miss the social historical component. The underlying allure of the Sunday roast is more about tradition and family memories than it is about gastronomic attributes. I suppose it depends on the ambiance of the dining establishment. It's not an acquired taste, but rather an acquired experience.

Blacklock Shoreditch in Shoreditch is where to obtain it.

2. Afternoon Scones and Cream Tea

The afternoon cream tea experience has sophisticated, high-society antecedents dating back to the nineteenth century. It was a staple of royalty meals back then. It was introduced by the upper class as a filler meal for individuals who were hungry before supper. The finger-sized cucumber sandwiches and cakes of the time are still popular today.

Earl Grey tea and scones with clotted cream and fresh strawberries are ideal. You can also select from a selection of elegant-looking desserts and pastries reminiscent of Victorian high society. Afternoon cream tea is often served about 3:00 p.m.

It's available at Fortnum & Mason in Piccadilly.

1. Traditional Full English Breakfast

The traditional foundation of a full English breakfast is sausages, bacon, baked beans, fried eggs, tomatoes, and mushrooms, but it would be incomplete without black pudding and hash browns. The traditional English cuppa (cup of tea) rounds out the meal, however some prefer coffee, cappuccino, green tea, or herbal tea.

There are, in fact, healthier breakfast options. In place of the customary fried items, some cafés offer avocado rye bread toast, kale, spinach, or rosemary sweet potatoes. Whichever you choose, it's so popular that it's rare to find a London cafe that doesn't serve it. The truly comprehensive full English breakfast—hash browns, black pudding, and all—is more commonly available outside of the city center, closer to residential streets and local settlements.

Terry's Café London or The Sportsman (outside of the city center) are good places to get it.

Chapter 11: Exploring Historic Sites Across the UK

We've compiled a list of 38 of the top historical places to visit in the United Kingdom. These historical sites can be located in several of the country's most populous and well-known cities.

Belfast Castle

Belfast Castle, located about 120 meters above sea level, offers panoramic views of the city. This fortress, which was initially erected by the Normans in the 12th century, was officially reopened to the public in November 1988.

Belfast Castle endured numerous alterations and sackings during the next several hundred years. As a result, this castle is rich in history, which you may read about at the visitor center.

Shankill Road

During The Troubles (from the late 1960s to 1998), the Shankill Road became well-known. During this time, there was a lot of sectarian bloodshed on Shankill Road between Catholics and Protestants.

Conflict no longer dominates this unique road, and the area is now a famous tourist destination. You can see colorful paintings and peace walls here. This history can be best appreciated by taking one of the city's famous Black Cab tours.

The Cadbury World

Cadbury World is one of Birmingham's must-see historical sites, located just south of the city center in the West Midlands. As the name implies, this museum is dedicated to the famous Cadbury family, who are well-known throughout the world for producing some very delectable chocolate. In 1824, this family began with a single business selling chocolate drinks and cocoa.

The Warwick Castle

Warwick Castle, which is conveniently positioned between Royal Leamington Spa and Warwick, is steeped in British history. This king-built castle served as a vital bastion during the War of the Roses and the English Civil War.

Not only that, but Warwick Castle is one of the most impressive Mediaeval castles in the United Kingdom, and it has been continuously inhabited since the Middle Ages! Special events and guided tours are held here on a regular basis.

The Duke of York Picturehouse

The Duke of York's Picturehouse is the UK's oldest operating purpose-built cinema! This Brighton and Hove cinema is over 100 years old and yet preserves many of its original Edwardian characteristics.

The Sea Life Center

The Sea Life Centre, which was originally known as the Brighton Aquarium when it first opened in 1872, is not only the United Kingdom's oldest aquarium, but also the world's oldest.

A lot has happened here since it first opened. The aquarium housed a music venue called The Florida throughout the 1950s and 1960s. The Who, among other musicians, performed a monthly Wednesday night event for the equivalent of only 15p!

The Brunel's SS Great Britain

Brunel's SS Great Britain, often regarded as Bristol's best historical site, is a magnificent steamship with various chambers that history buffs can tour. The historic ship's galley, dining salon, and surgeon's quarters are among them.

Clifton Suspension Bridge

Much of Bristol's history can be traced back to Isambard Kingdom Brunel, a world-renowned engineer noted for his ground-breaking work during the Industrial Revolution. Brunel created the 76-meter-high Clifton Suspension Bridge, which is definitely one of Bristol's most iconic sights.

Castell Coch

Castles abound in Wales. In reality, there are almost 600 of them, 427 of which are still standing! Castell Coch (Red Castle) is one of the most intriguing. This Victorian castle, located to the north of Cardiff, was erected on top of 13th-century ruins.

National War Memorial in Wales

The Welsh National War Memorial is located in Cardiff's Alexandra Gardens. This memorial, which was finished in 1928, serves as a vital reminder of those who fought and perished during World War One. A commemorative plaque was later added to remember those who died during World War II.

Chester's Walls

Chester's city walls are the longest and most complete in Britain. They're also the oldest, with some pieces dating back nearly 2,000 years. Walking the walls will also allow you to discover more about Chester's rich and illustrious history.

The Chester Cathedral

The Chester Cathedral is an incredibly stunning Medieval structure in Chester. This must-see historic destination combines a dynamic community of worship, a historical monastery, and an architectural masterpiece. As a result, tens of thousands of tourists visit this Cheshire cathedral each year.

Palace of Holyroodhouse

The Palace of Holyroodhouse, the official residence of the British monarch in Scotland, stands majestically at the end of Edinburgh's historic Royal Mile. This palace is primarily known as the residence of Mary, Queen of Scots.

A tour of the Palace of Holyroodhouse includes 14 unique apartments as well as the spectacular ruins of the 12th-century Holyrood Abbey. There are also beautiful royal gardens on the premises.

The Edinburgh Castle

Edinburgh Castle is one of Western Europe's most interesting and captivating historic structures, as well as one of the continent's oldest defensive buildings. This castle has served as a royal home, military garrison, prison, and fortification over the years. You'll learn everything about these fascinating facets of the castle's history when you visit.

Many tourists trek up to Edinburgh Castle for the beautiful views alone, since its high vantage point provides panoramic vistas of the Scottish capital of Edinburgh.

The Necropolis cemetery.

The stunning 37-acre Necropolis cemetery is filled with remarkable architecture, sculptures, and fascinating stories about the 50,000 people who are remembered here. This Victorian cemetery in Glasgow's core attracts visitors from all over the world.

The Glasgow Cathedral

Glasgow Cathedral, which was built between 1136 and 1484, is today Scotland's largest place of worship. One of the most popular things to do here is visit the crypt, which was created in the mid-13th century and includes St Mungo's grave. Much of Glasgow grew up around this shrine, helping to create this popular city into the one it is today.

Regular services are held, and there is no admission cost; however, donations to the building's upkeep are encouraged. There are other one-hour tours offered.

The Kirkstall Abbey

Kirkstall Abbey, which dates back to 1152, is one of Leeds' most historically significant sites. Despite being about 900 years old, the remains are still mostly intact and make an excellent photo location.

Thornton's Arcade

Thornton's Arcade, Leeds' oldest arcade (a covered hallway with arches along one or both sides), was erected in 1878 by Charles Thornton. Leeds is widely recognized for its arcades sprinkled throughout the city center, and this is without a doubt one of the most intriguing!

King Richard III Visitor Center

King Richard III ruled England from 1483 to 1485, when he was assassinated in the Battle of Bosworth Field in the East Midlands. An archeological excavation unearthed Richard III's skeleton in 2012, and radiocarbon dating was utilized to authenticate his identity.

Two years later, the King Richard III Visitor Centre opened, with this museum recounting the tale of the king's life, as well as how his body was discovered in the first place. This visitor center has received almost 40 honors since its inception!

The Leicester Cathedral

Leicester Cathedral, built on the site of a Roman temple, has been at the heart of the city's cultural and religious life since the Middle Ages. Over 500 years after his death, King Richard III's remains were discovered nearby and reburied in the cathedral.

The 220-foot spire, which was constructed in 1862, is one of the most remarkable aspects of this cathedral in Leicester.

The Royal Albert Dock.

Liverpool has one of the busiest ports in the world. The Royal Albert Dock is at the center of this in many respects, and it is a cornerstone of English heritage. These docks dominated worldwide trade in the 18th and 19th centuries. Today, this magnificent waterfront harbor offers a variety of attractions while proudly presenting its unique history.

The Liverpool Cathedral

Liverpool Cathedral, expertly integrating modernist and Gothic architecture, sits triumphantly in the heart of the city center. This is the largest cathedral in the United Kingdom and the sixth largest in the world. If you enjoy stunning architecture, the Liverpool Cathedral is a must-see historic attraction.

Parliamentary Chambers

The Houses of Parliament, located on the north bank of the River Thames in downtown London's Westminster, are a sight to behold, having been established in the early 11th century. This UNESCO World Heritage Site was previously the abode of the Kings of England before becoming the epicenter of political debate in the United Kingdom.

There are several tours available that will take you inside this world-famous edifice, covering the inner workings of both the House of Commons and the House of Lords. Visitors can even observe debates taking place for free!

Winston Churchill War Rooms

The Churchill War Rooms, considered one of London's must-see sights, served as the British government's nerve center throughout WWII. From then, Churchill and his government collaborated to ensure the Allied victory.

When you're at this underground area, you definitely get a sense of the tension that everyone would have felt. Regular tours are given, which take you through the War Cabinet Room, the Map Room, and other areas.

Westminster Abbey

Westminster Abbey, a World Heritage monument with almost 1,000 years of history, is one of Britain's most important historical sites, particularly in terms of royal history.

This church has hosted the coronations of 39 English and British monarchs, as well as at least 16 royal weddings, since 1066. The state funeral for Elizabeth II was held at Westminster Abbey in September 2022.

Throughout the week, Westminster Abbey is open for services and tours. You may explore this intriguing and beautiful church, which serves as the final resting place for almost 3,000 historically prominent Britons, on one of these excursions.

Highgate Cemetery.

Highgate Cemetery, one of the most famous cemeteries in the world, is located in the London borough of Camden.

This cemetery is well-known due to the large number of prominent persons buried there. There are at least 850 noteworthy people buried in Highgate Cemetery, the most well-known of which being German philosopher and communist father Karl Marx. Among the other notable inhabitants are novelist George Eliot and painter Henry Moore.

The grounds are also beautiful to explore, with plenty of mature trees, wildflowers, and wildlife.

The Chetham Library
Did you know that Manchester is home to the English-speaking world's oldest public library? Since its inception in 1421, Chetham's Library has remained in the city center. This library was once a college of priests and then a jail during the Civil War before becoming a public library in 1653.

The Victoria Baths
The historically significant Victoria Baths were characterized as "the most splendid municipal bathing institution in the country" and "a water palace of which every citizen of Manchester can be proud" when they first opened in 1906. This historical place is well-known throughout North West England.

The Hadrian's Wall
Hadrian's Wall, which stretches 73 miles from coast to coast, was originally built by Roman Emperor Hadrian to defend the northwest region of the Roman Empire.

Today, you may explore history as far back as the wall itself, as well as the often breathtaking views on either side. Forts can be found throughout the north of England, particularly near Carlisle and Hexham.

The Newcastle Castle
Newcastle Castle is an excellent reminder of Northern England's often turbulent past and military history. This castle is where the city's tale began - and where its name originates from.

Armies would often convene at this stronghold, and criminals would be imprisoned. You can discover about the history of this castle while exploring ancient passages, chambers, and apparently limitless hidden stories.

Ye Olde Trip to Jerusalem

Many classic English pubs vie for the honor of being the country's oldest. We'd have to say that Ye Olde Trip to Jerusalem has the most compelling case. Although sources and dates differ, many believe that the site of this historic Nottingham bar dates back to 1189.

The name is also rich in history, with Richard the Lionheart and his troops rumored to have congregated in the bar before heading to Jerusalem for the Crusades.

Wollaton Hall

Wollaton Hall, a remarkable feat of Elizabethan construction, is recognized for its grand proportions and for holding the UK's largest dedicated natural history museum.

When visiting Wollaton Hall, there is something for everyone to do all year. You may not only tour this royal house, but also the Grade II-listed walled garden and the Nottingham Industrial Museum, which are all nestled among 500 acres of lovely parkland near the village of Beeston.

Warsend Cemetery

The Warsend Cemetery is the final resting place for around 30,000 Sheffield and surrounding region residents. The Warsend Cemetery Heritage Park contains this cemetery. The picturesque River Don gently flows at the foot of the hill, as do a diverse variety of flowers that have developed and blossomed over the last 150 years.

Abbeydale Industrial Hamlet

The Abbeydale Industrial Hamlet is an excellent venue to learn about the steel industry, which had a significant impact on Sheffield's and South Yorkshire's history. This historical monument allows you to immerse yourself in steelworks dating back to the 1700s.

Bargate

This spectacular Grade-I listed mediaeval gatehouse in the heart of Southampton was built around 1180 and functioned as the city's primary entrance at the time. Today, Bargate is frequently lauded as England's most magnificent and complicated doorway.

Bargate has seen its fair share of history over the years. During the 15th century, the structure was used as a jail, and later as a guildhall and the location of a popular market.

Tudor House

Many people see Tudor House as Southampton's most important historic structure. This timber-framed edifice in the city's Old Town boasts nearly 800 years of fascinating history.

Tudor House, which is also Grade I listed, is an excellent venue to learn about its past residents as well as the greater history of Southampton.

Meanwhile, the contemporary garden recreates a Tudor knot garden, featuring plants that would have been found during the Tudor period.

Hafod Morfa Copperworks

Swansea's Hafod Morfa Copperworks was once one of the most major Industrial Revolution sites. This location was covered in a complex maze of structures and slag heaps during the 19th and 20th centuries as a byproduct of the copper smelting operation that took place here.

Though work no longer takes place, many of these copperworks, notably the Musgrave Engine House and the Vivian Engine House, have been restored. On the site today, no less than 15 noteworthy structures survive.

Swansea Castle

While virtually little of Swansea Castle exists, the surviving structures and ruins serve as a reminder of the once-imposing fortification. This location has had a castle in some form since at least the early 12th century, and a Grade-I heritage listing was given in 1952.

The castle is occasionally exposed to the public, such as during St David's Day in 2012. A initiative has been undertaken to try to make the castle more accessible to visitors on a more permanent basis.

Chapter 12: Essential London Food Guide: Popular English Delicacies

While traditional British cuisine may not have the best image around the world, there are some delicious London food options you should try on your next trip. London has a lot of delicious food. I've created a list of iconic London meals that you must taste on your next trip to the UK in our London food guide.

I've also added some great places to eat in London that serve these delectable selections. The majority of popular cuisines in England are savory, but that doesn't mean we don't excel at desserts as well. Save space for dessert because I also have a UK national cuisine guide to London's greatest ice cream shops.

MASH AND BANGERS

I'm starting with bangers and mash because I freaking love it. It's straightforward, honest fare that can be found in most UK pubs. You can't go wrong with bangers and mash if you're looking for the best meal in London.

When purchasing this UK national dish, there are a few things to keep in mind. To begin, what kind of sausages does the restaurant serve? Examine the various regional sausages available in the UK—trust me, not all are created equal! The gravy is the next thing to check for because bangers and mash aren't complete without it. When choosing between plain and original gravy, always choose the onion gravy.

The sausage and mash is frequently served in a massive Yorkshire pudding. If you see it on the menu, order it—it will alter your life! Perhaps not, yet Yorkshire pudding is one of the most traditional must-try London dishes. It's an egg, flour, and water batter baked in the oven and eaten with a roast beef supper. Long ago, someone wise decided to prepare a Yorkshire pudding with sausage, and so Toad In the Hole was formed.

I digress—my point is that on your classic British culinary tour, you must consume sausage and mash or Toad in the Hole.

'Fish and Chips'

Fish and chips is a typical London cuisine that can be eaten any day of the week, however it is generally served on Friday. Because Brits like to shorten everything, we call fish and chip shops "chippies" in the UK. For instance, you might say, "Let's go to the chippy for tea."

Fish and chips are at the top of most people's lists when it comes to amazing food in the UK. Almost any bar in London will provide the dish—look for beer-battered fish and chips. Poppie's of London serves the best of the best.

Remember to get your chippy tea with mushy peas, salt, and vinegar.

AN ENTIRELY ENGLISH BREAKFAST

Another must-eat cuisine in the United Kingdom is a full English breakfast, also known as a "full English." What exactly is a full English breakfast? This varies greatly, but the mainstays are:

Back bacon in two portions
two ham sausages
1 or 2 fried eggs
Baked beans (Henry Heinz)
Fried or plum tomatoes
Mushrooms
The black pudding
Toast or fried bread

Hashbrowns are occasionally available, but not always. If you dine later in the day, you may be offered brunch, which is all of the above except the toast is replaced with bread and butter and the hashbrowns are replaced with chips. Bottomless brunches are so popular in London that you should sample this typical English eating experience at least once.

It's essentially a heart attack on a platter, and the clogged arteries are worth it. Black pudding is a traditional London dish, but it's not my favorite, so I usually skip it.

The Shepherdess serves the best breakfast in London.

Sunday Roasts

Sunday roast is one of the most popular cuisines in England that I miss the most now that I live overseas. A classic roast supper, together with a full English breakfast, is the most traditional British dish in the UK. It's essentially a less formal Christmas supper served every Sunday—instead of turkey, Brits use roasted chicken, beef, or a leg of lamb. Every Sunday, roast supper is served around the country.

A carvery is one of the best spots in London to try a Sunday roast. A carvery is a business where you can buy a roast meal any day of the week—pay and wait in line to choose from three or four different types of meat, ranging from turkey, chicken, and hog to lamb, beef, and ham. Inform the chef of your preference, and they will carve slices and serve them with Yorkshire pudding. Continue down the line, filling your plate high with roast potatoes, mashed potatoes, veggies, cauliflower, and cheese, then drowning everything with gravy!

When it comes to the gravy, there will most likely be options for vegetarian, regular, onion, or lamb gravy. The lamb gravy has a minty flavor, which I discovered the hard way after making my dinner unpalatable because I despise mint sauce!

For an outstanding Sunday roast, go to The Spaniards Inn.

Indian Curry

I'm going to stick my neck out there and claim that British Indian curry is the most popular and possibly the most beloved UK national meal in London. We love Indian food in the United Kingdom. So, why do I call it British Indian curry rather than Indian curry? Because they're different—even the name "curry" is a corruption of the Tamil word "kari," which meaning seasoning.

Curry became popular in the United Kingdom following World War II, when numerous Indian immigrants arrived. They opened restaurants selling Indian food in order to find work in postwar Britain. Because the ordinary Brit won't be able to handle much heat, they altered traditional recipes to suit their customers. As a result, British Indian classics like Chicken Tikka Masala and Lamb Rogen Josh were created.

Head to Brick Lane, one of London's most unusual dining destinations, to experience some of the best curries in the country. The neighborhood has been gentrified and is quite hipster, but it is also full of wonderful curry establishments, so you may choose where to dine.

Mash and Pie
We're now getting into some traditional English cuisine! The potatoes and gravy in the pie and mash (or pie and chips) plate! Is there a pattern emerging here? Almost all British dish comes with potatoes and gravy, hehe. A classic British lunch will always include "meat and two veg" as well as potatoes and, more often than not, gravy!

Pie and mash is a traditional London dish, and there is just one establishment in London where you can obtain it: Godard's Pie Shop. Pie with liquor, a wonderful London cuisine specialty, is served here. Godard's features the best pies and other classics, such as jellied eels—yes, you read it correctly. Eels in jellied form!

Bubble and Squeak
Bubble & squeak is a typical English dish that many Brits adore, yet it is rarely served in restaurants. Bubble & squeak is created with leftovers from a roast meal, so it might be tricky if the stars align.

We have a deep-rooted tradition of "make do and mend" in the UK, which stems from living on rations during and after WWII. This reuse and repurposing mindset extended from socks to never wasting food. So any leftover potatoes and vegetables from Sunday dinner would be used for bubble and squeak on Monday. Mash everything together, shape into patties, and fry—usually served with a fried egg, leftover beef, or a couple of bacon rations.

It's a shame bubble and squeak isn't more popular in the UK because it's so tasty! Borough Market, a little bistro, is my favorite place to enjoy bubble and squeak. You won't be sorry if you order it for breakfast on a bap (bread bun) with an egg.

High Tea

Did you realize that even UK national food is classified? While traveling, I observed this since some London dishes are considered normal, while others are considered high-class.

Don't be perplexed by the word "tea," as it can refer to various things:

Tea: A beverage produced from black tea leaves that is served with milk.

Also, tea: Something to consume about five or six o'clock in the evening for your evening meal.

High Tea is a hybrid of the two—it's usually something that wealthy people eat between lunch and supper and is known as dinner or tea depending on where you're from. High tea is more than simply a traditional London meal; it's an entire experience! High Teas are served in venues such as the Ritz, Claranges, and the British Museum. This traditional British dish is only available between two and four p.m., so check the schedule ahead of time.

Jam, Rolly Polly, with Custard

Now comes dessert, or as we like to call it, "afters." Jam rolly polly with custard is one of the best England national culinary dishes presented for dessert.

You know how the British like to drown their food with gravy? We do the same with our dessert, except instead of gravy, we bathe it in sizzling hot, creamy custard! While custard can be eaten cold, I don't recommend it because the topping is better served warm.

If you can't locate jam rolly polly, try one of these famous London dishes instead:

Bread pudding with butter
Toffee Sticky Pudding
The Treacle sponge
Dick spotted
The sponge with jam

Anything including the words sponge or pudding will imply a hot cake topped with fruit that tastes like a warm hug.

Chapter 13: Navigating Manchester: A Comprehensive Guide

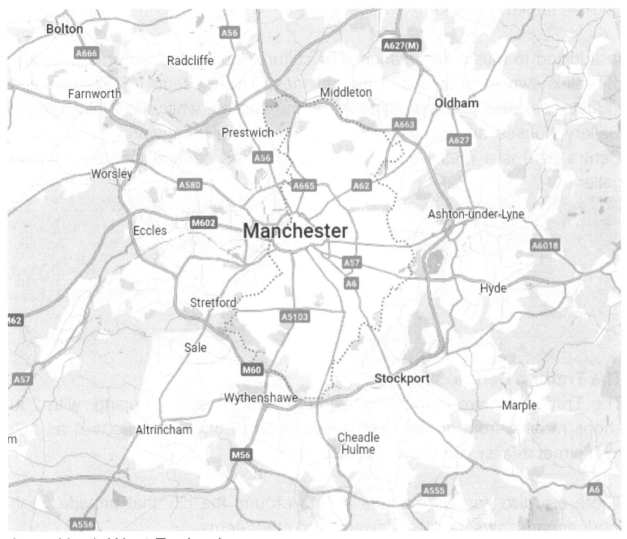

Area: North West England
Population: 464,000 people
Area: 115 square kilometers

Manchester is one of the largest cities in the United Kingdom, located in the north-west of England. It has a young, lively population and is a center for the arts, media, and higher education. Manchester United, one of the largest football teams in the world, is also based in the city.

For the last 50 years, Lowry Manchester has been a powerhouse of British music, producing influential bands like as The Smiths, Oasis, Joy Division, and the Chemical Brothers. There are fantastic music and nightclub venues, including the MEN Arena, the world's busiest indoor music venue, and the famed Hacienda.

In addition to music, the Manchester cultural landscape features a variety of well-known museums and art galleries. The Museum of Science and Industry provides precisely what the name implies, while the Whitworth Art Gallery houses an exceptional collection of British artworks. The Lowry Centre (left) is a massive structure that houses several theaters and art galleries.

The Trafford Centre
The Trafford Centre is the crown gem of Manchester shopping, with 230 shops ranging from department stores to small boutiques, as well as any high street retailer you could possibly want.

There are also various markets in and around the city that provide fresh food, apparel, gifts, textiles, flowers, and other items.

There are practically hundreds of restaurants in Manchester that can provide you with the perfect dinner regardless of your preferences. Classic British fare, Spanish tapas, Greek delis, Italian cafés, Michelin-starred French restaurants...Manchester has everything.

The famous Curry Mile, with over 70 Asian restaurants, is a particular feature. The single road contains the greatest concentration of curry places in the UK and should not be overlooked.

It couldn't be easier to get to Manchester. Manchester Airport is the largest in northern England, with planes arriving from all over the world on a regular basis. Manchester also has railway and road connections, making it simple to commute in and out of the city.

However, a large bus network and a tram system provide quick and inexpensive transportation throughout the city.

Old Trafford Sport is one of the most significant effects on life in Manchester, as the city is home to two of the world's largest football teams, as well as an internationally recognized aquatic center and velodrome.

Manchester United is perhaps the most famous and successful football club in the world, while Manchester City is presently the richest club in the world and is rapidly expanding. During the football season, both famed stadiums, Old Trafford and the City of Manchester Stadium, host weekly matches at low prices for students.

Football, however, is not the only sport played in Manchester. The city hosted the Commonwealth Games in 2002, with participants competing in the aquatic center, which features two Olympic-sized swimming pools, and the velodrome, which is now the National Cycling Centre.

Chapter 14: Cultural Marvels in London: Museums, Events, and Accommodation Suggestions

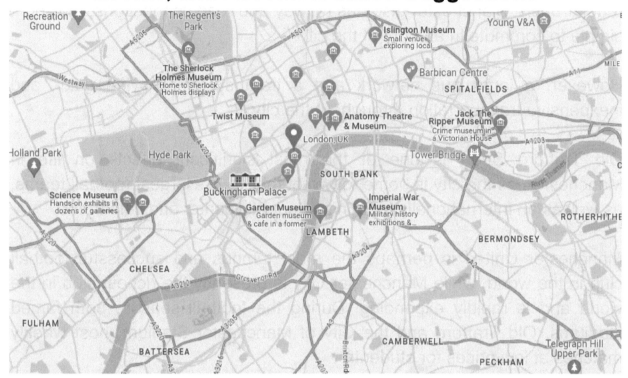

London is one of the world's most popular tourist destinations, with award-winning cultural attractions, a jam-packed events calendar, and a community at the forefront of music, art, and design.

From world-class museums to small indie music venues, the city has something for everyone.

That tremendous amount of variety, however, is difficult to filter through, so we've selected the greatest cultural attractions in London so you can truly strike the ground running on your vacation to the city.

The V&A Museum is one of the best cultural attractions in London.
The Victoria & Albert Museum in Kensington is the world's leading museum of design and applied and decorative arts.

It is also the largest, with over 2.2 million pieces spread across 145 galleries, as well as several guest and temporary exhibitions.

It's an incredible place that is rightfully regarded as one of the most important cultural attractions in London and the world.

Cromwell Rd, SW7 2RL, London

Tate and Tate Modern
The Tate and Tate Modern are two of Europe's most important art galleries.

The Tate holds the country's National Collection of art from the 1500s to the present day, and the Tate Modern is at the forefront of modern and contemporary art, attracting world recognized artists from around the world as well as the finest of British.

There are 70,000 pieces of artwork across the organization's venues, making it a must-see for art aficionados visiting the city.

The Tate Modern's beautiful views of the city and contemporary art displays make it an ideal date place for art-loving couples looking for a romantic and cultural encounter.

Millbank, London, SW1P 4RG

Tate current's current address is Bankside, London, SE1 9TG.

Natural History Museum
The Natural History Museum in London is one of the world's largest.

It houses 80 million objects and chronicles the story of the planet's 4.6 billion-year history.

It's a really magnificent museum with numerous intriguing displays and exhibitions, including large and full dinosaur skeletons.

Without a sure, one of the best museums to see in London.

Cromwell Rd, South Kensington, London, SW7 5BD

Shakespeare's Globe

Shakespeare's Globe, located on the banks of the Thames, is a must-see for theatergoers.

The theatre is a recreation of the historic theatre where William Shakespeare's plays were played.

Not only is it an amazing architectural project, but it also hosts world-class concerts.

Visiting The Globe theatre with your family may be a fun and instructive opportunity to learn about Shakespeare's plays and the history of theatre.

21 New Globe Walk, London, SE1 9DT, United Kingdom

Natural Portrait Gallery

The National Portrait institution is another world-class art institution in London.

It houses the world's biggest collection of portrait paintings, with over 220,000 distinct pieces of art spanning 1,400 years.

It was one of the first of its sort when it originally opened, and as a result, it has a world-famous reputation.

St. Martin's Pl, London, WC2H 0HE

West End Shows

The West End of London is one of the world's best theatre districts.

There is something for everyone, including family-friendly classics like The Lion King and Frozen, as well as more adult classics like Les Miserables and more modern performances like "Get Up, Stand Up!" that chronicles the narrative of Bob Marley's life.

The West End is a cultural hotspot in London, with new-wave performances and cutting-edge concepts sprouting on a weekly basis.

Various addresses in central London

Clubbing in London is at the forefront of the electronic music scene, alongside cities like as Berlin.

The city's nightlife culture is thriving, with some of the world's most recognized nightclubs drawing the world's greatest electronic music DJs on a monthly basis.

Printworks, Fabric, XOYO, Heaven, Ministry of Sound, and Electric Brixton should be on your radar for cultural events in London.

After a night of clubbing in London, there are lots of exquisite accommodations to pick from, offering a pleasant and fashionable stay in the city.

Attend a performance
Some of the world's greatest famous artists were born in England's capital, and the city has been at the forefront of innovative music for decades.

London boasts a jam-packed music calendar, with spectacular music venues strewn across the city.

From massive arenas like the O2 and Wembley to smaller scale legendry venues like Koko and Camden Roundhouse.

Barbican Centre
The Barbican Centre in the City of London is a cultural hub, holding theatre performances, concerts, film screenings, and various exhibitions.

It is the largest in Europe and so attracts cutting-edge performances.

The London Symphony Orchestra and BBC Symphony Orchestra are housed in the Grade II-listed structure.

Silk St, Barbican, London, EC2Y 8DS

British Museum
The British Museum is a magnificent cultural institution with one of the world's largest collections of human, art, and cultural displays.

There are 13 million pieces in all, with numerous guest displays.

It's one of the top cultural day activities in London.

Great Russell St, London, WC1B 3DG

Sherlock Holmes Museum
The narrative of the famed fictional detective Sherlock Holmes is told in the film Sherlock Holmes.

The museum is located on Baker Street, the same street chosen as the residence of Sherlock Holmes in Arthur Conan Doyle's novels.

The museum is a step back in time, recreating the setting of the novels, which have subsequently been adapted into TV shows and films.

221b Baker St, London, NW1 6XE

London events
The list of cultural events in London is so long that we could fill a dictionary with recommendations and ideas.

From large-scale events bringing hundreds of thousands of people to local gigs, concerts, and shows, there is practically something going on all the time in London, both day and night.

There are cultural events like as the Notting Hill Carnival and large music festivals such as SW4 and All Points East, as well as festive celebrations such as Winter Wonderland in Hyde Park and Bonfire Night celebrations.

When planning your vacation to London, we recommend keeping an eye on the following websites:

Gigs - https://www.songkick.com/metro-areas/24426-uk-london
Club events - https://ra.co/events/uk/london
West End Shows - https://www.londontheatredirect.com/

Where to Stay
Sanctum Luxury Serviced Apartments
When ticking off all of these amazing day activities in London and then maybe dancing into the night, you want to make sure you have a comfy place to rest your head.

Sanctum has three Luxury Serviced Apartment complexes in London that provide exceptional access to many of the city's best cultural attractions.

The locations are near Regent's Park, Maida Vale, and Kilburn. All are within striking distance of some of the world's greatest cultural destinations highlighted in this guide.

They range in size from studio apartments to 5 bedroom suites.

Many activities in the UK revolve on the capital. London is brimming with energy and innovation, with world-class attractions and an events schedule to rival any location on the planet. In London, there is something for everyone, including cultural attractions for the entire family.

What is certain is that you will never be short of cultural activities to do in London or events to attend. We hope you found our tour informative; now get out there and soak up some culture in England's capital.

Chapter 15: Adventurous Escapades in South Wales

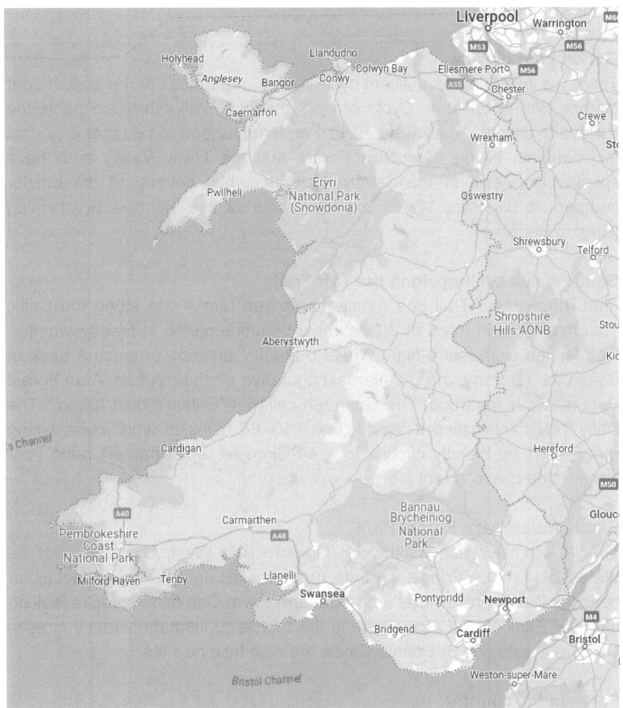

Find out what you can do in South Wales. Within two hours of London and the Midlands, there is world-class mountain riding, the best coastal hikes, and beaches ideal for surfing. Why are you not showing up to play?

South Wales offers a wide range of activities for individuals, couples, and groups of friends.

Get on your bicycle.

There are plenty of magnificent cycle routes, regardless of the size of your clan or cycling aptitude. Cycle or walk the Taff Trail, which connects the Valleys to Cardiff. The Valleys have wonderful rugged terrain that is perfect for mountain biking. Cwmcarn Forest and the Garw Valley both have spectacular views of the Severn Estuary, while several of the crazier courses at BikePark Wales provide vistas of the Bannau Brycheiniog (Brecon Beacons).

South Wales cycling along the Taff Trail

The Three Parks Trail is a mostly traffic-free family ride along the Celtic Trail that takes in three of Wales' most beautiful parks. In Maesycwmmer, look for the eight-metre-high 'Wheel o Drams' artwork, or catch a peek of Sultan the Pit Pony, the UK's largest figurative earth sculpture. Afan Forest Park is highly regarded. The Guardian called it "Britain's best biking." The Daily Telegraph called it "world-class." Its 60 miles of world-class biking range from kid-friendly circuits to a 44-kilometer epic that will rattle your fillings. You can also rent a bike.

South Wales' Afan Forest Park

The 14-kilometer beach between Ogmore and West Aberthaw may be Wales' best-kept walking secret. Its Jurassic cliffs drop down to spectacular beaches like Dunraven Bay near Southerndown. One minute you're looking out over Exmoor, the next you're in the middle of intimate bluebell forests. Ogmore Castle and St Donats Castle are also historic sites.

Parks in the country

Cwmcarn, located less than an hour from the Severn Bridge, is a must-see for hardcore mountain bikers. There are also several treks in the park, including a 9-mile walk, the 0.9-mile/1.5-kilometer Nant Carn Walk, and the 1.2-mile/1.8-kilometer Bluebell Walk. Please keep in mind that there are some uneven ground, and kissing gates may make these walks challenging for families with pushchairs. Throughout the year, a comprehensive events program for children is offered, including themed woodland walks.

Caerphilly's Cwmcarn Mountain Bike Park

Have a fantastic day in Parc Cwm Darran. There are numerous spectacular cycling and foot excursions to be had across former colliery lands. The restored lake is part of a large natural marsh, and there are lots of animals to see along the designated walk. There is an obstacle course for older children and a playground for younger children.

Parc Bryn Bach is a 340-acre lakeside park in the countryside. Explore a nature route around the lake or hop on your bike to take advantage of the extensive riding facilities. The adventure playground will appeal to children, while adults will enjoy soaring through the sky, crawling through caves, coasteering, archery, orienteering, and a variety of watersports.

Throughout the year, Dare Valley Country Park hosts a variety of family events and fun days. For those with younger children, the Bwllfa Trail is a wonderful option. The round walk is about two miles/3.5 kilometers long and offers spectacular views of the lake as well as the opportunity to see a variety of species. At the lake, the path splits into two, including a shorter accessible route for pushchairs and wheelchairs.

Cosmeston Lakes and Country Park, near Penarth, is an excellent site for fitness and wildlife viewing. Bryngarw Country Park near Bridgend has 100 acres of parkland to explore, or take a ride on the cycle track. Stroll around Porthkerry Country Park, which features woods, cliffs, and nature trails.

Recreational facilities

Parkwood Outdoors Activity Centre offers abseiling, hiking, canoeing, and stand-up paddle boarding among other activities. Show off your athletic prowess at the Summit Centre in Bargoed. The climbing walls have 180 alternative routes to the top. Caving, motorcycling, canoeing, and kayaking are among the other activities available. The outdoor play area will appeal to younger children. The center offers weekend and holiday activities for families, as well as lodging for group residential excursions.

Taff Valley Activity Centre offers quad biking. A specialized 150m children's circuit is available for juniors aged seven to eleven. Aside from gorge walking in the picturesque Bannau Brycheiniog (Brecon Beacons), other activities include an assault course, archery, laser shooting, and clay pigeon shooting.

Taff Valley Activity and Quad Bike Centre

Visit the Adventure Outdoors Activity Centre in Porthcawl for an activity break. Take a family trip for youngsters aged seven and up, or spend time with friends, including hen and stag groups. Rock climbing, gorge scrambling, watersports, paintballing, and completing the assault course are just a few of the activities available.

Swimming and other water sports

There are numerous chances for water sports or simply swimming around. Consider kayaking in Parc Bryn Bach or paddle boarding in Llandegfedd Reservoir.

Porthcawl's Rest Bay

Rest Bay Porthcawl is ideal for intermediate surfers because to its large area and decent waves, while novices can be assured of a lesson due to the neighboring beaches' ability to manage most wind directions. Look up surfing in Porthcawl.

Another enjoyable activity to attempt is stand up paddleboarding (SUP). Island SUP Ltd is headquartered in Barry Island and provides lessons for people of all skill levels. The National Lido of Wales, Lido Ponty, is a terrific spot for a family adventure, with hand boats, stand up paddle boarding, and zorbing wheels, as well as plenty of chances for swimming and sunbathing.

Smaller children will enjoy Cyfarthfa Park's splash pad. Boating, watersports, and wildlife viewing are all available at Cwmbran Boating Lake.

Cardiff white water rafting

Cardiff International White Water offers a mountain of adventure to Cardiff Bay, amplifying the enjoyment factor to 11. It's popular with kids and first-timers alike, but pro paddlers adore it as well because it condenses the rough-and-tumble of river rafting into a fierce 254m run.

The Wye Valley has 100 miles of navigable water to explore by canoe. Various canoe operators provide family-friendly tours that range in length from half a day to five nights. Stay under canvas or in a B&B.

Chapter 16: Exploring the UK's National Trails: History and Scenic Walking Routes

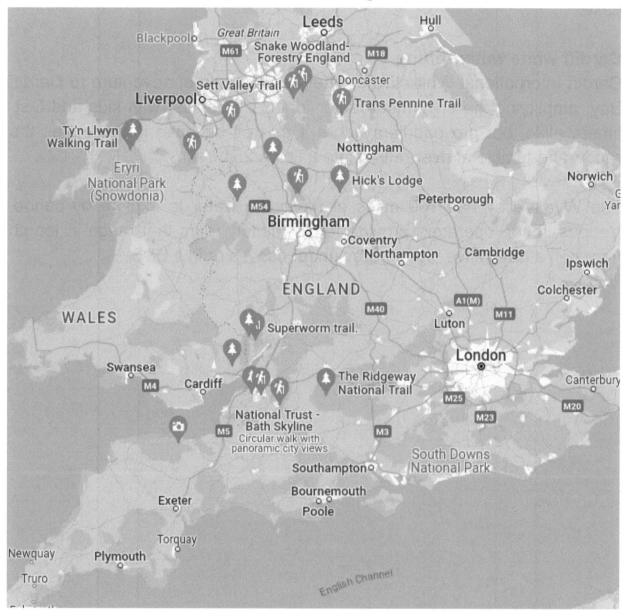

The National Trails of England and Wales, as well as Scotland's Great Trails, create a network of approximately 3,000 miles of long-distance trails. With our comprehensive reference of the UK's top long-distance walking routes, you can learn more about their history, the landscapes they pass through, and vital facts and data.

How many National Trails are there in the United Kingdom?

England and Wales have 16 National Trails while Scotland has 29 Great Trails. These long-distance hiking, biking, and horseback riding trails take you through some of Britain's most beautiful scenery.

What exactly are National Trails?

National Trails are long-distance trails that travel through some of England and Wales' most scenic and historic landscapes. The trails are designated by the government and adhere to a set of standards that distinguish them from other walking routes. They are well-marked (look for the distinguishing acorn sign) and are kept up by one or more trail officers as well as volunteers.

The historic 81-mile-long Hadrian's Wall Path to the epic 630-mile-long South West Coast Path are among the 16 National Trails. The Cleveland Way explores untamed heather moorland, the Offa's Dyke Path crosses the English-Welsh boundary, and the Glyndwr's Way travels through a terrain notable for its links with 15th-century warrior Owain Glyndwr.

Some sections of the National Trails in England and Wales are accessible by bike or horseback.

What are the Great Trails of Scotland?

Scotland's Great pathways are characterized in the same way as the National Trails of England and Wales, as long-distance pathways located among some of the country's most noteworthy landscapes. The routes are at least 25 miles (40 kilometers) long and are frequently completed over several days. They are well-marked, largely off-road, and have plenty of conveniences along the way.

There are 29 Great Trails, which are mostly utilized by walkers but also by cyclists, horseback riders, canoeists, and kayakers.

England and Wales National Trails

In England and Wales, there are 16 National Trails. Learn more about each path, including a brief route description, how long it is, the landscapes it passes through, and its history.

Cleveland Way, 109 miles (175 kilometers)
Route: This 109-mile route begins in Helmsley in the North York Moors and winds across heather moorland before following the Yorkshire coast south from Saltburn-by-the-Sea to Filey. The total ascent of the route is 5,562m, which is the equivalent as climbing Ben Nevis four times from sea level.

Rugged hills and heather moreland, coastal cliffs, fishing communities, and old monuments make up the landscape. Urra Moor (454m) is its highest point, and it is home to prehistoric remnants like as barrows and a rock marker carved into a face.

After nearly 16 years of effort, the path was designated as a National Trail in 1969, becoming England's second oldest National Trail.

Website: http://www.nationaltrail.co.uk/cleveland-way

The Cotswold Way is 102 miles (164 kilometers) long.
The Cotswold Way is a 102-mile National Trail in south-west England that runs from Chipping Campden to Bath, generally clinging to the edge of Britain's most famous hills but occasionally plunging down to visit the picturesque Cotswold villages. Walkers are exposed to an extraordinary panoramic vista of 16 counties from a single vantage point.

Landscape features include wildflower meadows, beech woodland, traditional Cotswold towns and villages, and significant historic sites.

The route was designed by Ramblers' Association members over 50 years ago, but the long-distance footpath was not officially opened until May 2007.

National Trails: www.nationaltrail.co.uk/cotswold-way

England Coast Path (when finished), 2,800 miles

Route: When finished (2020), this coastal route around England will be the longest in the UK and one of the longest in the world, reaching an amazing 2,800 miles (4500 km).

Coastal cliffs, beaches, seaside villages, tidal estuaries, and salt marshes make up the landscape.

The route was supposed to be completed in 2020. Four portions of the path have been officially finished as of this writing:

National Trails: www.nationaltrail.co.uk/england-coast-path

Glyndr's Way, 135 miles (217 kilometers)

Route: This 135-mile route begins in Knighton, a tiny market town in Powys on the English-Welsh border. It travels west through Machynlleth before turning east through Powys to Welshpool, just a few miles from the border.

Open moorland, rolling farmland, woodland, and forests make up the landscape.

The Trail was named after Prince of Wales Owain Glyndr. In 1400, the Welsh nationalist leader led a rebellion against England's Henry IV. In the year 2000, the Glyndr's Way was classified as a National Trail.

Website: http://www.nationaltrail.co.uk/glyndwrs-way

The Hadrian's Wall Path is 85 miles (137 kilometers) long.

Hadrian's Wall Path follows this historic defense barrier built by Roman Emperor Hadrian for 85 km. The coast-to-coast path is normally walked from east to west, beginning at Wallsend on Tyne and Wear's east coast and ending at the Solway Firth on Cumbria's west coast.

The trail traverses Cumbria, Northumberland, and Tyne and Wear, passing through towns, rivers, estuaries, wild uplands, and mild pasturelands.

Hadrian's Wall was built in the second century AD by the Romans and served as a protective barrier for 300 years. Hadrian's Wall and the Antonine Wall, another Roman barrier built in Scotland, are both designated World Heritage sites. Hadrian's Wall Path was designated a National Trail in 2003.

Website: http://www.nationaltrail.co.uk/hadrians-wall-path

The North Downs Way is 153 miles (246 kilometers) long.
This National Trail stretches for 153 miles across the North Downs from Farnham in Surrey, through Guildford, Dorking, and Rochester, to Dover on the south Kent coast.

The trail winds through downland with chalk-based soil and calcareous grassland, including the Surrey Hills and Kent Downs AONBs. Boadleaf woodland and open pasture are common, as are a number of villages and towns.

The North Downs Way National Trail, which follows the historic Pilgrims Way, was established in 1978.

Website: http://www.nationaltrail.co.uk/north-downs-way

Offa's Dyke Path (177 miles/285 kilometers)
Offa's Dyke Path extends for 177 miles (285 kilometers) from Sedbury Cliffs in Chepstow to the beach town of Prestatyn on Wales' north coast.

The path passes through valleys and along ridgelines, as well as agriculture and small communities. Despite the fact that the Offa's Dyke Path traverses the full length of the English-Welsh border, the massive earthwork itself comes and goes. It occasionally charges through peaceful ancient woods, a fortified ditch, and a steep slope up to 2.5m (8 ft) high. At times, it is nothing more than a line through a field.

History: In the 890s, 100 years after the alleged date of construction, Alfred the vast's historian Asser stated that King Offa had built a vast dyke from sea to sea to isolate Wales from his own kingdom of Mercia. While archaeologists debate whether the dike was ever completed, erected all at once, or even built by Offa at all, walking along its most spectacular sections reveals a genuinely magnificent linear fortification comparable to Hadrian's Wall.

In 1971, Offa's Dyke Path was designated as a National Trail.

Website: offas-dyke-path.nationaltrail.co.uk

Peddars Way and Norfolk Coast Path 130 mile (208 km)
Route: This relatively flat route begins inland in Suffolk at Knettishall Heath and runs virtually straight to the Norfolk shore at Holme-next-the-Sea. It then turns south, passing through several medieval ports before arriving in Hopton-on-Sea.

Heathland, forest, low river valleys, agriculture, beaches, sand dunes, salt marshes, and nature reserves make up the landscape.

Peddars is assumed to stem from the Latin word pedester, which means "on foot." The Peddars Way is based on a Roman route. In 1986, the Peddars Way and Norfolk Coast Path were designated as National Trails.

Nationaltrail.co.uk/Peddars Way and Norfolk Coast Path

The Pembrokeshire Coast Path is 186 miles (299 kilometers) long.
This mostly clifftop walk has a total rise of 11,000 meters (35,000 feet). Pen yr afr on Cemaes Head is the path's highest point, standing 175 meters above sea level.

Landscape: With sandy beaches, rolling clifftops, charming fishing communities, and breathtaking views, Wales' south-west coast is ideal for exploring on foot.

The Pembrokeshire Coast National Park was created in 1952. The Pembrokeshire Coast Path was designated a National Trail over 20 years later, in 1970.

National Trails: www.nationaltrail.co.uk/pembrokeshire-coast-path

The Pennine Bridleway is 205 miles (330 kilometers) long.
The 205-mile (330-kilometer) Pennine Bridleway, created exclusively for horse riders and mountain bikers, follows ancient packhorse trails, drovers roads, and bridleways through the Pennines.

The Pennine Hills, which span Derbyshire and Cumbria, offer a spectacular landscape. The bridleway mainly follows valleys, hillsides, and across moorland.

Mary Towneley, who rode 250 miles on horseback from Corbridge in Northumberland to Ashbourne in Derbyshire in 1986, conceived of the Pennine Bridleway. After a route analysis, the walk was designated as a National Trail in 1995.

National Trails: www.nationaltrail.co.uk/pennine-bridleway

The Pennine Way is 268 miles (435 kilometers) long.
Route: This 268-mile route begins in the Peak District and travels north along the Pennines, passing through the Yorkshire Dales and Northumberland National Park before arriving in the Scottish Borders.

The Pennine Way traverses public pathways through valleys and communities, over hills and mountains, and across moorlands and bogs. It is not the longest route, but it is undoubtedly the most difficult.

The Pennine Way is the oldest National Trail in England. The final leg of the Pennine Way was officially inaugurated in 1965, after been proposed by journalist and hiker Tom Stephenson in an article for the Daily Herald in 1935.

National Trails: www.nationaltrail.co.uk/pennine-way

The Ridgeway is 87 miles (139 kilometers) long.

The Ridgeway National Trail connects Overton Hill near Avebury in Wiltshire to Ivinghoe Beacon in Buckinghamshire and is 87 miles long.

The path passes through rolling chalk downland, villages and towns, and various archaeological sites, including Neolithic long barrows, Bronze Age round barrows, Iron Age forts, and chalk white horses.

The Ridgeway is claimed to be Britain's oldest route, having been used by prehistoric travellers, shepherds, and soldiers. In 1972, the path was recognized as a National Trail.

Website: http://www.nationaltrail.co.uk/the-ridgeway

South Downs Way, 100 miles (160 kilometers)

The South Downs Way runs 100 miles from Winchester in Hampshire to the East Sussex coastal resort of Eastbourne.

The route winds across the South Downs, passing through scenic villages and past Bronze Age barrows, ramparts, and iron Age hill forts. The track has a total elevation gain and loss of 4,150m (13,620ft).

The trails of the South Downs have given wayfarers with a drier and safer alternative to the lowlands below for over 8,000 years. The South Downs Way was the fifth National Trail in England and Wales, opening in July 1972.

Website: http://www.nationaltrail.co.uk/south-downs-way

The South West Coast Path is 630 miles (1014 kilometers) long.
The South West Coast Path is England's longest waymarked footpath (until the England Coast Path is completed). The route follows the coastlines of England's four most south-westerly counties - Dorset, Cornwall, Devon, and Somerset - from Minehead to Poole Harbour.

Despite the lack of mountains on this long-distance coastal trail, walkers who finish the entire route will gain an amazing 35,000m of elevation due to the undulating shoreline. Beaches, clifftops, seaside communities, and estuary crossings are all possible.

History: In the nineteenth century, coastguard patrol workers walked most of the shoreline here to prevent smuggling. In 1978, the path's final segment was designated as a National Trail.

Website: www.nationaltrail.co.uk/southwest-coast-path

The Thames Path is 184 miles (294 kilometers) long.
Route: Tracing the UK's most famous river, this 184-mile trail begins in the Cotswolds and meanders east to the heart of London.

Landscape: The track follows the riverbank through wildlife-rich meadows, rural villages, and ancient towns, culminating in an on-foot bisection of England's capital city (just 1,438m of rise on the entire trail).

The trail was designated a National Trail in 1996.

Website: http://www.nationaltrail.co.uk/thames-path

The Yorkshire Wolds Way is 79 miles (127 kilometers) long.
The Yorkshire Wolds Way runs for 79 miles from the Humber estuary through the Yorkshire Wolds chalk hills and north to the Cleveland coast.

Riverside walkways, wooded slopes, dry valleys, undulating hills, and arable land make up the landscape.

The Yorkshire Wolds Way was designated as a National Trail in October 1982.

Website: yorkshire-wolds-way.nationaltrail.co.uk

Chapter 17: Unveiling England's Ten National Parks: Hiking Trails, Stargazing, and Wildlife Exploration

England has a lot of landscape to offer, with breathtaking chalk cliffs, old woodland, foggy moorland, glorious lakes, and rolling green fields, and lots of room to clear our minds, breathe, and reconnect. Some of the nicest scenery is located in designated national parks, which offer numerous possibilities to climb, walk, ride, and bike.

From stargazing beyond our stratosphere to simply immersing yourself in nature's sounds, here's what to expect from each of England's ten national parks, beginning with the most northerly and working south.

Northumberland

Northumberland is England's least populated national park, covering 405 square miles. Choose a walking route that is appropriate for your level of fitness, and keep an eye out in the woods - this is one of the few sites in

England where you may still see red squirrels. A part of the Unesco-listed Hadrian's Wall - the Roman wall that runs coast to coast - runs through the park's south.

Visit Kielder Observatory, which is accessible all year, to see "some of the darkest skies in the world" and to see the Milky Way and other cosmic beauties. This park is one of England's last real wildernesses. The ideal months to visit are April to May, when lambs can be seen, and August, when the moors become purple with blossoming heather.

Hiking and water activities are popular in the Lake District.
The Lake District, one of Britain's most visited national parks, is famed for its beautiful hill climbs and water-based activities. There are plenty of chances for boating, paddleboarding, kayaking, and fishing in the lakes, tarns, and beaches here.

The region is also rich in literary ties. Have you ever wondered what prompted Beatrix Potter to pen The Tale of Peter Rabbit? Then you (and any children) will enjoy connecting the surrounding surroundings with the stories of Beatrix Potter's World. Interested in learning why Wordsworth "wandered lonely as a cloud"? Then visit Cockermouth's Wordsworth House or Grasmere's Dove Cottage and Wordsworth Museum. Lakeland's magnificent hills and reflected lakes have inspired these writers and many more creatives.

With a slew of creative eateries and gorgeous day spas (the outdoor hot tub at Low Wood Bay has stunning views of Windermere), it's difficult to leave. The villages get crowded in the summer, so if you don't mind the water being a little colder, the best time to visit is in the fall, when it's less crowded and the autumn colors are beginning to shine.

The North York Moors have spectacular atmospheric views.

The North York Moors are made up of windswept moorland, dales (valleys), and coast, which is especially lovely in August and September when the heather blossoms. The majority of the moorland is open access area, which means you can wander away from the trails. It's best visited by car, as you'll drive along ridgetop roads above lush green valleys, spotting weathered stone crosses that trace the paths of ancient highways.

If you don't have a car, you can take the steam train from Pickering to Whitby, the UK's gothic capital, and then walk along the walking paths that connect the stations along the way. Because it doubles as Hogsmeade Station in the movies, a stop at scenic Goathland is certain to be popular with Harry Potter enthusiasts.

Hikers seeking for a challenge will like the Yorkshire Dales.

The Yorkshire Dales are one of the best places in England for trekking and cycling. Hundreds of miles of trails lined with drystone walls wind through picturesque valleys and picture-postcard communities where sheep still graze on the greens. England's best examples of karst scenery, formed by precipitation dissolving the underlying limestone bedrock, can be seen in the limestone terrain of the southern Dales.

The popular Yorkshire Three Peaks Challenge, a 24-mile trek that must encompass all three peaks and be finished in 12 hours, is held in the Dales. The 30-meter-high Ribblehead Viaduct, an extraordinary work of Victorian engineering that connects Settle and Carlisle, is nearby. Visit between April and May, when tourists are outnumbered by lambs.

The Peak District National Park is the greatest for climbers and cavers.

The lovely Peak District, England's first national park, is the southernmost point of the Pennines and a popular day excursion from Manchester. There are hills, valleys, moorland, and escarpments, but no summits. The slopes are filled with rocky outcrops and grand buildings like Chatsworth House and Haddon Hall, while ancient stone settlements are folded into wrinkles in the terrain. The Dark Peak is dominated by exposed moorland and gritstone, while the White Peak is dominated by limestone dales to the south.

Climbers visit the gritstone outcrops of Stanage Edge or the Roaches to ascend the cliffs and boulders, and cavers visit because there are many subsurface formations. Those who like to explore cave networks rather than scramble through them can join tours at Poole's Cavern's enormous limestone tunnels or Treak Cliff Cavern's mining experience.

Boating and bird-watching are popular activities on the Broads.

The Broads are a protected wetland in Norfolk (and a minor piece of Suffolk) that consists of shallow lakes, coastline, and navigable windmill-lined canals. The area is filled with nature, so if you enjoy bird watching, butterflies, or hoping to sight a seal pup, here is the place to go.

On a boat journey, you can see the many habitats of reed beds, fens, and marshland - tourist boats leave daily from towns throughout the Broads (Wroxham is a suitable inland base), or you can charter one yourself for a more hands-on view of life on the water. This is also a popular kayaking, canoeing, paddleboarding, and sailing location.

Take a long-distance hike in the South Downs.
The South Downs National Park has almost 600 square miles of terrain sculpted by centuries of farming. Take any of the car-free trails, bridleways, walks, or even disused railway lines for breathtaking vistas that span the Weald and all the way to the seaside. The South Downs Way traverses the chalk and flint range from Winchester in the west to the beach town of Eastbourne in the east. The journey takes about a week to complete, although the greatest part is the approach into Eastbourne over the top of the white cliffs and Beachy Head, which is an easy day walk.

It is possible to take public transportation to various parts of the route, rent a bike somewhere along the way, or simply sit and admire the vistas that inspired writers such as Virginia Woolf and Jane Austen. The South Downs are beautiful at any time of year, but the months of May to October are ideal for exploring.

Keep an eye out for wildlife in the New Forest.
The New Forest is neither new nor entirely forest, consisting of heathland, woodland, bogs, farming, and shoreline. It has hundreds of miles of walking and cycling paths, as well as historic attractions such as Buckler's Hard, Hurst Castle, and Beaulieu.

Nature, however, takes center role here, and you may see ponies, cattle, or donkeys strolling nonchalantly into the road. They are released loose in the forest by commoners, who are local landowners who have the authority to allow their animals to graze in the national park. Pigs are often introduced in the fall to clean fallen acorns. There are also five distinct species of deer in the park, however they are more difficult to identify than the ponies. Visit Bolderwood, near Lyndhurst, to see fallow deer from the observation platform. Rare birds nest in the heathlands, and many species of butterflies can be seen. Begin at the New Forest Centre in Lyndhurst, which, together with adjacent Brockenhurst, serves as a suitable starting point for exploring the area. You may even visit on a day trip from London by train, though you'll wish you could stay longer.

Exmoor, Europe's first Dark Sky Reserve, is ideal for beginning astronomers.

Exmoor has a diverse scenery of stony river basins, lonely moorland, and coastal cliffs where life is in sync with the rhythms and hues of the seasons. It's a touch addictive, and you might not want to leave. Mountain bikers will discover a plethora of hard trails and bridleways to ride throughout the park, while on-road cyclists will enjoy some of the park's stunning views.

Exmoor was Europe's first declared Dark Sky Reserve due to its unparalleled astronomy prospects. To get the most of the experience, download its Dark Skies Pocket Guide or attend the yearly celebration in October. Visit the dramatic seaside town of Porlock, as well as the twin villages of Lynton and Lynmouth, which are linked by a Victorian cliff railway, with Lynton at the top and Lynmouth and its picturesque harbor on the coast.

Dartmoor is the ideal national park for wild camping.

Dartmoor is known for its extensive moorland interspersed with impressive granite tors (rock outcrops or stacks, generally on a hill) and deep forested river valleys with tinkling streams. While the landscapes may appear bleak, there is evidence of human activity dating back to the Bronze Age in this region.

Hiking, cycling, horseback riding, climbing, and white-water kayaking are all popular outdoor sports, and there are plenty of rustic pubs and country-house hotels to stay in when the fog comes in. Follow one of the national park's themed walking trails to get a greater sense of the countryside, and keep an eye out for the distinctive Dartmoor ponies grazing on the moors. Wild camping is permitted in many areas of Dartmoor - check the authority's excellent interactive map before venturing out - but whatever you do, be aware that mist and rain might descend unexpectedly.

Chapter 18: England's Top Ten Beach Escapes

The English beach is known for its honking, beeping amusements, loud stag parties, and persistent gusts that require erecting a windbreak to keep the sand out of your sandwiches.

That's just one side of the English coast. The other side is spectacular, with untamed stretches of beach stretching to the horizon, seafood adventures down the shoreline, barreling waves, buffeting winds for kitesurfing and windsurfing, and sand so white it could compete with the Caribbean.

Whether you prefer typical coastal resorts, urban beaches, or long, calm sands, you'll find a beach in England that matches your expectations. Here's our guide to the top sand and shingle beaches in England.

1. Norfolk's Holkham National Nature Reserve and Beach
Beautiful Holkham Hall, in addition to being one of England's most spectacular country estates, also looks after the stunning Holkham National

Nature Reserve and Beach, possibly Norfolk's most exquisite strip of dune-backed beach.

It is accessed via a long journey across the marshes, as are all beaches on the north Norfolk coast, yet what awaits at the end would not appear out of place on America's Atlantic coast - boundless sand and tufted dunes fanned by steady sea breezes. Make time to see Holkham Hall, a beautiful Palladian villa created to hold the first Earl of Leicester's Grand Tour treasures.

The Lynx Coastliner bus connects a succession of marsh-backed beaches surrounding Holkham, from undiscovered Brancaster to the lovely coastal village of Wells-next-the-Sea. Sanders Coaches' Coasthopper operates east from Wells all the way to the Victorian resort of Cromer.

2. East Sussex's Brighton Beach

Brighton Beach may not be known for its sand or tranquility, but its mix of piers, seaside amusements, faded (and restored) seafront hotels, and kissme-quick nightlife is the living embodiment of the English seaside. Brighton's popularity as a destination for international students, clubbers, and the LGBTIQ+ community only adds to the excitement.

On summer weekends, it may be difficult to find a towel on the steep ramp of pebbles leading down to the water, but the promenade runs for miles, the pier is packed with rides and arcade machines, fish-and-chip shops abound, and there's plenty to do inland, from the wedding-cake-like Royal Pavilion to the quirky shops and cafes tucked away on the lanes behind the beach.

After braving the summer throng, go for the hills, notably the South Downs, for some well-deserved peace and quiet. This stunning swath of high chalk grassland begins just north of Brighton and is covered by the lovely South Downs Way walking trail.

3. Woolacombe Beach (Devon)

In the opinion of holidaymakers, Devon's beaches are second only to Cornwall's sands, and charming Woolacombe Beach near Barnstaple is a particular stunner. From dawn to dusk, three miles of vast golden sands, dependable surf breakers, and a backdrop of rolling green hills keep families entertained. The secluded setting in north Devon keeps the tourists at bay, though it does get crowded in the summer.

If you get tired of the sand, there are walking routes crisscrossing the verdant hills of the North Devon Coast Area of Outstanding Natural Beauty just inland from the beach.

4. Viking Bay, Broadstairs, Kent.
The charm of this small cove in Broadstairs, Kent, stems in part from its adorable, cliff-enclosed curve of sand, and in part from the voyage back in time it provides sunbathers. Italian-owned gelaterias serve real gelato behind 1950s facades on the roads that slope down to the beach, while an old-fashioned puppet performance entertains the tots out on the sand.

As the afternoon fades into the evening, explore the superior eateries in the alleyways above the beach - the meal at the Little Sicilian is authentically Italian.

Planning tip: The Kent coast rail route connects London to Broadstairs, looping around to adjacent Ramsgate and Margate, both of which have sandy beaches. Margate is loud and vibrant, with a well-known amusement park, whilst Ramsgate is more refined, with a large public beach and some attractive secondhand shops.

5. Blackpool Beach - Lancashire, Blackpool
Blackpool Beach, Northern England's answer to Brighton Beach, is long, sandy, and lapped by mild breakers, making it ideal for families who flock to paddle in the shallows and walk along the vast, wave-patterned beach during low tide. One of England's most famous entertainment strips is located behind the beach, giving hours of seaside fun.

Choose from coastal bars, fish-and-chip eateries, and garish arcades crammed with slot machines, or the thrills and spills of Blackpool Pleasure Beach and the vistas from Blackpool Tower. It has everything you'd expect from an English seaside, but the noise and congestion may drive some people away.

6. Kynance Cove on Cornwall's Lizard Peninsula

Cornwall's beaches are similar to those of the Caribbean and South Pacific, but without the palm trees and with fried scampi instead of barbecued conch. Summer crowds can be so dense on the sandy strips in popular tourist destinations like Penzance, St Ives, and Porthcurno that football fields are used as overflow parking.

We recommend quieter beaches in Cornwall, such as the Lizard Peninsula's wave-lashed, rock-strewn Kynance Cove, where fingers of white sand curl between rugged outcrops, churning white horses fill the air with spray, and the steep walk down from the car park deters fair-weather beachgoers.

Cornwall is England's best surfing destination, with some of the best waves between October and April, when the tourist crowds thin. The most famous breaks in North Cornwall are at Newquay and Bude; for beginners, the broad beach at Polzeath includes a surf school and plenty of space to train.

7. Northumberland's Bamburgh Beach

What could be better than a beach with a castle? Beaches in England get larger and wilder (and a touch colder in summer) as you travel north, but the beaches in Bamburgh are breathtakingly beautiful, backed by the looming ramparts of Bamburgh Castle, which was used by English kings until being renovated by Victorian industrialist William Armstrong.

The beach faces the Farne Islands, which were teeming with wildlife and home to a thriving monastic community until Henry VIII's catastrophic feud with the Catholic church, and walking pathways continue along the shore to other coves, caves, and castles.

8. Southwold - Suffolk

Suffolk has plenty of seaside towns, but eccentric Southwold stands out for its calm demeanor, dainty town center, and pretty collection of beaches, from the groyne-crossed sands near the pier to the dune-flanked Denes Beach, which feels like a wilderness despite being just a stroll from the High Street.

The village behind the sand is also charming, with a central lighthouse, the interesting satirical arcade games of the Under the Pier Show, and delightful wafting aromas from the Adnams Brewery.

Southwold is an excellent location for exploring the Suffolk Coast's bird-filled nature areas. Bitterns, curlews, and marsh harriers are just a few of the species seen at RSPB Minsmere and Dunwich Heath's beach-fronted coastal wetlands.

9. Whitby Beach (Yorkshire)

Whitby Beach makes the list not only because of its beautiful sand, but also because of its environment. This broad, shallow strand is flanked by a row of rainbow-colored beach huts and Whitby buildings that rise steeply to the ethereal ruins of Whitby Abbey.

Among other things, this is where the world's most renowned vampire, Dracula, made landfall in England as he chased his would-be bride in Bram Stoker's Dracula. It's a lovely location that appeals to both families and goths and horror aficionados.

After you've seen the beach and the abbey, proceed to the upliftingly beautiful footpaths of North York Moors National Park for some quiet contemplation.

10. West Wittering Beach, West Sussex.

Kitesurfers and windsurfers flock to the indented strip of shoreline facing the Isle of Wight like moths to a flame. The beaches of Bournemouth and Sandbanks near Poole are popular destinations for surfers, but we recommend avoiding the crowds at nearby West Wittering, at the mouth of Chichester Harbor in West Sussex.

This beautiful Blue Flag-rated beach features fine sand, a ring of dunes, and shallow waves excellent for surfing, windsurfing, kiteboarding, and stand-up paddleboarding.

Chapter 19: Unveiling the 33 Best Beaches in the UK: From Sandy Bays to Sun-soaked Retreats

Whatever the season, the beaches of the United Kingdom are among the best attractions the country has to offer. But it's during the summer when those beaches really shine. What could be better than fresh sea air, soft sand under your toes, thunderously crashing waves, and warm weather? Maybe the weather bit is a touch ambitious, but when all of those things come together, life really doesn't get any better.

The United Kingdom is home to dozens of breathtaking beaches just waiting to be discovered. These islands have it all, from wide, sandy crowd-pleasers conveniently located near glittering seaside towns to isolated coves with incredibly pure water accessible only by boat or trek. Whether you're looking for picnic areas, nature watching, or vistas you'd never think were in the UK, our curated guide to the UK's finest beaches is below.

1. Devon's Woolacombe Sands

Woolacombe, one of north Devon's most popular hangouts, is a beast of a beach with miles of continuous golden sand - construct gigantic sandcastles and play hide & seek in the dunes. This gorgeous harbor is popular with surfers and families, and it also offers rock pools for children to explore. Grab a bite to eat at one of the seaside cafés, or head to nearby Ilfracombe for a more substantial meal.

What you should know

During busy times (see dates here), there is a lifeguard service.

Arrival

Barnstaple, the nearest train station, is a 30-minute drive away.

Stay

The Watersmeet Hotel, located on the peaceful end of Woolacombe Bay, offers breathtaking views of the sea and Lundy Island. The hotel has a pool, although visitors are more likely to use the private steps to Combesgate Beach. It's riddled with rockpools and is rarely crowded.

2. Bamburgh Beach, Northumberland

The northeastern coast of England can get canny freezing, which presumably explains why its great lengths of stunning shoreline have been criminally disregarded by holiday-goers. Bamburgh's immaculate 1.5-mile-long white sand beach is one of the greatest in the area, and it rests beneath a magnificent eleventh-century castle that was recently used as a movie set for the latest Indiana Jones film. The location is also great for boat trips to the Farne Islands, which are just off the shore and where you may see seals, puffins, and possibly dolphins, as well as the charming medieval settlement and the RNLI's Grace Darling Museum.

What you should know

Despite the fact that the world's first lifeboat was developed and tested in Bamburgh, there is no coastguard on the beach these days.

126

Arrival

Chathill is the nearest station.

Stay

The Bamburgh Coach House, an airy two-bedroom conversion a mile down the road from the hamlet, is one of several charming holiday houses in the area managed by Coastal Retreats. There is a large yard and the bedrooms have fantastic sea views.

3. Kynance Cove, Cornwall.

Kynance Cove is one of Cornwall's most photographed beaches, thanks to its white sand, crystal blue waters, and stunning rock formations. At high tide, it virtually disappears, but if you time it properly, the receding waves will reveal a spectacular network of coves and caverns with names like the Ladies Bathing Pool and the Drawing Room. The descent from the car park is steep and takes about ten minutes; treat yourself at the bottom with crab sandwiches from the popular Kynance Cove Café.

What you should know

Are you coming this summer? It gets extremely busy, and the National Trust car lot is frequently filled by 11 a.m. - arrive early to ensure a spot. Between Easter and September, dogs are not permitted.

Arrive

This one requires a car as it is just under an hour's drive from Penzance.

Stay

A cozy cabin that accommodates four people is very near to the Kynance Cove Café. It's furnished in relaxing beach colors, has a wood-burning stove, and its own picnic bench in the garden - what more could you want?

4. Barafundle Bay, Pembrokeshire, Wales.

Another award-winning beach in Wales, Barafundle Bay, drew international recognition when it was rated one of the greatest in the world. Visitors will reach a picture-perfect beach after following the scenic half-mile journey from Stackpole Quay, where little turquoise waves lap up against a crescent of sand. The secluded cove is ideal for swimming, and the Pembrokeshire Coast Path provides additional paths for ramblers. Visit the tea cafe at Stackpole Walled Gardens (a ten-minute drive away) for refreshments with a feel-good factor. People with learning difficulties can gain work experience and training at this communal garden and farm.

What you should know
There are no amenities on site, so bring whatever you need and take it with you. Also, make cautious to verify the tide times and leave early to avoid becoming stuck.

Arrival
Lamphey rail station is a 13-minute drive away.

Stay
If you like charming country pubs, reserve a room at The Stackpole Inn. Downstairs, a wood fire warms the restaurant, which serves Welsh-reared steaks with locally produced food. Upstairs, the bedrooms are stylish and cozy, and the traditional Welsh breakfast is not to be missed.

5. Pentle Bay, Tresco, Isles of Scilly
This next beach will require some effort to access, but it will be well worth it. Pentle Bay is an isolated length of dazzling white sand lapped by glassy-blue waves on the Isles of Scilly, an unspoiled archipelago off the coast of Cornwall. The magnificence of this shoreline has not gone unnoticed, as the Wall Street Journal named it one of the best four under-the-radar beaches in the world. Despite this, it's still relatively calm - perhaps the frigid water helps.

What you should know
Abbey Gardens, the nearest bathrooms, are a ten-minute walk away.

Arrival

The flight from Newquay to the Isles of Scilly takes 30 minutes, followed by a 20-minute boat ride from St Mary's to Tresco and a 25-minute walk to Pentle Bay. (Trust us, you won't be sorry.)

Stay
The New Inn, located on the opposite side of the island but only a 20-minute walk from Pentle Bay, is more than just a bar, with an AA Rosette-awarded restaurant and modern, comfortable rooms, some with their own sun terrace overlooking the swimming pool.

6. Holkham Beach, Norfolk

Holkham, easily one of the best-looking beaches in the UK, would be overrun with people if it were just a little closer to London. The beach, which makes you feel a million miles away from civilization, has justifiably starred in many a film and pop video, including All Saints' smash hit "Pure Shores." An expansive sandy length is backed by a lush nature reserve with a maze of well-marked walking routes; explore the pinewoods and saltmarshes to view orchids, sea lavender, and unusual birds.

What you should know
Wells-next-the-sea has the nearest bathrooms, which are a short drive away. For further amenities, park at Holkham Hall, which also has a play area, café, and museum.

Arrival
Sheringham, the nearest train station, is a 45-minute drive away.

Stay
The Victoria Inn boasts 20 freshly polished rooms with a beautiful contemporary-cottage ambiance. Walk through the walled rose gardens, dine in the café for fresh shellfish and samphire from the Holkham coastline, or walk the few minutes to the beach's magnificent sands.

7. Whitby Sands, North Yorkshire

Whitby Sands, located just a few minutes' walk from the idyllic former fishing town of Whitby, provides a perfect British seaside setting, complete with bright beach huts, a beautiful stretch of white sand, and miles of the big blue. Magpie Café's battered fish is so popular that lines often snake down the street. Have you been to Whitby if you haven't been to Fortune's Kippers? These fish fans have been smoking scales for over 139 years, and they do a darn fine job at it. Purchase a smoked kipper from their shop over the bridge from Whitby Beach.

What you should know
In the summer, dogs are not permitted.

Arrival
Whitby is the nearest train station.

Stay
La Rosa is unlikely to be found anywhere else in the UK, let alone in Whitby. The hotel has embraced the 'Alice in Wonderland' theme, adapting it for a grown-up audience with whimsical decor in each room. It was a former haunt of Lewis Carroll when he visited the seaside. Breakfast is delivered in a hamper to your door and is best consumed beneath your quilt.

8. Rhossili Bay, Gower, Wales.
Rhossili Bay is remote but not unnoticed, with titles like 'best beach in Europe' and 'top ten beaches in the world' among its accolades. The steep, winding walk down to the coast from Rhossili village is stunning, with panoramic views over three miles of golden sand and, on clear days, to the coastline of North Devon. The beach itself is all about nature, but there are facilities nearby: visit the National Trust shop and visitor center near the village, or stop by the Bay Bistro for homemade soups and sandwiches if you've forgotten your packed lunch.

What you should know
Dog-friendly all year round.

Arrival

Closest train station is Gowerton, a 37-minute drive away.

Stay

The views from The Worm's Head Hotel are so staggering, you'll barely notice the dated decor. We're not fussed about a few mad carpets when every room has a view over the cliffs of Rhossili Bay. Take advantage of the view with their restaurant's cliff-top terrace – bagsy a table and settle in for some proper pub grub.

9. Camber Sands, Sussex

Camber Sands is so wide and golden you'll be transported to other shores. In fact, this Arabian-looking beach has been used for a number of desert film locations, including Carry On Follow That Camel. The sandy shore stretches for almost five miles before it starts to turn into shingles towards the eastern end. From the western side, it's four miles to the pretty town of Rye, where cobbled streets, proper pubs and rickety old houses make for a charming day trip.

What you should know

Dogs on a lead are allowed on the beach, although there are restricted zones from May to September.

Arrival

Closest train station is Rye, a 12-minute drive away.

Stay

The duneside boutique hotel The Gallivant's restaurant sources virtually all of its ingredients from within a ten-mile radius. Residents of the 20 bedrooms can lounge by log fires, read in the book-lined snug, or prop up the bar – which is dog-friendly, by the way.

10. Summerleaze, Cornwall

One of Bude's best-loved beaches, Summerleaze is the embodiment of the classic British seafront. Perfect for families who want more home comforts, cute beach huts are available to hire in a range of prices – splash out on a seafront hut out of season from £35 for a week. At low tide, a paddling pool emerges, as does an expanse of golden sand for walks along the coast. And there's no need to bring a packed lunch – the family beach has brilliant bars and restaurants within walking distance.

What you should know
Dogs should stay on a lead from 10am to 6pm.

Arrival
Closest train station is Okehampton, a 50-minute drive away.

Stay
The Beach (yes, that's the hotel's name) balances style and charm with slick contemporary rooms and a traditional Victorian terrace overlooking Summerleaze beach. The restaurant showcases the best of Cornish produce, while the beach bar comes to life with live music on Sunday afternoons.

11. Blackpool Sands, Devon
The small entry fee for Blackpool Sands is worth it for a spotlessly clean coastline despite a high number of visitors, while families will appreciate the modern and well-equipped facilities. The wide pebble beach is one of the cleanest in Devon and is sheltered by pine trees and evergreens, while rocks at the far corners provide shade. Feeling brave? Visitors can hire kayaks for £18 per hour.

What you should know
The entry is around £8, but changes depending on the season – call 01803 771800 for up-to-date prices, and barbecues are allowed after 5pm.

Arrival
Closest train station is Totnes, a 30-minute drive away.

Stay

Views don't get much more stunning than those at Gara Rock. The secluded hotel and restaurant is perched on the coastline just 30 minutes by car from Blackpool Sands. Inside, the artsy decor features grand open fires, cosy seating areas with sheepskins and board games. The kitchen celebrates local produce including Dartmouth kippers, vegetables from its onsite allotment and locally foraged ingredients.

12. Watergate Bay, Cornwall

You'll find big waves at this lively bay, which makes it a magnet for surfers and thrill-seekers. The family-friendly spot is buzzing with extreme sports activities all year round; take surf lessons from Extreme Academy, or just spectate from your deckchair on the two-mile-long sandy shoreline. Events take place throughout the year. And dog owners can rejoice – there's no seasonal ban and pooches are always welcome.

What you should know

Lifeguards are on watch during peak periods (check here for dates).

Arrival

Closest train station is Newquay, a 10-minute drive away.

Stay

Set slap-bang in the middle of the beach, the family-run Watergate Bay Hotel is the beating heart of the bay. The second generation of owners took over in 2004, and the 69-room hotel saw an £8 million redevelopment, transforming it into a hub of activity and relaxation. Expect luxury rooms with beach-chic decor (some featuring freestanding baths with sea views) and a jam-packed events programme.

13. Beer Beach, Devon

Fishing still dominates this shingle beach; boats, nets and buoys are spread all over the pebbles. It makes for a wholesome day out for visitors, who can find their sea legs on a mackerel fishing expedition, visit the jaunty fishmongers that sits on the slipway, or just hole up in one of the stripey deck chairs on the shore. The adjacent village is charming and picturesque, but the best lunch is found at the beachfront cafe, which serves up a nostalgic menu of sandwiches (hello, prawn Marie Rose cut into triangles), ice cream and cracking views of the jagged chalk cliffs.

What you should know
Everyone loves Beer. Best to visit off-season for maximum chill.

Arrival
Closest train station is Axminster, a 20-minute drive away.

Stay
Glebe House is the former family home of owner Hugo, and together with his wife Olive they have transformed the rural Georgian abode with a metropolitan maximalist makeover. Expect mismatched wallpaper, modern artwork and an accomplished kitchen knocking out rustic dishes and homemade charcuterie (so don't get too attached to the cute pigs that welcome you on the way in).

14. Porthcurno Beach, Cornwall
Small but perfectly formed, this little turquoise bay is the stuff that dreams are made of. At least that's what the 'Poldark' location scouts thought: they used this beautiful beach on the western foot of Cornwall as the location for a dream sequence in season two. But it's not just actors that like to hang out here: dolphins and basking sharks are sometimes spotted in the calm waters, too. The soft, white-shell sand and freshwater stream also make this a popular beach with families. On the granite cliffs above, you'll also find the legendary Minack Theatre, quite possibly the most attractive open-air theatre in the UK.

What you should know
There's a dog ban from Easter to October 1, and lifeguards keep watch during summer months only.

Arrival
Closest train station is Penzance, a 25-minute drive away.

Stay
Surrounded by ferns and foxgloves and sweeping lawns to the sea, Cove Cottage is one of the most delightful retreats in Cornwall. The tiny B&B offers romantic getaways, complete with four-poster beds and private flower-filled terraces. There's chintz and geraniums by the bucketload and we're totally on board.

15. Scarista Beach, Isle of Harris, Scotland
One of the most dazzling beaches in the Hebrides, even on a cloudy day Scarista Beach is breathtaking – visit in the sunshine and you'll struggle to pull yourself away from the sugary-soft sand and inviting water. Despite its remote location, there are some top foodie trips nearby. Pop into Scarista House, the Georgian manor set on the edge of the sand for a fancy afternoon tea, or drive ten minutes south to The Temple Café, a cute, hand-built stone-and-timber café with a counter full of tempting cakes.

What you should know
There's no signage or parking, but that helps to keep this hidden paradise safe from the majority of tourists.

Arrival
One hour 25-minute bus ride from Stornoway.

Stay
For dramatic views, starry skies and cosy fires, book a stay at the Oran Na Mara. Perched to the north of Scarista beach, its curved walls make the most of the azure sea views with floor-to-ceiling windows, and winter offers a chance to see the Northern Lights from its secluded patio area.

16. Gwynedd's Morfa Nefyn Beach
The distant peaks of the Yr Eifl (Rival Mountains) provide a lovely background to this beach on the Lln Peninsula's lonely North Coast. The

sandy beach, sheltered by low cliffs, is a fantastic sun trap with crystal blue seas and excellent rock pools. The ancient Coch Inn is part of a tiny cluster of buildings near the beach's head and serves traditional pub fare.

What you should know
A neighboring National Trust car park provides parking. There is no coastguard stationed here.

Stay
The Old Boat Store is a cosy self-catering apartment with fantastic sea views and a wonderful nautical motif suiting its heritage. It sleeps five people in the main Captain's Room and the bunk bed-filled Crew Room, and it has an open-plan living area and a small gravel yard (equipped with a BBQ).

17. Dorset's Durdle Door and Lulworth Cove
Water smashed through a stack of rocks on the Jurassic Coast over 10,000 years ago, becoming one of the most beautiful landforms in the UK. Durdle Door is now a magnificent archway that frames the crystal-clear waters beyond. The rock structure is best enjoyed in conjunction with a visit to adjacent Lulworth Cove. A 30-minute walk along the coastal road will take you to a secluded white pebble beach that is nearly completely circular, providing a haven of tranquility as you watch the boats bobbing in the emerald water.

What you should know
During the summer months, the parking lot can fill up quickly; cycle or arrive early to get a spot.

Arrival
Wool, the nearest train station, is a 15-minute drive away.

Stay

Travel light by booking a wooden camping pod at Durdle Door Holiday Park. The pods, which are only 200 metres from the beach, provide picnic tables, heaters, and electricity, but you must bring your own bedding.

18. White Park Bay, County Antrim, Northern Ireland.

This magnificent three-mile stretch of white sand is nestled away in a peaceful place on the generally rugged shoreline that surrounds the Giant's Causeway. Despite the popularity of Northern Ireland's first World Heritage Site, the bay's remote location ensures that it is never overcrowded, even in fine weather. When the conditions are ideal, you may even hear the sand on the beach'singing,' an exceedingly unusual event in which the sand particles vibrate together and make a weird humming sound. There are additional fossils scattered across the beach, as well as a Neolithic cairn in the nearby dunes.

What you should know

The beach is unsafe for swimming due to strong rip currents.

Arrival

Coleraine is the nearest train station, from which daily buses travel to the beach.

Stay

The Fullerton Arms is a clean and cozy family-run inn directly on the seashore, with modern minimalist rooms available at a reasonable price and a superb restaurant featuring a variety of local mussels cooked in various ways.

19. Tankerton Beach, Kent.

Tankerton Beach has it all: rolling grassy slopes, a long promenade, attractive beach huts, and, of course, the sea, with the added advantage of Whitstable, one of the UK's buzziest coastal towns, just a 20-minute walk away. When you've had your fill of the pebble beach, head into town to refuel. Share a drink and mezze at the popular beachside tavern JoJo's, or feast on fresh seafood at the rustic and respected Whitstable Oyster Company.

What you should know
It is a dog-free zone from May 1 to September 30.

Arrival
Whitstable is the nearest train station.

Stay
The Marine Hotel is the seaside refuge of dreams, with the beach directly on its doorstep. Splurge on a superior sea-view room, which features sophisticated, classic furnishings and double doors that swing open onto a private balcony with a view of the ocean.

20. Llandudno's North Shore Beach, Wales
The North Shore is Llandudno's best-equipped beach, with a bandstand, Victorian pier, and summer donkey rides. For generations, it has been a popular beach resort, and many traditions, such as the Punch and Judy show, which appears on the promenade in fine weather, have survived.

What you should know
Climb Great Orme for breathtaking gull's-eye views of the seashore.

Arrival
Llandudno train station is a 9-minute walk away.

Stay
With a chintzy room at the Osborne House Hotel, you can embrace the Victoriana atmosphere. Inside, it's all frills, antiques, and chandeliers, with no hint of driftwood. Expect exquisite sea-facing accommodations with diverse decor acquired from all around the world. It's not your standard coastal hotel, according to the owners.

21.West Wittering Beach, Sussex

West Wittering beach is a clean resort with abundant facilities, including three blocks of toilets, drinking-water taps, and shower blocks. It is surrounded by bushy dunes and green marshland ideal for bird-spotting. After a refreshing dip in the surf, warm up with a cup of coffee at the beach café or travel five minutes to East Wittering, where eateries serve a greater selection of lunch and dinner options - we recommend Drifters for craft beer, homely meals, and veggie alternatives.

What you should know
The Hinge has dangerous currents, so don't go splashing around there.

Arrival
Chichester, the nearest train station, is an 18-minute drive away.

Stay
Millstream Hotel, a traditional British getaway, is located back from the bustling beach amid wonderfully manicured gardens. The bedrooms are opulent, and the two-AA Rosette restaurant is a must-see.

22. Portstewart Strand, Northern Ireland

There are rolling dunes and virgin sands between the mouth of the River Bann and Portstewart. And designated drivers rejoice: the two-mile stretch is one of the few spots in Ireland where cars may still drive directly onto the beach. It's not for everyone, but it's extremely popular with families who want to picnic on the beach. After that, pack up and walk 30 minutes to Three Kings Coffee Company for a decent flat white, sourdough sandwiches, and seriously amazing pancake stacks.

What you should know
The National Trust facilities are open from 10 a.m. to 5 p.m.

Arrival
Castlerock train station is a 6-minute drive away.

Stay

Saltwater House, with its plumped Egyptian cotton linens and optional nutritional treatment service (complete with Instagrammable chia smoothie bowls), wouldn't look out of place on Santa Monica's seaside. A glance out the window of your stylishly designed home, on the other hand, will remind you that you're in the UK, since there are stunning views of the Portstewart Strand and the Atlantic Ocean.

23. Formby Beach, Merseyside
The lovely, family-friendly Formby beach is surrounded by a network of dunes that migrate at an alarming rate of four meters per year, making it one of the National Trust's fastest-changing shorelines. The shifting sands are revealing prehistoric footprints: walk along the beach to find them, then look out to sea for breathtaking vistas of the Irish Sea. The woodlands that border the beach are managed to protect the habitat of the red squirrel - visit the National Trust's website to download 'squirrel walks'. While you're here, take a 30-minute trip to Crosby Beach to see Antony Gormley's landmark public artwork 'Another Place'.

What you should know
There are facilities on Victoria Road, and some of the woodlands have pushchair-accessible routes.

Arrival
Formby is the nearest station.

Stay
Watkinssons Farm is more on the rustic end of the glamping scale, which is why we like it. It has cozy bell tents overlooking a wild meadow, a roaring log burner, a basketful of logs, and a good double bed.

24. Compton Bay, Isle of Wight
Beach bums will be happy hanging out on the sandy shelves or surfing the waves of Compton Bay, but extend your legs across the lush grassy banks and you might see some dinosaurs. When the tide goes out, head to the east of the Compton Bay car park at Hanover Point and seek for large

three-toed Iguanodon foot casts near the base of the cliffs. It's a ten-minute drive to Freshwater, where The Freshwater Coffee House delivers a nice flat white, or a 30-minute drive south to Ventnor, where Stripped serves OTT burgers and a cheeky cocktail.

What you should know
In the summer, there are on-site restrooms and a food truck.

Arrival
Newport is a one-hour bus trip away.

Stay
Tiny Homes Holidays' collection of adorable tiny houses is far from complete. Every dwelling, each with its own charming design and name, is like an eco-friendly Tardis, full with sustainable features like solar electricity, composting toilets, and recycled water. During your stay, participate in equally adorable classes like spoon-whittling and willow-weaving.

25. Camusdarach Beach, Scotland
If craggy Scottish coastline is your thing, Camusdarach Beach is a must-see. This ribbon of pillow-soft white sand is cradled by clear-blue waves and framed by stunning, jagged rocks and is one of the cleanest, most tranquil beaches on the western coast. What's the catch? There aren't many amenities, but the surrounding town of Morar (an eight-minute drive away) provides home comforts in the form of cafés, restaurants, and motels. Continue north to Mallaig, where the Jacobite steam train (as shown in the Harry Potter films) stops. Eat in the renovated dining cars or stay in the refurbished carriages.

What you should know
Bring a picnic lunch because there are no facilities other than a small parking lot.

Arrival

Morar, the nearest train station, is a 10-minute drive away.

Stay
The Wee Lodge has no TV, no internet, and no phone, and they make no apologies about it. It does, however, include a comfortable double bed, the sound of birds singing, and a lovely view of Loch Morar. This isolated getaway on the grounds of a working farm is the ideal spot to unwind and recharge your batteries.

26. Marazion Beach, Cornwall
This beach, in addition to the usual suspects - lifeguards, sand dunes, and rock pools - offers views of the whimsical St Michael's Mount, a little island reachable by a cobbled causeway at low tide. It's crowned by a twelfth-century castle, which houses a mummified cat and a piece of Napoleon's cloak, among other things. I don't know what will tempt you to cross the cobblestones if that doesn't.

What you should know
Have you missed the low tide? Don't worry, you can get a ferry return (from April to October; £2.50 adults, £1.50 under-18s).

Arrival
Penzance, the nearest train station, is a ten-minute drive away.

Stay
The Marazion Hotel has been welcoming guests since the 1700s, so it should know a thing or two about hospitality. Since then, the old coaching inn has been repainted, and bright, seaside-y rooms await. After you've finished creating sandcastles, relax at the hotel's Cutty Sark tavern and restaurant, or curl up with a nice book next to the wood stove in the lounge.

27. Studland Bay, Dorset
You might see a few beach balls at Studland Bay, which is a favorite naturist destination in the UK. If skinny-dipping isn't your thing, head to the south, where you'll find lush heathland and a woodland region with walking

trails where you may view wild deer and birdlife. Studland, the ridiculously cute village that inspired Noddy's Toytown, features a number of restaurants, including the Michelin-starred Pig on the Beach, where simple British cuisine are cooked from ingredients farmed on-site or obtained within a 25-mile radius.

What you should know
There are plenty of amenities, including public wi-fi at the Knoll Beach tourist center.

Arrival
Corfe Castle train station is a 15-minute drive away.

Stay
At Pig on the Beach, the refurbished country manor estate that houses the popular aforementioned restaurant and spa treatment rooms located in a wild meadow, there's quirky furniture and crazy wallpaper galore.

28. Morecambe Beach, Lancashire.
In these parts, Blackpool gets all the attention, yet the stretch of beach around this charming if little faded Lancashire seaside town has the greatest span of intertidal sand flats in the UK (with a whopping five miles of sandy and shingle coastline). Stroll along the promenade to see the TERN Project, an award-winning sculpture trail with steel gannets, cormorants, and razorbills strewn along the beachfront.

What you should know
During peak season, from May to September, dogs are not permitted on the beach.

Arrival
Morecambe station is a short distance from the beach.

Stay

The Midland Hotel, a 1930s art deco classic that has recently been painstakingly refurbished, is directly on the seaside and has rooms with sea views, a sun terrace restaurant, and a stunning circular bar.

29. Luskentyre Beach, Isle of Harris

If you go to Luskentyre out of season, you might have miles of bright-white sand all to yourself. This is one of Harris's largest beaches, just a short drive north of Scarista, and travelers come here to relax on empty coastlines between the blue sky and turquoise water.

What you should know

The facilities are limited, although there are restrooms near the car park. All year, dogs are welcome.

Arrival

Stornoway is 90 minutes away by bus.

Stay

The tiny B&B Shore Cottage isn't the most glamorous place to stay, but what it lacks in style, it makes up for in location. This secluded refuge, which appears to be poised on the edge of the world, is only a ten-minute walk from Luskentyre beach and provides a comfortable base from which to explore the remainder of the island.

30. Cromer Beach, Norfolk.

Aside from the tranquil beaches and crystal-clear rock pools, the majestic Victorian pier is the primary draw here. It's refreshingly free of the usual beach tourist kitsch, instead housing a flourishing theatre with regular soul nights, comedy acts, and creative productions to keep tourists and locals entertained. After the show, go to No. 1 Cromer for the fresh local crab and delectable deep-fried cockle popcorn.

What you should know

Visit during low tide for the best sand action.

Arrival

Cromer is the nearest train station.

Stay

The Gunton Arms is a charming historic tavern located four miles from the shore and a short drive from Cromer. Venison from the adjacent deer park is cooked over an open fire in the pub's kitchen and served with goose fat roast potatoes.

31. Saunton Sands, Devon

Saunton Sands is a three-and-a-half-mile stretch of gold sand flanked by dunes with tufts of green and a row of colorful beach cottages that is popular with families and dog lovers. There's plenty of space for dogs to run around without stepping on the toes of sunbathers, surfers, and beach loungers. There's also a strong sense of community here, with regular beach clean-ups and BBQ days, as well as stunning D-Day festivities that include military rallies and battle reenactments.

What you should know

Swim with caution as there may be riptides near the cliffs.

Arrival

Barnstaple, the nearest train station, is a 20-minute drive away.

Stay

Stay at Saunton Sands Hotel, a beautiful white 1930s Art Deco structure that presides over the vast sandy vista, for the greatest view of the beach. The renovated spa is an excellent reason to stay, and the supervised children's play area with two hours of free childcare is a godsend for parents.

32. Footdee Beach, Aberdeen, Scotland

This broad sandy beach provides a classic seaside feel while being only half a mile from the amenities of Aberdeen city center. As one would anticipate, it is frequently crowded; cyclists and skaters visit the promenade, while water sports enthusiasts frequently hit the waves. On the beachfront, you'll find an amusement park, a leisure park, and a retail park, while the Aberdeen Maritime Museum is located further inland.

What you should know
There is no lifeguard on the beach, and dogs are not permitted between groynes 5 and 13.

Arrival
The beachfront is a 15-minute walk from Aberdeen Station.

Stay
Girdle Ness, only 20 minutes from the city center, is a still-operational lighthouse with surrounding cottages that once housed the lighthouse keepers. Northern Lights Apartments now rents them out as holiday houses, with wonderful uninterrupted views of the North Sea and plenty of dolphin-spotting opportunities.

33. Chesil Beach, Dorset
Put those buckets and spades away; you won't need them here. Chesil Beach is an 18-mile stretch separated from the mainland by a shallow lagoon that is as rocky as it is gorgeous. It's a stunning building that's best seen from the Tout Quarry Nature Reserve and Sculpture Park on the Isle of Portland. Visit the neighboring Crab House Café to refuel, where freshly captured crabs are served with a hammer and bib, and fresh oysters grown on the café's own beds are eaten within minutes of leaving the water.

What you should know
Near the bridge going to the Fortuneswell end of the beach, there is a visitor's center with facilities and a café.

Arrival
Weymouth or Upwey train stations are around a 20-minute drive away.

Stay

The Manor House is a small green paradise on the seaside with delicate, classically elegant rooms. The sixteenth-century manor home has been lovingly refurbished and now houses a restaurant serving modern British meals made with local ingredients.

Chapter 20: Exploring Ireland: Navigating by Car, Bike, or Public Transport

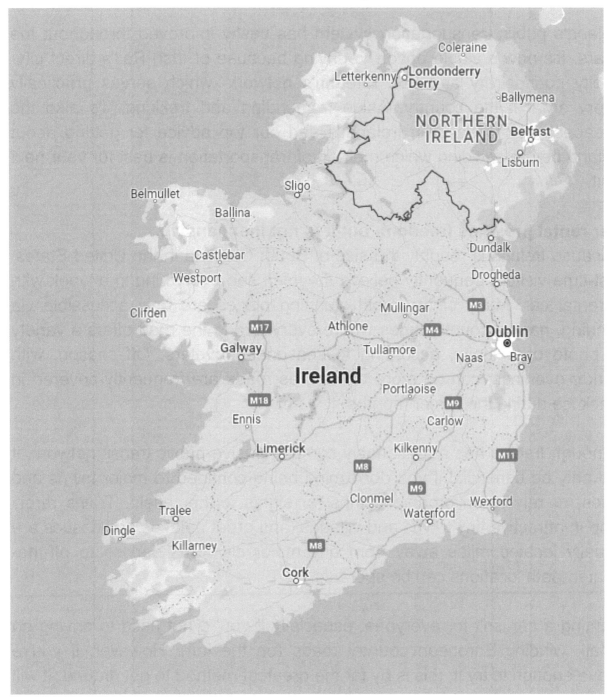

Despite its high cost and lack of environmental credentials, vehicle rental has long been the primary form of transportation for independent travelers to Ireland. Visitors are opting for alternate means to experience the country's stunning coasts, lush countryside, and ancient historical monuments, owing to rising automobile rental charges, tolls, parking fees, and a fuel supply crisis.

Ireland's public transportation system has vastly improved throughout the years. It's now a viable option to driving because of Irish Rail's direct city-to-city connectivity and Bus Éireann's network, which serves practically every area in the country. Aside from riding and trekking, it's also the cheapest way to travel in Ireland. Read our top advice for getting about Ireland before deciding which method of transportation is best for your next visit.

Car rental provides freedom, but it is not inexpensive.
Because Ireland is roughly the size of South Carolina in the United States, first-time visitors frequently believe they can see everything in a week with a rental car. Many of the most stunning places are only accessible via winding, narrow country lanes where every turn in the road offers a variety of photo opportunity, according to seasoned travelers. Off season, with darker evenings, can be more difficult, as roads are frequently covered in black ice during the winter months.

Although Ireland has a reasonably comprehensive public transit network, it will only be beneficial if you don't mind being confined to major towns and cities, or relying on organized trips for sights further afield. Trains rarely stop in attractive tiny towns and villages, and great palaces and castles are usually located miles away from any major city. Bus service to off-the-beaten-path locations can be sporadic.

Renting a car isn't for everyone, especially if you're not used to driving on small, winding European country roads (on the left). However, if you're brave enough to try it, this is by far the greatest method to get around. It will provide you the most freedom and provide you with more options than any other mode of transportation. Simply put, renting a car allows you to see more of Ireland.

Weekly rental fees for a manual-transmission compact vehicle start about €160 and rise considerably in the summer. Out of season, rates are significantly lower.

Unless your stay in Ireland exceeds 6 months, you only need your own valid driver's license (that you've had for at least 6 months) to drive in Ireland. The rules and limits for car rental are similar to those in other European countries and the United States, with two key exceptions: Most rental car companies in the Republic will refuse to rent to you if you are (1) under the age of 25 or beyond the age of 74 (there is no maximum age limit in the North), or (2) if your license has been valid for less than a year.

Driving Laws, Tips, and Warnings Highway safety has become a serious problem in Ireland in recent years. For such a small country, the amount of traffic fatalities is high—Ireland consistently ranks toward the bottom of European league tables for accident rates. In an effort to rein in Irish drivers, the Republic has implemented a penalty "points" system similar to that used in the United Kingdom and the United States. Visitors will not receive points on their licenses, but they may be punished if they speed or commit other driving violations.

In the Republic of Ireland, all distances and speed restrictions on road signs are in kilometers, but in Northern Ireland, they are in miles. Take cautious if you're driving through the borderlands—the border is unmarked, so you could accidentally cross from one side to the other. It's easy to become disoriented and speed up by inadvertently.

Getting acclimated to left-side driving, a left-handed stick shift, tiny roads, and a foreign scenery are all challenges, especially if you're driving alone—it's beneficial if you can bring someone along to assist you navigate. Some people even utilize techniques like affixing a large arrow to the dashboard to remind you that the left lane is your default.

A GPS navigation system can be quite helpful in navigating the countryside, especially in remote areas. Almost all rental companies provide them.

Roundabouts (also known as traffic circles or rotaries in the United States) can be found on most main roadways and take some getting accustomed to. When approaching a roundabout, always yield to traffic arriving from the right and follow traffic to the left, notifying before exiting the circle.

A flashing amber light at a pedestrian traffic light is one indicator that may be confusing to US cars. This usually always comes after a red light and signifies to yield to pedestrians but proceed once the crossing is clear.

The Republic has a limited number of road types. National (N) roads, which connect major cities, are rarely more than two lanes in each direction (and are often as little as one American-sized lane). Motorways (M) are major highways, the equivalent of Interstates in the United States. Most pass through towns, making cross-country travel lengthier than expected. Regional (R) highways typically feature one lane of traffic in each direction and connect smaller cities and towns. Finally, there are rural or unclassified roads, which are often the most scenic back roads. These can be poorly marked, narrow, and rough, but they frequently pass through lovely landscape.

Both the Republic of Ireland and Northern Ireland have strict anti-drunk driving regulations. The legal limit for alcohol is 35 micrograms per 100 milliliters of breath. What that translates to varies from person to person, but even one pint of alcohol can push you over the limit. The main rule is to avoid drinking and driving.

In a Nutshell: Traffic Regulations
- Driving on the left side of the road is required.
- Except in Northern Ireland, where road markers are in miles, road signs are in kilometers.

- The left lane is the traveling lane on highways. The right lane is designated for passing.
- Seat belts are required by law for all passengers. Children must ride in kid seats that are appropriate for their age.
- Children under the age of 11 are not permitted to sit in the front seat.
- Give way to traffic coming from the right when entering a roundabout (traffic circle).
- Another guideline of the roundabout: always go left (clockwise) around the circle.

Speed restrictions in urban areas are 50kmph (31 mph); 80kmph (50 mph) on regional and local roads, also known as non-national roads; 100kmph (62 mph) on national roads, including divided highways (known as dual carriageways); and 120kmph (75 mph) on freeways (known as motorways). Renting -- Customers who book in advance from their home country usually get the best rates from rental businesses. Ireland is a small country, and during peak season, it can run out of rental cars—but not before it runs out of affordable rental cars. Keep in mind that weekly rentals are usually always less expensive than day rentals, and that the vast majority of accessible rental automobiles are equipped with manual transmissions (stick shifts). Automatics are available, although at a higher cost. Another word of caution: petrol in Ireland is highly expensive.

To rent a car in Ireland, you must be between the ages of 25 and 75. The only documents you should bring are your driver's license and photo identification, such as a passport, as well as a printout of your reservation, if you have one.

When making a car reservation, make sure to inquire if the price includes all taxes, including VAT; breakdown assistance; unlimited mileage; personal accident or liability insurance (PAI); collision-damage waiver (CDW); theft waiver; and any additional insurance options. If not, inquire about the cost of these extras, as they might have a significant impact on your bottom line. If you use your credit card to pay for the rental, your CDW and other insurance may be covered; check with your card issuer to ensure that there are no restrictions on that coverage in Ireland. (Not all cards provide insurance coverage for automobile rentals in Ireland.) Some travelers enjoy living recklessly and forego optional insurance. However, if you do not purchase CDW, many rental firms may require you to pay for any damages on the spot when you return the car, making even the smallest ding or scratch a very pricey experience. To avoid problems, snap cellphone images of your car with a time stamp so that any dents and dings are recorded and you are not charged for them.

If your credit card does not cover the CDW, try purchasing third-party Car Rental Collision Coverage. Travel Guard (www.travelguard.com; 1800/826-4919 in the United States and Canada) will insure you for approximately $8 to $10 each day. Insurance 4 Car Hire (www.insurance4carhire.com; 0344/892-1770) in the United Kingdom provides comparable coverage.

Parking -- In Dublin, you're better off without a car. Traffic, a scarcity of parking spaces, and one-way streets all conspire to make you hate owning a car. Almost every street in Dublin charges for parking. Look for signs pointing you to ticket machines; there should be one every few blocks. Multistory car parks are also available in several major towns; in central Dublin, they cost roughly €2 per hour and €23 for 24 hours.

In contrast, parking is frequently easy and free in most villages and small towns. Look for public parking areas, which are generally free and located on the outskirts of town centers.

Special security measures are constantly in place in Belfast and other northern cities. Control zone signs state that no vehicle should be left unattended in the zone at any time. That means if you're traveling alone, you can't leave your car; if you're traveling with someone else, one of you must stay in the car while it's parked. Unlocked cars are also subject to a fine in the North for security concerns.

Before you arrive in Ireland, plan your driving schedule.

Airports are the most important vehicle rental hubs. If you don't have a few weeks to travel the entire country, there are several options for making the most of your time. First, verify with your car rental provider to see whether a different drop-off location is permitted, and plan to use alternate airports, like as arriving in Dublin and departing from Shannon. Then, from east to west, journey across the country, focusing on either the northern or southern counties as you go. Travel south to visit Kilkenny, Cashel, Cork, Kerry, and Clare. Head north to see Belfast, the Antrim Coast, Donegal, Mayo, and Galway. If you want to explore Northern Ireland, be sure your car insurance covers travel in the United Kingdom before you leave.

The first rule of public transportation is to purchase a Leap card.
The first step in moving about Ireland on all publicly subsidized transportation is to purchase a Leap Card online. It provides significant reductions on bus, tram, and rail prices across the country and is a much safer option than paying cash every time.

Intercity travel by train is the greatest alternative.
Many people are now taking the train across Ireland because vehicle rental is so expensive. The clean rail grid provides a dependable intercity link between cities. Irish Rail (known as Iarnród Éireann in Gaeilge, the Irish language) has reduced fares for passengers under the age of 24, but it still provides exceptional value for anyone using a Leap Card, with discounts of up to 30% and a price cap for multi-journeys.

The DART allows you to explore Dublin's outskirts.
The DART (Dublin Area Rapid Transit) is a lightweight electric rail system that connects Dublin to its seaside suburbs, while a separate diesel train system provides commuter service to towns further away. Connolly Station in Dublin serves Northern Ireland and Sligo, whereas Heuston Station serves metropolitan hubs in the midlands and southern counties. Another set of lines connects the cities of Galway, Limerick, and Cork individually.

The extensive bus network can transport you practically anywhere.

While the train provides good intercity service, its network is limited in comparison to the sheer size and volume of destinations served by public and private buses. By using the train as a jumping off point, you can enjoy the speed and comfort of rail to reach to transportation hubs before switching to the bus network for shorter journeys. The Leap Card is also accepted by Bus Éireann (the national bus service), Dublin Bus, and a few independent operators. It also means you can get off at any point along the route and catch the next bus without purchasing a new ticket.

Bus Éireann operates an Expressway Service, which is similar to the rail network but incorporates airports. Rural services span scenic places, and the route can be as enjoyable as the destination. The 350 bus route in County Clare runs along the Atlantic coast of the Burren National Park and passes by the Cliffs of Moher, while the 237 runs through a string of charming seaside towns in County Cork. Similar services are offered for Dingle, the Ring of Kerry, Connemara, and the Beara Peninsula, but check timetables carefully because they are not as frequent. Private operators provide year-round Hop on Hop off (HOHO) bus services in Dublin and Belfast, while places such as Galway and Cork provide seasonal city HOHO trips.

The Luas makes it simple to tour Dublin City.
The modern tram service in Dublin has been a part of the city's life and streetscape for several decades and is the best method to get around the capital. The Luas (Irish for "speed") Green Line runs from north to south, while the Red Line runs from east to west, and both lines intersect in the city center. It provides a cost-effective means to travel from the city to the outskirts, and yes, the Leap Card is accepted.

Taxis and private hire services are available.
In Ireland, major rideshare companies such as Uber and private taxis exist; registered taxis have ranks outside transportation hubs and in metropolitan areas. Private bus services and tour operators frequently provide bespoke services that can be cost effective for larger parties and families.

Services for ferries

Spending time on one of Ireland's many small yet nicely constructed islands is one of the best vacation experiences. Most ferry services, including the popular Doolin-Aran Islands link, reduce or cease operations beginning in November. However, Connemara has a year-round ferry and plane service.

Drivers can cross the Shannon on a ferry to get from County Kerry to County Clare.

Boat rental

Visitors who wish to travel at their own leisure and choose the less trafficked road or waterway on the Shannon can hire a boat from Lough Derg to Lough Erne or wherever in between. There are drop-off and pick-up points for boat rentals along the 362 km (225 mile) stretch of diverse landscapes and charming settlements.

Hiking and cycling

Off-road hiking and cycling trails abound in Ireland, and the number of options rises year after year. Disused railway lines in Mayo and Limerick provide stunning settings for treks, while the Beara Peninsula in County Cork serves as the starting point for Ireland's longest trip.

Ireland has easily accessible transportation.

The accessibility of Ireland for those with mobility difficulties has increased in recent years. The websites of transport operators such as Dublin Bus, Go-Ahead Ireland, Iarnród Éireann (Irish Rail), Bus Éireann, and the Luas provide detailed information about wheelchair accessible and tailored accessibility. When it comes to traveling throughout Ireland with a baby, children under the age of five who are accompanied by a Leap Card holder can travel for free on Bus Éireann (including Expressway), Luas, Irish Rail, and Dublin Bus. Unless a wheelchair is currently necessary, space will be made available for prams and strollers.

Chapter 21: Navigating Ireland: Comparing Cars, Tours, and Public Transport Options

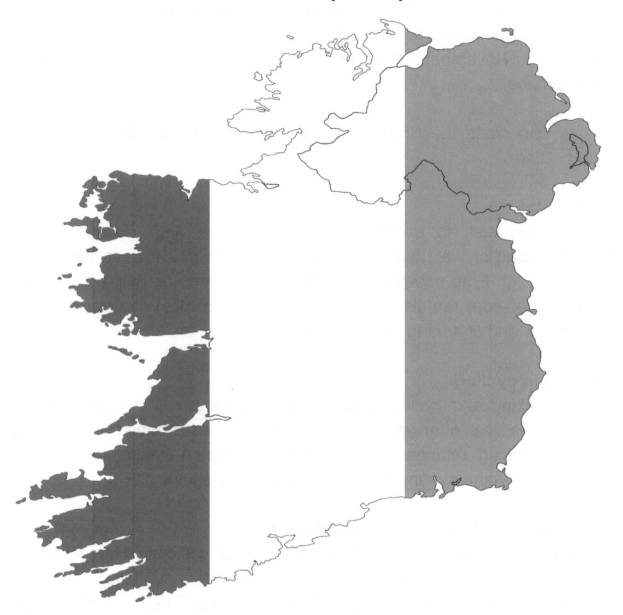

It can be difficult to decide how to navigate around Ireland.

Especially if this is your first visit and you are unfamiliar with the terrain.

The following information is based on my many years of traveling around Ireland, making every mistake possible along the way!

1. You have vehicle, bus, train, tour, and tram (kind of) alternatives.

Ireland's public transportation system differs per county. All of the above can be found in Dublin (the capital), and the first four can be found in most'main' cities and towns (for example, Killarney). More information is provided below.

2. If you're unsure, stick to your intended path.

I'd urge that you don't even consider how to move around Ireland until you've created a rough itinerary. The reason for this is that you may not be able to achieve what you want to do without a car (of course, your road trip may be totally viable by public transportation).

3. Each mode of transportation has advantages and disadvantages.

Most people (including myself) believe that driving is the greatest way to move around Ireland, however every mode of transportation has advantages and disadvantages. It's worthwhile to examine the advantages and disadvantages of each, as this will ultimately help you decide.

4. Budget is frequently a deciding factor.

Budget is the deciding factor in how people travel throughout Ireland 9 times out of 10. Renting a car in Ireland is frequently prohibitively expensive, and if you're traveling on a budget, taking buses and trains will significantly reduce the cost of your vacation.

The ideal way to navigate about Ireland boils down to three factors.
Choosing how to get around Ireland is not something to be taken lightly. Your primary form of transportation, whether a car or a bus, will have a significant impact on your trip.

When making your decision, you should consider three factors:
- Your expertise
- Your financial situation
- What you'd like to see

1. Your experience.

The most important factor to consider when deciding how to move around in Ireland is how the kind of transportation you choose will effect your whole travel experience.

Will having to drive every day cause you stress and ruin your holiday if you're anxious behind the wheel and driving in Ireland for the first time?

Perhaps you enjoy driving and think that driving the Ring of Kerry or the Antrim Coast will be the highlight of your trip?!

Alternatively, if getting about Ireland should be as stress-free as possible for you, you could be better off booking on an organized trip!

2. Your financial situation

Another important factor to consider while deciding on the best way to travel throughout Ireland is your financial situation.

If you're traveling alone, renting a car can be costly. However, if you travel in a group, it works out nicely and reasonably. Large group excursions can be reasonably priced, however smaller group tours might be costly.

3. What you'd like to see

Another helpful technique to assist you choose the best way to move around Ireland is to make a list of all of the places you wish to visit.

If you're only visiting major towns or cities in Ireland, for example, public transportation will suffice.

If you want to go off the beaten path, a rental car or a private driver (both of which are pricey) are your best bets.

The advantages and disadvantages of traveling throughout Ireland by automobile, tour, and public transportation

When considering how to move around in Ireland, consider the advantages and disadvantages of each means of transportation.

The benefits and drawbacks of traveling around Ireland by bus, train, automobile, and tour are listed below.

1. Taking a vehicle trip around Ireland

Traveling by automobile is arguably the greatest way to see Ireland (which is why our self-drive Ireland excursions are so popular!).

A car allows you to go wherever you want, whenever you want, without having to rely on public transportation or tour operators.

Advantages

Driving throughout Ireland has considerably more benefits than drawbacks. The major benefit is freedom; being able to go wherever you want whenever you want makes this a very appealing means of transportation for many.
- Flexibility and freedom
- It simplifies the process of planning a trip to Ireland.
- And you may adjust it as you go if you want. It can be inexpensive if there are a number of you to split costs.

Disadvantages

The main downsides of driving around Ireland are that it will be pricey for lone travelers and will certainly make the journey needlessly unpleasant for some drivers.
- It might be costly if you are on your own.
- Driving while apprehensive can make the trip stressful.

2. Getting around Ireland by bus, train, and tram

In Ireland, public transportation can be hit or miss. It's generally good in the major towns and cities, although services deteriorate as you travel further afield.

Here are the advantages and disadvantages:

Advantages
If you're traveling alone and want to move about Ireland on a budget, it may be the cheapest alternative.
- Trains and buses travel frequently in Ireland's busier towns and cities.
- It can be beneficial if combined with private tours.

Disadvantages
- Public transportation might be unreliable at times.
- Train tickets, in particular, can be costly if not purchased in advance.

3. Touring Ireland with a tour company
Another common method of getting around Ireland is to use a tour company that organizes all-inclusive trips of the country. These are very popular and vary in terms of party size and trip length.

One word of caution: if you're planning a tour of Ireland in advance, make sure to conduct plenty of study. Make it abundantly clear what is and is not included.

Advantages
- They will do all of the labor.
- There's no need to worry about car rental, itinerary, or anything else.
- It's less demanding.
- You'll be traveling around Ireland with a group of individuals with whom you'll (hopefully) have a good time. Most organized tours have knowledgeable guides.

Disadvantages
- Tours, particularly larger ones, are notoriously rigid.
- They can be costly (smaller trips are typically significantly more expensive than larger tours).
- You might be stuck with a bunch of individuals who bother you (hopefully not).

4. Hiring a personal driver

If you're wondering how to travel throughout Ireland on a tight budget, hiring a private driver is undoubtedly the best option.

If you choose to go this path, do a LOT of research. You'll be locked in a very tiny room with this person for lengthy periods of time, so you need to select someone who will enhance your experience rather than hamper it.

Advantages
- If you choose the correct guide, you will have access to a wealth of information.
- The driver will normally take the route you specify.
- A private driver is also a good alternative if you wish to undertake part of your tour with a guide and part on your own.

Disadvantages
- The most expensive mode of transportation in Ireland
- You must conduct extensive research to guarantee that you receive the most bang for your buck.
- If you end up with a guide you don't like, you'll be locked in a small area with them every day, which isn't ideal.

5. Merge means of transportation

Combining means of transportation is, in my opinion, the greatest way to move across Ireland.

This is especially helpful for those of you who want to avoid renting a car.

1. The mix of public transportation and organized tours
For those of you who cannot (or do not want to) rent a car, a mix of public transportation and organized tours will be a viable option.

Assume you travel into Dublin and stay for three nights. You can easily move around on foot and by bus, LUAS (tram), and DART (train).

You spend two days exploring the city and taking one of the many day trips available from Dublin (for example, Meath).

You take the train to Galway and stay for many days. You can spend the first day exploring the city. Day two was spent on an organized tour to Connemara, while day three was spent on a day trip to Clare.

2. Combination of rental car and public transportation
Another effective combination is to use a rental automobile in conjunction with public transportation. Assume you travel into Belfast. The first day is spent exploring the city.

Then you rent a car for a few days and drive along the Causeway Coastal Route to Donegal.

Or suppose you fly into Shannon. You pick up a car near the airport and go to Kerry. You spend a few days exploring the numerous peninsulas before returning the car and driving to Killarney.

You spend the day exploring the national park before boarding the train to Dublin. You could also take a train to Waterford or Tipperary.

My thoughts on the best method to navigate around Ireland.
Choosing how to get around Ireland can be stressful because it has such a large impact on the rest of your stay.

The simplest approach to choose the best mode of transportation for you is to consider:
- Your expertise
- Your financial situation
- What you'd like to see

After you've considered the above, you'll want to create a rough itinerary - they'll take the tension out of the process.

Chapter 22: The Complete Guide for Tourist Driving in Ireland

When most tourists visit Ireland, they will be driving on the wrong side of the road, and things can get scary right away. They will drive on the left side, with the steering wheel on the right. This may be startling at first, but it will become second nature in no time.

Because Irish roads are narrow and twisty, make cautious to drive at a comfortable speed. If someone follows you from behind, don't panic; simply pull over and let them pass. Driving in Ireland should not frighten you; we swear it's not that awful!

Can Visitors Drive in Ireland?

They certainly can! You can drive with your standard driving license if you are from the United States or Canada. If you are from another country, you will almost certainly need to obtain an International Drivers License, which you may do relatively easily in your home country.

However, there are age limitations, and most businesses refuse to hire automobiles to drivers under the age of 25. Furthermore, if you are over the age of 75, you may be requested for additional information and may find it difficult to rent a car.

Because most individuals in Ireland drive manual cars, automatic autos are more expensive to rent.

What are Ireland's driving laws?

Driving laws in Ireland will be extremely similar, if not identical, to those in other countries. There are a few minor exceptions that will take some getting used to. Roundabouts are uncommon in the United States, although they are ubiquitous in Ireland. When approaching a roundabout, stay in the left lane if heading left or straight through, and enter the right lane if turning right.

It's also vital to keep in mind that if you come to an unmarked crossing, the person on the right has right of way.

There are gas stations all around the country. In most cases, you fill up your automobile before paying, but there are some areas where you must pay before filling up your car.

Cars with the letters L, N, or R in a white box on their windows are also common. This suggests they are inexperienced drivers. A driver in the process of acquiring their permission is denoted by the letter L. The letter R is the same in Northern Ireland. N denotes a driver who has only recently obtained his or her full license.

Drink driving is very strictly enforced in Ireland, and if you consume one full pint, you will be over the limit. So, if you intend to have a few beers in the evening, don't bring your car!

Is it difficult to drive in Ireland?
Driving in Ireland is not difficult, but it does take some getting used to. Even though it is much more expensive, renting an automatic car is a smart idea if you are not comfortable driving a stick shift.

The most common occurrences to occur are flat tyres from being too close to the curb on the side of the road or broken mirrors from hitting branches. Cars and roads in Ireland are much smaller thus it can be a little bit daunting!

We would highly recommend driving portions of the Wild Atlantic Way which is a coastal route of Ireland and extends from the Northern tip of Donegal to the Southern town of Kinsale. It's one heck of a drive but offers some extremely magnificent views around Ireland and some pretty small roads!

Staying safe when driving in Ireland
Always check which gas you are putting into your automobile, petrol stations sell unleaded and diesel gas at practically every pump. The wrong one could inflict damage to your car. Also, most cars will notify you which side the petrol can be filled, there should be an arrow next to the gauge.

Focus on staying near (but not too close) to the line in the middle of the road. That will help you adjust to driving with the steering wheel on the right.

On a freeway, do not stay in the overtaking lane. You will be forcing traffic to pass you in a slower lane, which is unusual in Ireland. Pull out, overtake, then pull back into the left lane.

Be mindful of the road categories and speed limitations on each road, M= Motorway N= National Road R= Regional Road.

On some country roads, the speed restrictions could be as high as 100kph/60mph. That doesn't necessarily mean it is safe to drive at that speed. Trust your wits and don't drive at that speed if you feel that it is incorrect for a meandering country road.

Overall, U-turns are not safe and should not be attempted. An American family sadly lost their life attempting this in Ireland in 2017.

You can NOT turn unless there is a green light or a filter light. In some jurisdictions, you can turn right on a red light but that is not the case in Ireland.

Don't forget to secure your car when you are gone from it even if it is for a brief amount of time.

Do not leave anything valuable visible in your automobile.

On the M50 motorway around Dublin, there is a barrierless toll bridge called eFlow. It charges you for passing but you do not stop. You can pay the €3.10 charge in any large petrol station in the country simply saying your license plate number to the cashier. The fee might build quickly if you don't pay it before 8 pm the next day! This is exceedingly uncommon though, practically all other tolls are paid at on the spot at toll bridges.

Using these recommendations you should be able to have a fun and safe experience when driving in Ireland. Enjoy!

Chapter 23: Irish Bucket List: Exceptional Stays and Luxury Accommodations

My Irish bucket list includes unique stays, holiday homes, and several luxury hotels in Ireland, ranging from lighthouses to beach villas, lakeside lodges to penthouse suites.

Did you know that Ashford Castle boasts an exclusive Hideaway Cottage, or that Lough Eske Castle has a private Lake Lodge? Last year, I stayed at the Cliff House Hotel, but I had no idea they had a beautiful Beach House!

I fell in love with the thatched cottages at Sheen Falls Lodge Hotel, as well as the remote Inis Meáin Suites, and there are some lovely Airbnbs and private residences worth mentioning as well.

Ireland's best luxury hotels

I've chosen penthouse suites with butlers, lighthouses with breathtaking sea views, beautiful beach cottages, a treehouse in Wexford, and dinner on the Orient Express!

As you can see, I have not only chosen luxury hotels in Ireland, but also some unusual places to stay. These are my personal selections, and this is my bucket list, so you may find some of my picks odd.

It is important to note that not all facilities may be running as indicated; please verify with the specific hotel or vacation home to see if there are any restrictions in place.

1. Adare Manor in Limerick County

Adare Manor reopened to amazing acclaim after a two-year renovation and has already received multiple honors, including the best resort in Europe and the fifth best resort in the world in the Condé Nast Traveler Readers Choice honors. The 840 acres of gorgeous countryside, luxurious rooms, and award-winning spa will astound you.

This five-star luxury resort also has a Michelin-starred restaurant, The Oak Room. There are numerous accommodations to choose from, and even staying in one of the Classic accommodations merits a spot on this list.

If you really want to spoil yourself, the Dunraven Suites, which were previously the private apartments of the Earls of Dunraven, are located in the ancient Manor House, while the opulent Signature Suites include a complimentary minibar that is refreshed daily and your own private Manor Butler.

2. Tigh Thor is a 5-bedroom luxury residence in Dingle, Co. Kerry. Kerry.

The newly refurbished Tigh Thor is certainly one of the most exquisite residences on The Dingle Peninsula - simply looking at it gives me serious decor goals.

It is highly attractive due to the amount of light, contemporary furnishings, and open plan living space with views of Dingle Bay. There's also a cozy couch if you want to read a book in peace, and don't forget about the outdoor hot tub.

3. Ashford Castle's Hideaway Cottage in County Mayo

Is there anything more romantic than vacationing in a castle from the 13th century? I remember driving across the moat for the first time and seeing Ashford Castle for the first time; it felt like I was inside a fantasy.

Ashford Castle, named a National Geographic Unique Lodge of the World, is without a doubt one of Ireland's top luxury hotels. In addition to opulent furnishings and a variety of eating options, you may engage in a variety of recreational activities or unwind in the gorgeous spa.

Staying in any of the 83 rooms is a bucket list event in and of itself, but the Hideway Cottage is truly one-of-a-kind. This lakeside property, a former boathouse, is surrounded by private grounds and is only minutes from Ashford Castle. You can dine privately in your cottage, alfresco on the pier (weather allowed), or at any of the Castle's dining options throughout your stay.

When you arrive, you'll find a welcome basket and a fully stocked bar, as well as a 24 hour concierge service and complimentary Jack Murphy Jackets and Wellingtons to take home as a memento of your beautiful stay.

4. Cliff Beach House in Co. Waterford

I stayed at The Cliff House Hotel last year and had a great time. Many consider it to be one of Ireland's greatest luxury hotels, and I couldn't agree more. The ultimate romantic escape, this five-star boutique hotel in the little coastal village of Ardmore offers only 39 rooms.

I had a fantastic supper in its Michelin-starred restaurant, which was one of the nicest meals I've ever had. I only wish I had more time to enjoy the pool and spa. Its location, positioned on a cliff overlooking the Irish Sea, is breathtaking. Please bring me back....

All rooms feature sea views and are tastefully decorated, but the split-level Cliff Veranda Suites are stunning if you truly want to go all out. The living area is on the ground floor, while the bedroom is upstairs, overlooking the cliffs. Glass doors from floor to ceiling open onto a big private veranda with ocean views and luxurious sun loungers.

The Cliff House also offers luxurious self-catering solutions for families and groups. The Cliff Cottage is a three-bedroom contemporary residence, while the Cliff Beach House, with six bedrooms, is one of Ireland's most luxurious vacation rentals.

5. The Lighthouse, Enniscrone, Co. Clare, Sligo

The Lighthouse Penthouse, with its 360° living area and breathtaking ocean views, is without a doubt one of the most distinctive locations to stay in Ireland. The two-story penthouse features four bedrooms, making it suitable for both a passionate pair and a family or group of friends.

Its chic interior design has a polished Italian porcelain floor, premium leather couches, and a 50-inch TV. The video above reveals that there is no better place to enjoy the sunset over Killala Bay than near the magnificent Enniscrone Beach.

6. Fiddle + Bow Lodges and Cottages, Doolin, Co. Clare

Fiddle + Bow is a one-of-a-kind hotel that launched in Doolin in the summer of 2019. It is a beautiful boutique hotel with only 12 beds, a loft, and 11 self-catering lodges and cottages.

While the hotel rooms are stylish, it was the lodges and cottages that drew my attention. They are all tastefully decorated and have stunning sea views, with Hazel Lodge and Elphin Cottage standing out in particular.

7. Dromoland Castle in Co. Clare

Since the 16th century, Dromoland Castle has welcomed visitors. Many years ago, I spent a lovely weekend here in a deluxe tower room. These are located in the hotel's towers and provide a fairy-tale-like atmosphere.

You can even go all out and book one of the luxurious suites. This opulent five-star hotel is steeped in history, grandeur, and romance, ensuring a regal experience.

8. Stargaze at the Finn Lough Bubble Domes in County Cork. Fermanagh

You may have seen photos of similar domes beneath the Northern Lights in Lapland or Norway, but you only need to travel to Co. Fermanagh to gaze at the stars from the comfort of your own four-poster bed.

With a 180-degree glass dome, you will feel immersed in nature, although from a heated dome that includes an ensuite shower, a Nespresso coffee maker, bathrobes, and full breakfast. There is also a spa and a restaurant on the premises. Keep in mind that you are paying for a one-of-a-kind experience, so don't anticipate five-star treatment.

9. Dine on the Orient Express at Glenlo Abbey Hotel in County Wicklow. Galway

Glenlo Abbey, which sits on a 138-acre estate on Lough Corrib, has been inviting visitors since 1740. The on-site amenities are remarkable, with falconry, archery, fishing, golf, and the Abbey movie theater.

There are numerous room types to select from, including junior suites in the historic Manor House and many grand suites with four-poster beds. The Pullman Restaurant, which is housed in two historic Orient Express coaches, is the pièce de résistance. Dining on the Orient Express has always been on my bucket list, but I think this is the closest I'll ever go...

10. Monart Destination Spa, Co. Wexford

If you want a luxurious spa getaway in Ireland, go no further than Monart. When you arrive, you can put on your robe and never take it off until you leave - many people even dine in their robes!

It is one of the most pleasant hotel stays I have ever had, but you must plan a tranquil night with few nightcaps to fully appreciate it. There are several spas in Irish hotels, however there is only one destination spa hotel in Ireland - Monart.

The rooms aren't as luxurious as some of the other hotels featured here, but you're not going to stay in Monart for the hotel rooms. There are two deluxe rooms with four poster beds, a free standing bath, and a separate spa-style shower with garden views if your money allows.

11. Dromquinna Manor's Hideaway, Co. Kerry
The Hideaway is ideal for couples looking for the ultimate getaway. You will be staying in a custom-made African safari tent on the grounds of Dromquinna Manor, overlooking the lake. The term 'tent' does not appropriately represent your accommodation, which includes a beautiful en-suite bedroom and private veranda. It is camping, but not as you know it.

The Hideaway has its own entry through a private gated yard, ensuring complete solitude. Every morning, a great breakfast basket will be served to your tent, and you can dine in The Boathouse in the evening. This is my vision of paradise, and I can't wait to go!

12. Top Airbnb with stunning sea views in Lahinch, Co. Clare
Look no further for the Holy Grail of seaside holiday cottages along the Wild Atlantic Way. With beautiful floor to ceiling windows overlooking Liscannor Bay and the Cliffs of Moher, this modern 2-bedroom home has a 270-degree view of the sea.

The open plan living space features polished concrete floors and a rotating stove in the center. This has to be one of the nicest Airbnbs in Ireland, and it's high on my Irish bucket list!

13. Mount Juliet Estate offers traditional experiences.

This summer, I had the pleasure of staying in Mount Juliet and thoroughly enjoyed it. There are several excellent Manor House hotels in Ireland, but Mount Juliet stood out. Even the name sounds romantic - I suppose it conjures up images of Romeo and Juliet.

The Manor House is gorgeous, and its surroundings are breathtaking. It is situated on a ridge above the River Nore and encompasses 500 acres of woodlands, parks, and gardens. It also has a Michelin-starred restaurant, The Lady Helen, a pool, spa, and the most stunning walled garden.

One of my favorite aspects about Mount Juliet is the variety of outdoor activities accessible. Why not cross falconry and horseback riding off your Irish bucket list? Both are available on Mount Juliet Estate. This summer, I rode a horse for the first time, and I couldn't have picked a more picturesque setting. I also had a lot of fun with falconry.

Mount Juliet Estate offers a variety of lodging options. We stayed in one of the Manor House's garden rooms, which were excellent; alternatively, Hunters Yard provides more modern and cheaply priced rooms, or if you are traveling with family or friends, you may choose one of the beautiful self-catering lodges.

14. Dolphin Beach Lodge is located in Clifden, County Clare. Galway

Dolphin Beach Lodge is the ideal Connemara escape. The design is fantastic, located just yards from the beach and with panoramic views of the bay from practically all living rooms.

The three-bedroom lodge is adjacent to the hosts' Country House, which runs as a luxury bed and breakfast. During high season, there is a one-week minimum stay - but after seeing the interiors, you won't want to stay for less!

15. Away from it all at Inis Meáon Suites in the Aran Islands.

Inis Meáin is the most remote of the three Aran Islands, and a stay at the magnificent Inis Meáin Suites is the ultimate escape. Explore the beaches, go on cliff walks, and meet the Irish-speaking locals on this 5km x 3km island.

There are only five private suites, and each has been built to mirror the surrounding scenery with wood, lime, stone, and wool. A 10-metre-long window affords unbroken views of the island and Galway Bay, and there is a secluded south-facing seating area outside if you want to take in the scenery outside.

The onsite restaurant has received multiple honors and serves a four-course dinner that changes nightly and is based on the best local ingredients. A breakfast box and a HotPot Lunch are delivered daily to your suite, as well as an Exploration Kit containing bicycles, binoculars, a fishing rod, walking sticks, beach towels, maps, and books of interest.

AranIslandferries provides daily ferries to the island, but for the ultimate pleasure, you may charter a private helicopter, which can land on the site of the restaurant.

16. Sheen Falls Lodge's thatched cottages

Sheen Falls Lodge has a beautiful setting overlooking the Sheen Waterfalls and is a short walk from the scenic town of Kenmare on the Ring of Kerry and the Wild Atlantic Way.

It is a Relais & Chateaux hotel with great food and wine, as well as a variety of activities such as kayaking, paddleboarding, archery, fishing, horseback riding, clay pigeon shooting, and falconry. If you prefer to unwind, use the spa or indoor heated pool.

You may be familiar with the lodges at Sheen Falls Country Club, but did you know that the Sheen Falls Lodge Hotel also has thatched cottages? These Hansel and Gretel-style houses are reached via a private gate, have a large lawn, and stunning interiors.

Little Hay cottage includes a spiral staircase leading to the bedrooms, and your bedroom balcony offers views of Kenmare Bay. There are three two-bedroom cottages and one four-bedroom house to select from, and all have access to the activities and facilities at the Sheen Falls Lodge Hotel.

17. Stay at the Armada Hotel's Wild Atlantic Suite in Spanish Point, Co. Clare

It's no surprise that the 4-star Armada Hotel is one of Clare's most popular hotels, with the Cliffs of Moher, Aran Islands, and the Burren on your doorstep, as well as the traditional Johnny Burke's Irish bar on site.

I have the option of staying in the Seascape Suite or the Wild Atlantic Suite. They each boast beautiful views of Spanish Point Beach, as well as a library, record player, and telescope. The Seascape Suite features a feature soaking tub with a view of the ocean, while the Wild Atlantic Way Suite offers a four poster bed and a fireplace. Decisions, decisions, decisions.

18. For a family reunion, rent Luttrelstown Castle exclusively.

Is there anything better than renting this beautiful 15th-century Irish castle exclusively for your family when covid restrictions are lifted? In this 567-acre estate, you will be served by a private team. Afternoon tea, high dining meals, golf, fishing, and even falconry or air rifle shooting are available.

19. Lough Eske Castle's lake lodge

Lough Eske Castle is one of Ireland's top luxury hotels, but its private two-bedroom hideaway, Lake Lodge at Lough Eske, appears to be a small slice of heaven. This quiet two-story lodge at the Castle gates overlooks Lough Eske and keeps all of its original character, but with Scandinavian style furniture and all modern creature comforts.

You can cook in the fully equipped kitchen, but if that's not your idea of a vacation, you can eat at Lough Eske Castle. Guests also have access to the Castle's Spa, swimming pool, and other amenities.

If you want to stay in Lough Eske Castle, the Tower Suite in the original 18th century wing is an excellent bucket list alternative! It is divided into three floors, with a twisting staircase leading to an open-concept bathroom on the top floor.

20. The Merrion Hotel's Seven Star Steal

The Merrion Hotel is a five-star luxury hotel in Dublin that is also a member of The Leading Hotels of the World. It not only has Ireland's first two-star Michelin restaurant, but it also has an 18-metre pool, spa, and gym.

This fantastic seven-star deal includes a four-course meal at Restaurant Patrick Guilbaud with a surprise tasting menu, followed by a stay at the Merrion Hotel with breakfast. Prices start at €225 per person.

21. The Europe Hotel's Superior Lake View Room

When I asked on Instagram for recommendations for your favorite luxury hotels in Ireland, The Europe Hotel came up frequently. It is said to be THE place to stay in Killarney, surrounded by the Lakes of Killarney, with a sumptuous spa and award-winning eating options.

The outside terrace of the Brasserie Restaurant, as well as the fine dining Panorama Restaurant, provide stunning views of the lake.

There are numerous room kinds to choose from, but a superior lake view room is the ultimate bucket list experience. These bright, roomy rooms face south and include an own balcony with outdoor furniture to take in the breathtaking lake views.

22. Pamper yourself at Powerscourt Hotel Resort & Spa in Co. Wicklow.

I've had the good fortune to stay at the Powerscourt Hotel on several occasions. I'm not sure if it's the location at Powerscourt Estate or the excellent facilities on offer, but I usually feel like I'm in a 'resort', miles away from home, despite the fact that it's less than an hour away. Bicycles are available at no cost for exploring the estate, the neighboring Powerscourt Waterfall, and the Wicklow countryside.

I've had informal eating in the Sugar Loaf Lounge and dinner in the Sika restaurant, but it's the 20-metre Swarovski crystal-lit swimming pool and the luxurious ESPA that always take my breath away.

All of the rooms are attractively equipped and feature novel features such as recessed televisions in the bathrooms. Superior rooms offer a furnished outside balcony, which is ideal for taking in the views of the Wicklow Mountains.

23. Take a culinary break in Virginia Park Lodge, Co. Cavan.

Richard Corrigan, a Michelin-starred chef, prepares delectable rural meals at Virginia Park Lodge, an 18th-century hunting lodge. It is well-known as an exclusive hiring site for weddings and other celebrations, but it is also available for individual bookings from Sunday to Thursday.

There is a large range of housing options available, including apartments, cottages, and even Woodland Huts. This is glamping at its finest, with French double doors, thick oak floors, and a Shaker-style galley kitchen.

24. The Hideout, a Romantic Tree House in Wexford County

Are you seeking for a one-of-a-kind place to stay in Ireland? This lovely tree house should suffice! This completely insulated tree house, featured on RTÉ's The Big DIY Challenge, comes with a wood fire and many big windows to enjoy the best sunset views.

You may even enjoy a BBQ on the outside deck while stargazing through the skylight in the loft-style bedroom. The house is fully equipped with modern electronics, and the bathroom pod includes a regular toilet and a spacious two-person shower.

25. Ballyfin Demesne, County Laois
When it comes to luxury hotels in Ireland, Ballyfin Demense is unrivaled! Condé Nast Traveler named it one of the greatest hotels in the world. "It was like stepping back in time without the inconvenience of no electricity," says Richard E Grant.

The personal attention...the welcome of the people, the environment, the food, I should be their public relations manager" - doesn't it sound rather special? This five-star luxury country estate has only 20 rooms and suites and is exclusively open to residents - it is ideal for an intimate getaway.

26. Lighthouse Keepers, Youghal, County Cork
When it comes to unique Airbnbs in Ireland, it doesn't get much better than this. Featured as RTE's Home of the Year and selected one of Ireland's best 50 places to stay by the Irish Independent, it doesn't get much better than this. This 200-year-old mansion was the home of every lighthouse keeper who staffed Youghal Lighthouse from the 1800s.

It was renovated for two years by the owners, and it is now a modern masterpiece that retains its charm and past. There are three bedrooms and two bathrooms, as well as underfloor heating and a conservatory with a hanging chair. If you still need convinced, read the reviews from prior visitors.

27. Stay in a Shelbourne Signature Suite.
The Shelbourne is not only one of our best luxury hotels in Ireland, but it is also a landmark in Dublin. For 200 years, it has been the social and cultural hub of the city, located directly on St. Stephen's Green. It also features an amazing dining selection, a health club, spa, and a 19-metre swimming pool.

The Signature Suites at the Shelbourne are ideal for history aficionados and culture vultures. They got their names from famous guests over the years, such as JFK, Michael Collins, and Éamon de Valera.

Each suite's story is expressed via thoughtful décor and curated artifacts, making it unique. Expect opulent furnishings (and a price to match) as well as beautiful views of St. Stephens Green.

28. Galgorm Resort & Spa, County Antrim

I've booked Galgorm Spa and Golf Resort four times and had to cancel each time due to availability, so it's definitely on my list! It is one of Northern Ireland's most exquisite spa hotels, with the sensation of a hidden refuge yet being only 30 minutes from Belfast.

The riverfront hot tubs and outdoor heated pools are popular on Instagram, but Galgorm is more than its one-of-a-kind thermal village. There are several dining alternatives, and the cottages look amazing - I can't wait to stay there personally.

29. Folan's Stone Cottage, Roundstone, Galway

Folan's Cottage is only a few meters from a peaceful sandy beach in Connemara. It is your picture-perfect Irish getaway, rebuilt in 2010 from two destroyed stone cottages. It is without a doubt one of the greatest Airbnbs in Ireland at the beach, with three bedrooms, a huge kitchen, underfloor heating throughout, and a south-facing patio with sea views.

In fact, it is so popular that it is always sold out between July and August, and is only rented by the week, Saturday to Saturday, the rest of the year.

30. Portrush, Co. Antrim Penthouse Apartment

I love the Causeway Coast, but I've never made it as far as Portrush, so I'd want to return and stay in this fantastic Airbnb. It doesn't get much better than a luxury apartment with a terrace overlooking the lovely Whiterocks Beach!

This popular vacation home is close to restaurants, pubs, and the best attractions on the Causeway Coast, including Dunluce Castle, which is only 5 kilometers away.

31. A family getaway at the Dunloe Hotel in County Kerry

The Dunloe Hotel and Gardens is a recent addition to my Irish bucket list, and it has to be one of Ireland's top luxury hotels for families. In addition to the 64 acres to explore, the hotel grounds include a fantastic outdoor adventure playground.

Families can also go kayaking on the estate's river, as well as complimentary pony trekking, tennis, and fishing. If you are fortunate enough to catch something, the kitchen will gladly prepare and grill your catch for dinner that evening.

During the summer, two popular movies ideal for children of all ages are screened each night. Popcorn and beverages will be supplied.

The hotel features spacious family accommodations that can accommodate two parents and three children, consisting of a double room with balcony and a separate room for children accessible only through an internal interconnecting door not accessible from the hotel corridor - I adore this idea! This motel is also pet-friendly.

Chapter 24: Where to Stay? Exploring Your Accommodation Choices in Ireland

A holiday in Ireland is certain to be full with interesting exploring, breath-taking views and plenty of 'craic'. You'll want a place to rest your head at the end of the day (or the early hours of the following!).

Whatever your chosen accommodation style is, or if you want to try something new, Ireland has it all: high-end hotels, beautiful B&Bs, wild camping, and everything in between.

HOW TO FIND A ROOM IN IRELAND

Ireland is a well-known tourist destination. Tourism Ireland reports that 11.2 million tourists visited Ireland in 2019. When you compare that to the country's population of 4.9 million, you can see how providing the legendary warm Irish welcome to tourists is an important and proud part of life in the country.

1. PLAN AHEAD

As a popular destination, it's always a good idea to reserve at least some of your lodging ahead of time, especially during high seasons like St. Patrick's Day, Summer, and Christmas. If you're flying from outside the EU, such as the US, you'll need to present an address or proof of a reservation at Immigration when you reach at the airport, so planning beforehand makes sense.

While we're talking about airport arrivals, scheduling your car rental ahead of time is another decision you'll be glad you took, especially after a long travel. Book with NewWay for an all-inclusive (no hidden fees) pick-up at Dublin Airport and you'll be on your way in no time. Learn more about our Dublin Airport car rental services.

2. CONDUCT YOUR RESEARCH

When it comes to accommodation, as with any other aspect of trip planning, research is essential.

There are numerous booking websites where you can begin your search. Many of these are presumably already familiar to you, such as:
- Booking.com
- TripAdvisor
- Trivago
- Airbnb
- Expedia

Here are a few Irish-specific websites you may not be aware of:
- Hotels in Ireland. The official webpage of the Irish Hotels Federation is useful for finding hotel accommodations.
- Ireland.com. Tourism Ireland's search engine providing a comprehensive variety of hotels, campsites, university accommodations, and everything in between.
- The Blue Book of Ireland. Unique country mansions, historic homes, luxury boutique hotels, and B&Bs are available.

3. DIRECTLY CONTACT THE ACCOMMODATION PROVIDER

While OTAs and aggregators like Booking.com are excellent locations to start your search, if you find the lodging of your dreams, it's worth contacting the owner personally. While rooms on the OTA may be unavailable, the proprietor may have some. It's also worth noting that businesses pay an OTA fee for each booking. Going directly to the source may result in a lower price for your accommodation.

1: A HOTEL

A hotel is usually the most expensive alternative, particularly in major cities. But that doesn't mean you can't discover a decent price. Hotels frequently provide discounts for midweek stays, for example.

Hotels in Ireland are classified from one to five stars, with five stars giving the highest level of comfort and service and one star providing the bare minimum. Some may have private bathrooms.

HOTELS WITH 5 STARS

If you like to splurge on your holiday accommodations and live like a rock star for a few days, Ireland has no shortage of world-class five-star hotels. You'll be spoilt with choice in Dublin, with a few famous favorites.

Charlie Chaplin, Grace Kelly (who had a suite named after her), and President John F. Kennedy have all stayed at the Shelbourne Hotel.

The Merrion Hotel is home to Restaurant Patrick Guilbaud, which has not one, but two Michelin stars for gourmet dining.

But you don't have to stay in Dublin city to get five-star service. There are five-star hotels all around the country.

HOTELS IN THE MIDDLE AND LOWER PRICE RANGES

If you want the convenience of a hotel but don't want to spend a fortune, there are plenty of mid-range, budget, and boutique hotel options to choose. The most convenient approach to conduct research is through one of the OTAs listed above.

Hotel costs vary greatly depending on a variety of criteria other than their star rating. The season and location are important considerations. A three-star hotel in Dublin city center, for example, is likely to be more expensive than a similar hotel in the isolated Irish midlands.

Of course, no matter which end of the market you shop at, some guidelines apply to any hotel. Smoking is prohibited in the workplace, enclosed public spaces, bars, restaurants, and public transportation in Ireland. It is legal in hotels, but only if you have reserved a smoking room. Otherwise, you can fairly trust that your room (and most likely your floor) will be smoke-free.

2: HOSTELS

Hostels in Ireland are now worth visiting even if you're a couple or have children, as they were traditionally catered to the single, young, and broke backpacker. While shared dorm rooms remain popular and offer some of the best value, many hostels also offer private rooms, family rooms, and even en suites for a fraction of the price of a hotel.

ARE IRELAND'S HOSTELS SAFE?
Hostels in Ireland are warm, entertaining, and secure places to stay. However, no matter where you stay, it's always a good idea to be cautious. Read reports from other travelers and take the typical precautions like avoiding leaving valuables laying around and using safety deposit boxes.

HOW MUCH DO HOSTELS COST IN IRELAND?
Hostel prices will vary depending on the reasons listed earlier, but if you're lucky, you might be able to locate a room for as little as €12 per night.

According to Hostelworld, the following are the average hostel costs in some of Ireland's most popular cities:

€44 in Dublin
€32 in Galway
Cork is €23
Doolin costs €22.
Killarney is €22.
Wicklow is €20.
Donegal is worth €14.

3: SELF CATERING
Self catering refers to vacation accommodations that are self-contained and provide facilities for you to prepare your own meals. It will feel like a home away from home, and in Ireland, it could be a traditional cottage, a seaside vacation property, or a convenient townhouse.

For many people, the advantages of self-catering accommodation are insurmountable. Cooking for yourself allows you to save money for other activities while also allowing you to experience local produce. Let's face it, who doesn't get a little giddy perusing the aisles of a new country's supermarket? There is also more space and freedom to keep a routine, making it an excellent choice for families with little children.

Self-catering accommodations can be found on the standard booking sites mentioned above, as well as on the following Irish sites:

- Discover Ireland
- Dream Ireland
- Visualize Ireland

4: AIRBNB

AirBnB is alive and well in Ireland as well, however if you've previously used Airbnb in Ireland, you should be aware that new restrictions enacted in 2019 have restricted the number of available units.

Ireland's long-running housing issue was aggravated when landlords began to remove long-term rental homes from the market in order to promote them as short-term vacation rentals on Airbnb instead. The new restrictions have made it more difficult for landlords with houses in areas with high housing demand to use Airbnb. As a result, there may be fewer assets available on the platform now than there were a few years ago.

5: BED AND BREAKFAST

From Airbnb to good old-fashioned bed and breakfasts!

If you enjoy learning about local history and culture, there is no better place to stay than with an Irish family in a bed and breakfast. With hundreds of superb B&Bs located throughout the country, you can meet the actual people of Ireland, have a home cooked breakfast, and receive fantastic value for money.

According to B&B Ireland, the average price per person sharing a B&B is €32-38, but this varies depending on the season and location.

DO YOU TIP IN IRELAND FOR BED AND BREAKFAST?

Tipping is not required or expected at most B&Bs in Ireland because they are small, family enterprises. Staff may be employed in larger B&Bs to provide food service or housework. You may desire to tip these employees, which is entirely fine but not expected.

WHERE CAN I FIND BED AND BREAKFAST IN IRELAND?
The major OTAs include search filters to help you find bed and breakfasts. For additional information, see B&B Ireland and Discover Ireland.

6: HISTORIC BUILDINGS AND CASTLES
Ireland's rich history and architecture are two of its main draws. You'll never be far from an amazing castle or old ruin as you tour the country, each with its own unique history. Not only that, but you may even sleep in some of these magnificent historical structures.

IN IRELAND, WHICH CASTLES ARE HOTELS?
Check out these renowned castles in Ireland that are also hotels, and who knows, you might be able to live like a king (at least for a few nights!):

Abbeyglen Castle, Galway Ashford Castle, Mayo Ballygally Castle, Antrim Ballynahinch Castle, Galway Ballyseede Castle, Kerry Cabra Castle, Castle Castle Leslie, Monaghan Clontarf Castle, Dublin Dromoland Castle, Clare Dunboyne Castle, Meath Fitzpatrick Castle, Dublin Kilkea Castle, Kildare Kilronan Castle, Roscommon Kinnitty Castle, Tipperary Waterford Castle, Waterford Wilton Castle

7: CAMPING
The weather in Ireland can be unpredictable and, let's face it, rainy, but the wealth of undisturbed natural beauty and scenery would entice even the most hesitant of outdoor sleepers.

CAMPING IN THE WILD
Camping outside of designated campgrounds, sometimes known as 'wild camping,' is permitted in many parts of Ireland. OSi's brief wild camping

guide highlights some of the most beautiful camping places you should consider.

CAMPSITES

If you're traveling with children, it's difficult to beat the distractions and fun that a campsite provides.

Pitchup.com has a comprehensive list of the best campsites in Ireland. In Ireland, prices start at €12.91 per night for two persons.

GLAMPING

Ireland provides a plethora of superb glamping options for those who wish to enjoy the great outdoors in style.

Glamping, or glamorous camping, provides outdoor sleeping with added conveniences such as decent beds and power. Luxury tents, yurts, and cottages of all shapes and sizes are available, and the sites are frequently linked with a variety of exciting activities such as watersports, yoga, climbing, horseback riding, and bicycling.

Glamping sites in Ireland can be found on Booking.com.

GET OUT THERE AND EXPLORE

Wherever you choose to stay on your Irish vacation, our best advice is to use it as a base from which to embark on your true adventures! The nice thing about Ireland is that you're never more than a short drive away from picturesque, calm Irish countryside, even if you're staying in one of the country's largest towns.

Chapter 25: Dublin Attractions: Exploring the City's Highlights

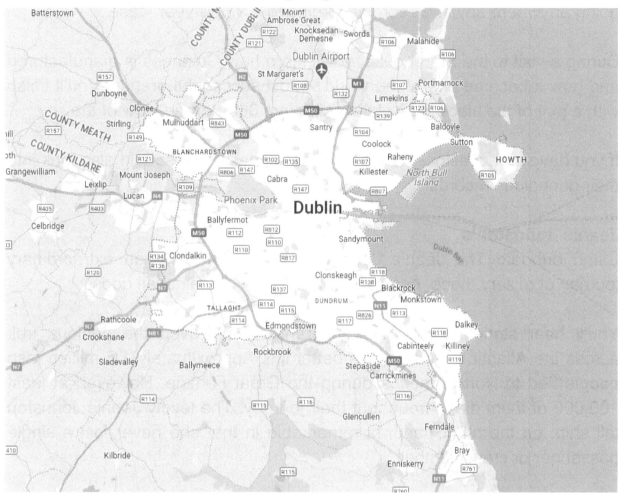

One of the most significant advantages of living in Dublin is the abundance of world-class galleries, museums, and cultural attractions right on your doorstep. Because of Dublin's rich history and culture, there are always intriguing locations to visit. The best part is that many of them are free. We've included some of the finest Dublin attractions below.

Book of Kells, Trinity College

The Book of Kells is a manuscript of the Gospels from the ninth century. It is extraordinarily ornate, one-of-a-kind, and immaculately kept. You'll also travel through Trinity College's famed Long Room Library, which is worth the trip on its own. This site, located in the heart of Dublin, should be one of the first on your list.

The Guinness Book of World Records

Guinness has had its headquarters at St James' Gate since 1759. It's not going anywhere anytime soon, according to a 9,000-year lease.

During a visit to the Storehouse, you'll learn how Guinness is manufactured and how it became one of the world's most successful brands. You'll finish with a pint of the black stuff while taking in a 360-degree view of the city.

If you have an ancestor who worked at Guinness, you should also look into their genealogy records.

Jeanie Johnston's

Climb onboard The Jeanie Johnston Famine Ship for an extraordinary journey of misery, hope, endurance, and triumph against all odds.

You'll hear stories about Irish emigrants who braved the perilous trek across the Atlantic in search of a better life. Approximately 1.5 million Irish people fled to North America during the Great Famine. However, at least 100,000 of them died throughout their journey. The lovely Jeanie Johnston tall ship, on the other hand, is remarkable in that she never lost a single passenger or crew member.

National Botanic Gardens

The National Botanic Gardens, open daily and free of charge, is home to some of Ireland's most lush and stunning floral pleasures. It is home to nearly 15,000 plant species, 300 endangered species, and six extinct in the wild.

Some of the most unusual items are housed in its exquisite Victorian-style glasshouses. Different excursions and exhibitions are frequently available in the grounds as well.

The St. Patrick Cathedral

This Church of Ireland cathedral is both stunning and historically significant. However, it is also a place of worship - 800 years after it was established.

Enjoy the beautiful architecture, bright stained glass windows, and a cup of coffee in the connected delightful park. Try to visit during a choral recital if possible. The cathedral's choir, like Christ Church Cathedral's, sang for the world premiere of Handel's Messiah in 1742. Their musical history continues to this day.

Christ Church

Christ Church is a short distance from St. Patrick's Cathedral. So, if you go to one, make sure to stop by the other.

Christ Church is a Viking cathedral that dates back 1,000 years. It has religious relics, Ireland's first Magna Carta, and Strongbow's grave, making it one of Dublin's most popular tourist destinations.

The Dublin Castle

Dublin Castle, built on the site of an earlier Viking settlement in the 13th century, was formerly the seat of British sovereignty in Ireland. It is now the site of Ireland's presidential inaugurations.

Its enormous buildings have witnessed decades of victories and tragedies, but it remains a steadfast feature on Dublin's shifting face. The castle is located in the midst of the city, although the entrance is easily overlooked. It's right off Dame Street, one of Dublin's busiest thoroughfares.

View the latest exhibition in the Coach House Gallery, attend a choir performance in the chapel, tour the State Apartments, or explore the gorgeous gardens. The Chester Beatty Museum, one of Dublin's best, is also located around back, thus this is a Dublin site that should not be missed.

The Phoenix Park

The Phoenix Park, Europe's largest enclosed city park, offers a respite from the rush and bustle of metropolitan life. Despite the fact that it is only a short distance from the city center.

The park is home to a diverse range of native vegetation and fauna, including a herd of fallow deer. Half of Ireland's animal species and 40% of its bird species are also found here. Key Dublin attractions such as Dublin Zoo, Farmleigh Estate, the President's House, and the Phoenix Park Visitor Centre are also located inside the park.

Witness History at the GPO
The General Post Office, one of Dublin's grandest Georgian structures, can be found on O'Connell Street. It was also a revolutionary stronghold during Ireland's most famous revolt against British control, the Easter Rising, in 1916. Today, the structure houses a museum that commemorates the events that occurred there.

You'll study the narrative of rise and the events that have occurred since through an immersive and engaging self-guided tour.

The National Leprechaun Museum is located in Dublin, Ireland.
The Leprechaun Museum in Dublin has been carrying on Ireland's storytelling legacy for over a decade. Visitors learn about the history of Irish mythology and stories through an immersive tour. They'll also have some fantastic stories to tell.

The Marsh Library
Marsh's Library, located next to St. Patrick's Cathedral, was Ireland's first public library. Little has changed since it was opened in 1707. Its dark oak interior, as well as thousands of books, have been meticulously kept.

Marsh's Library is a book lover's dream, with odd displays and exquisite books dating back to the Renaissance.

The St Michan's Church
St Michan's Church, founded in 1095, is the oldest church on Dublin's northside. What makes it truly unique is concealed beneath the floors. The mummified remains of some of the city's wealthiest and most powerful

families from the 17th, 18th, and 19th centuries can be found here. Among them is the mother of Bram Stoker, the Irish author responsible for Dracula.

St. Valentine's relics

Whitefriar Street Church appears simple and modest from the outside. Step inside, however, and you'll find a slew of holy shrines, including one housing St Valentine's relics. And what romantic wouldn't want to bow down to the patron saint of love himself?

Teeling Distillery produces whisky.

This tour, which is based in Newmarket Square in the city's south, allows you to discover the sights and sounds of Teeling's fully working distillery. You will also be able to sample the finished product.

Chapter 26: Exploring Ireland's 32 Most Iconic Landmarks

Ireland has a seemingly endless collection of notable landmarks.

Some, like the Cliffs of Moher and Blarney Castle, are globally famous, while others, like Jerpoint Abbey, are underappreciated.

In this guide, we've compiled a list of Irish landmarks that are well-known around the world as well as some that are less well-known.

Now, a brief disclaimer: this is not an exhaustive list of all of Ireland's monuments. That is a really large list.

1. Cliffs of Moher
The Cliffs of Moher in County Clare are one of Ireland's most recognizable natural monuments and a highlight of the Wild Atlantic Way.

They span for 14 kilometers (9 miles) along the craggy Clare coast in the Burren region. The Cliffs of Moher rise 390 feet above the rough Atlantic below at their highest point.

Although you may visit them on foot via the visitor center, a boat excursion from Doolin or Galway City is a more unique way to experience Moher.

2. Cashel's Rock (Tipperary)

Few Irish monuments seem as magical as the beautiful Rock of Cashel in County Tipperary.

The Rock of Cashel, a popular tourist destination in Ireland, is also known as 'St. Patrick's Rock.

During the fifth century, St. Patrick is said to have converted King Aenghus. But that wasn't its only claim to fame.

The place was previously the seat of the Munster High Kings! Many of the constructions that can still be seen today are from the 12th and 13th centuries.

3. Monasterboice High Crosses (Louth)
The Monasterboice High Crosses in County Louth are a historical site in Ireland.

Monasterboice is the site of a 5th century monastery settlement and is home to The Cross of Muiredach, possibly the most spectacular of Ireland's many Celtic Crosses.

It's one of three High Crosses on the property. There are two 14th-century churches as well as an antique round tower (shown above) that was used to see approaching assailants.

4. Newgrange, County Meath
Our next trip is the old Boyne Valley, where we will see one of Ireland's most ancient sites, Newgrange.

Newgrange is a UNESCO World Heritage Site that goes back to 3,200 BC and is part of the world-famous Br na Bóinne complex, which also includes Knowth.

Many archaeologists assume that Newgrange was built to serve an astrological religion.

Every year, on the winter solstice, a beam of light shines through a roof-box at the entrance to Newgrange, illuminating the interior.

The event requires participants to enter a "ticket lottery," with thousands of people from all over the world eager to view one of Ireland's most spectacular landmarks on its big day.

5. Skellig Michael (Kerry)

The Skelling Islands (Skellig Michael and Little Skelling) are two of Ireland's most unusual natural attractions, jutting out of the Atlantic off the coast of Kerry.

Skellig Michael is the more well-known of the two due to its use in a Star Wars film. It is also the only one that can be visited.

The Skelligs are like something from another universe, with a rich bird population, an early Christian Monastery from the 6th century, and several beehive huts that were formerly home to monks.

6. Antrim's Giants Causeway

For good cause, the Giant's Causeway topped our list of Northern Ireland's most iconic sites.

The Giant's Causeway, like Newgrange, is a UNESCO World Heritage Site, and it is said to be over 50 million years old!

The 40,000+ black basalt columns that protrude boldly out of the water are the most distinctive elements of this beautiful region of Ireland.

The columns are a sight to behold, set against the green cliffs of the Antrim Coast, and give the feeling that you're wandering in another planet.

7. Benbulben (Sligo)

Few natural sights in Ireland can halt you in your tracks like Sligo's table-top-like Benbulben.

The very unusual Benbulben, which is part of the Dartry Mountain range, was formed by various responses to limestone erosion.

It may be seen from many sections of the county, and its distinctive aspect never fails to capture the attention.

It's best seen on the excellent Benbulben Forest Walk, which takes around 2 hours and provides a close-up view of the mountain.

8. Dublin's Christ Church Cathedral

Christ Church Cathedral is an important landmark in Ireland because it is one of the first sites that many tourists visiting Dublin visit.

The cathedral, located in the heart of Dublin City Centre, was founded by a Viking ruler in the early 11th century, making it nearly as old as the city itself!

Manuscripts place the current location of Christ Church Cathedral around 1030. The current cathedral was constructed in 1172.

9. Mayo: Dun Briste

Downpatrick Head in County Mayo is home to the tall sea stack known as Dun Briste.

It, like many of the sites on the North Mayo coast, is one of many natural Irish sights that tourists often overlook.

Downpatrick Head's surrounding cliffs, with their unique rock formations, are an astounding 350 million years old.

When there's a strong wind and the waves are pounding against the cliffs, you'll feel as if you've arrived at the end of Ireland.

10. Mayo Slieve League

The Slieve League Cliffs, located on the Wild Atlantic Way, are probably Ireland's most iconic features after the Cliffs of Moher.

They are some of Europe's highest sea cliffs, with spectacular views on a clear day.

They're in Donegal, a short drive from the county town. During the off-season, you can drive straight up to the observation point.

11. Claire's Burren

The Burren National Park in County Clare is around 1,500 hectares in size, while the greater Burren region encompasses 200 square kilometers and contains everything from the Aran Islands to the Cliffs of Moher.

Despite being one of Ireland's most popular tourist destinations, many visitors leave disappointed because they arrive (bad pun, I know...) without a plan of action.

The Burren Drive takes you to Doonagore Castle and Father Ted's House, as well as Doolin Cave, Poulnabrone Dolmen, and the Aillwee Caves.

12. Kylemore Abbey (Ireland)

Kylemore Abbey in Connemara is perhaps one of Ireland's most famous sites, having appeared on over a million postcards.

Kylemore Abbey, built in 1867, has seen its fair share of romance, tragedy, and innovation throughout the years.

Kylemore is now occupied by Benedictine sisters, who have lived there since 1920. This is one of the most popular things to do in Galway, and it can get crowded at times.

If possible, aim to arrive when it first opens or just before it closes.

13. Wexford Hook Lighthouse

Hook Lighthouse in County Wexford is a must-see for anyone interested in historical structures in Ireland.

Hook Lighthouse, located on the rugged Hook Peninsula, is one of the world's oldest working lighthouses.

In fact, a lighthouse of some kind has existed in this location since the 5th century, when a Welsh monk named Dubhán founded a monastery just north of Hook Head.

14. Kilkenny: Jerpoint Abbey

Few Irish antiquities are as spectacular as the medieval Jerpoint Abbey in County Kilkenny.

If you're unfamiliar, Jerpoint Abbey is one of Ireland's best-preserved Cistercian abbeys, dating back to the 12th century.

The abbey existed for hundreds of years until King Henry VIII enacted the Monasteries Dissolution Act in 1536.

In 2023, the abbey is a joy to wander around, despite the fact that much of it is in ruins.

15. Mayo's Croagh Patrick

Croagh Patrick, a hill steeped in Irish mythology and history, is one of Ireland's most popular hikes due to the other-worldly views it offers on a clear day.

It's a short drive from Westport Town, where pilgrims have been making the ascent for hundreds of years.

The trek to the peak is difficult and takes 4 to 5 hours. The views of Clew Bay and its many islands, however, make the effort worthwhile.

16. Kerry's Muckross Abbey

Muckross Abbey, which was founded in 1448, is a popular stop on the Ring of Kerry.

Its history is stormy, and the abbey has been destroyed and rebuilt numerous times.

The friars who lived at the abbey were periodically raided. They, like many others, were hounded by Cromwell's army.

Even if you have no interest in ancient ruins, the abbey here is worth a visit. Mostly because of the ancient yew tree that stands in the center.

17. Cork's Mizen Head

Mizen Head in West Cork is Ireland's southernmost point and a great (but very windy!) site to visit at any time of year.

One of the reasons that the massive Mizen Head is one of Ireland's most recognized features is that it was frequently the final portion of Europe that many on transatlantic sea voyages saw.

It's located on the rugged and desolate Mizen Peninsula, and it features a mini-museum, a signal station, and a bridge that you may cross while staring out at the surrounding cliffs.

18. Limerick's King John's Castle

King Johns Castle may be found in Limerick City, where it is ideally placed on King's Island, overlooking the Shannon River.

King John's, like many Irish castles, is built on a historic location that was originally home to a Viking settlement.

Unsurprisingly, Kind John ordered the castle's construction in 1200, and it is thought to be one of Europe's best-preserved Norman fortresses.

19. Dublin's Guinness Storehouse

Another well-known monument in Ireland is the Guinness Storehouse. In any case, it's Ireland's most popular tourist attraction!

The factory, which stands proudly at St. Jame's Gate near Dublin's Phoenix Park, is on the same site where Arthur Guinness took out a 9,000-year lease in 1759.

You can take a self-guided or guided tour here, and both will end in the stunning Gravity Bar, which offers spectacular views of Dublin City and beyond.

20. Monastic Site of Glendalough (Wicklow)

Glendalough Monastic Site is a beautiful place to walk at any time of year, and it has drawn pilgrims, visitors, and locals for thousands of years.

St. Kevin created the Monastery in the sixth century as a refuge for him to get away from the world.

He spent a brief period of time in a cave near Upper Lake that is now known as St. Kevin's Bed. The Monastery has a round tower, a cemetery, and some ruins.

21. Kerry Carrauntoohil

Carrauntoohil is Ireland's tallest peak, standing at 2,407 feet.

It's part of the MacGillycuddy's mountain range, and the Devil's Ladder from Cronins Yard is the most popular way to get there.

This is not a walk to be taken lightly. The track takes about 6 hours to complete, but the terrain is challenging and weather can change quickly, so extreme caution is required.

22. Donegal's Fanad Lighthouse

The Fanad Lighthouse in County Donegal is a striking landmark, especially at sunrise or sunset.

It was created after a Royal Navy frigate was wrecked nearby at the end of 1811, killing over 250 people.

Despite its fame, several other ships, including the S Empire Heritage, have been wrecked nearby.

23. Derry's Free Derry Corner
The Free Derry Corner is one of Ireland's major historical sights, located in Derry's Bogside.

Despite its youth, the location has become synonymous with the city's violent past.

The Free Derry Corner narrative began on January 5, 1969, when a local activist spray-painted 'You are now entering Free Derry' on the corner.

Over the years, images of the corner have appeared in history books, films, and numerous news headlines.

24. The Cork Deck of Cards
The Deck of Cards in Cobh is one of several renowned sights in Ireland that rose to prominence thanks to social media.

The 'Cards' are a row of brightly colored residences situated against the backdrop of St Coleman's Cathedral and the neighboring harbor.

Seeing them from the position on the left above can be perilous and difficult, as the view is from atop a high wall.

25. Dunamase (Laois) Rock
The Rock of Dunamase in County Laois blends history with breathtaking valley vistas.

The site was chosen for its strategic location with a view of the surrounding area, and 'the rock' was built on the site of an early Christian community.

When the daughter of the King of Leinster married Strongbow, a Norman, in 1170, the Rock of Dunamase was part of her dowry (items of value brought by a woman to her marriage).

The fortress was robbed until Cromwell's army demolished it in 1650. It is now in ruins.

26. Glencar Waterfall (Leitrim)

Few natural landmarks in Ireland have sparked the imaginations of as many people as Glencar Waterfall in Leitrim.

If you're familiar with WB Yeats' works, you'll recall references to Glencar Lough and its waterfall.

It is now one of the more noteworthy sites along the Wild Atlantic Way, and it is a short walk from the local car park.

27. Dn Aonghasa (Ireland)

Few natural landmarks in Ireland gained as much attention as Dn Aonghasa in 2023 (Achill Island's Keem Bay also drew some interest!).

Because of its stunning coastline setting, the fort on Inis Mor was one of numerous Banshees of Inisherin filming locations.

Dn Aonghasa was initially built around 1100BC. It was re-fortified some centuries later, approximately 700-800 AD.

The rugged cliffs, the incredible power of the wind, and the crash of the waves below will send shockwaves through your senses if you visit.

28. Sean's Bar (Wexford)

Sean's Bar in Athlone Town, County Westmeath, is Ireland's oldest tavern, dating back to 900AD.

It's a short walk from both Athlone Castle and the Shannon River, and its age was confirmed during an excavation in 1970.

During the 'dig,' walls constructed with the wattle and daub technique were unearthed, which are thought to date back to the 9th century.

29. Waterford's Reginald Tower

Reginald's Tower, located in the heart of Waterford City, is now a Viking museum showcasing the city's rich history.

The 16-meter-high circular tower is Waterford's oldest civic structure, dating from between 1253 and 1280.

The tower is thought to have been named after one of the area's Viking lords, Raghnall Mac Gilla Muire, and it was used as an observation tower.

30. Wexford's Dunbrody Famine Ship

The Dunbrody Famine Ship is another prominent landmark in Ireland due to its proximity to Rosslare Harbour, which serves as the arrival point for many people taking the ferry to Ireland.

It can be found in the town of New Ross. If you're not aware with Famine Ships, they were vessels that transported people from Ireland to distant regions during the Famine.

The original Dunbrody Famine Ship was built in the mid-nineteenth century and set sail from Wexford for Quebec in 1845.

The replica was built in the 1990s with the help of the JFK Trust and the expertise of local ship builders.

31. Kerry's Dun Chaoin Pier

We're on our way to the Dingle Peninsula, then to one of Ireland's most recognized sights, due to incessant social media posts.

The one-of-a-kind Dun Chaoin Pier on the Slea Head Road is located in the village of Dun Chaoin, just a short drive from Dingle Town.

The Blasket Island Ferry departs from here, and parking is available at the small ticket shack (never drive down the curving route!).

You don't have to take the ferry to enjoy this location; you can see it and the Dingle coast from the grass above.

32. Birr Castle (County Offaly)

One of Ireland's more odd historical landmarks can be seen in the grounds of Birr Castle in Offaly.

The land has been the site of fortresses since 1170, and the current castle is inhabited by the same family that purchased it in 1620.

On the grounds, you'll find what was once the world's largest telescope. It was built in the 1840s and was used by people from all over the world for many years.

Chapter 27: Ireland Unveiled: Ten Fascinating Fun Facts

These Ireland fun facts will teach you everything you didn't know about Europe's third-largest island. When did the Irish language emerge? Why do Irish people enjoy watching the Eurovision Song Contest? What is the location of the world's oldest operational lighthouse? Here are our ten interesting facts about Ireland!

1. Halloween was invented in Ireland.

The eerie autumn festival Halloween originated as an Irish holiday. Samhain is a Celtic ritual that inspired the celebration. Large bonfires were formerly burned during this occasion to ward off evil spirits.

2. A harp is Ireland's national symbol.

Ireland is the only country in the world whose national symbol is a musical instrument: the Irish harp. This sign is well-known as the logo of the iconic Irish beer brand Guinness. Surprisingly, Guinness utilized the harp before it became Ireland's national symbol.

To obtain the trademark, the Irish government had to request a favor from the Guinness family. That wasn't a problem, Guinness reasoned, as long as the national harp was shown similarly to their own - something that remains true today.

Did you know that Lough Tay on the Wicklow Way, which was previously owned by the Guinness Family, is also known as the Guinness Lake because it resembles a pint of the black stuff?

3. Irish is one of the world's oldest living languages.

Ireland has two official languages: English and Irish. The Irish language, commonly known as Gaelic, is completely distinct from English. Word order is inverted, and characters that do not appear in the English alphabet are employed.

So, of course, one of our interesting facts about Ireland has to be about the Irish language! Gaelic is one of the world's oldest living languages. Although scholars vary on the precise dates, the Irish language is thought to have originated between 3,000 and 4,000 years ago. That means the Irish language is approximately as old as Chinese, Ancient Greek, and Hebrew.

4. The author of Dracula was Irish.
Despite the fact that Dracula is situated in Romanian Transylvania, the narrative was written by an Irishman, Bram Stoker. Stoker attended Trinity College in Dublin, as did Oscar Wilde, Samuel Beckett, and Jonathan Swift. In homage of the literary hero, Dublin organizes the Bram Stoker festival every year.

5. Vikings founded Dublin.
The Irish capital was founded by marauding Normans, not Irish. The Vikings established Dublin as a strategic settlement in the ninth century. They pillaged the nearby coastal towns before returning to their camp, which was most likely located exactly where Dublin Castle now sits.

6. The average Irishman consumes approximately 100 liters of beer every year.
This statistic about Ireland validates all stereotypes: each year, the country consumes an average of 100 liters of beer per person. This places the country in the top ten of the world's beer consumers. There is even a pub for every hundred people in Dublin.

7. Ireland has won the Eurovision Song Contest seven times.
The Eurovision Song Contest is a favorite pastime of the Irish. They have seven times won the European talent show (in 1970, 1980, 1987, 1992, 1993, 1994, and 1996). That is more than any other country has ever contributed to the competition!

8. There are more 'Irish' people living outside of Ireland than inside.

This is one of the facts about Ireland on which not everyone agrees. After all, there are numerous ways to determine whether or not someone is Irish. This only applies to those born in Ireland or to offspring of one or two Irish parents. Anyone who descends deep enough down the family tree will always find a wanted ancestor — as it turns out, Barack Obama's great-great-grandfather was an Irishman who immigrated to America in 1850.

As a result, there are nearly 35 million Americans of Irish heritage, which is more than seven times Ireland's population. A third of Australians are also of Irish descent. These familial relationships can be many generations old, yet the numbers don't lie: the Irish have spread all over the world!

You probably have a link to Co. Kerry if your surname is O'Sullivan, O'Connor, Shea, Murphy, McCarthy, Fitzgerald, O'Connell, or Donoghue. Learn more about the Kerry Way by taking a walking tour.

9. Ireland is home to the world's oldest operational lighthouse.
This lighthouse's black and white striped structure has been around for over 800 years, but light beacons were first deployed on this site in the fifth century. Hook Lighthouse is located in County Wexford on Ireland's south coast. It is one of the most popular attractions in the area. The lighthouse is still operational, but it hasn't been manned since the tower went autonomous in 1996.

10. In Ireland, there are no wild snakes.
After being beset by snakes, Saint Patrick, according to legend, chased them all off the island of Ireland. Indeed, no one who has ever visited Ireland has ever seen a snake. According to scientists, this has little to do with St. Patrick. Since the last Ice Age, there have been no snakes in Ireland. Except for in the zoo.

According to legend, St. Patrick banished snakes from Ireland from the summit of Croagh Patrick. On a walking tour of Connemara, you will pass Croagh Patrick.

Chapter 28: Hidden Gems of Ireland: Seven Overlooked Natural Marvels

Explore Ireland's lesser-known sites, such as mirror lakes and ancient castles, distant monasteries, stunning beaches, and secret waterfalls, in addition to the iconic landmarks. Nomad Ronan reveals his favorite treks and the greatest road trip to see them all.

While tourists throng to Ireland's iconic natural beauties, such as the Cliffs of Moher and the Ring of Kerry, equally stunning but comparatively desolate landscapes lie hidden off the tourist track. From deep forests to breathtaking valleys and sacred mountains, here are seven hidden gems worth exploring.

Slieve League (Donegal County)

A blackface sheep trots down the edge of Europe's tallest accessible sea cliffs as I stare down at the Atlantic Ocean, waves exploding on a rocky shoreline 1,900ft (580m) below me. Slieve League is the location. Despite being three times higher than the Cliffs of Moher (Ireland's most popular tourist attraction), this lonely corner of northwest Ireland sees only a fraction of the visitors.

Recognizing its unrealized potential, Irish authorities recently renovated it for USD $6 million. Visitors can now enjoy its renovated visitor center and 1 mile (1.6 kilometers) of new walkways. These smooth roads and staircases lead tourists up to the peak of the cliffs from the parking park, which gives panoramic views of the Atlantic. Visitors can take boat cruises that allow them to swim, fish, and scuba dive in the clean ocean that licks these cliffs if they are truly overwhelmed by the enormity of Slieve League.

Dooney Rock Forest (Sligo County)
When I visit Ireland, I always make a point of visiting this tranquil woodland on the banks of sparkling Lake Gill. There is, in my opinion, no place more calm and gorgeous on the earth. This tranquillity originates not just from its beauty, but also from the fact that it is devoid of crowds, while being only a short drive from the busy, historic university town of Sligo.

The massive rock that lends this site its name serves as a windbreak. Its tall woodland does as well. Between September and November, the leaves shed by such trees create a colorful carpet on the ground, ranging from gold to orange, pink, and purple.

Beautiful vistas are available all year along the 1mi (1.6km) stroll that loops along the lake's edge and back into the dense forest. After completing this short climb, tourists will understand why one of history's finest poets, Sligo's own W.B. Yeats, came here for inspiration on a regular basis.

Peaks embrace Lake Doo (Doo Lough) so tightly that it's as if they're attempting to keep its majesty from escaping. This rugged mountain route in Ireland's far west is breathtaking. It's not lovely in a manicured way; rather, its splendor is tinged with hostility, providing the impression that, while it's an incredible location to visit, survival in this isolated, rugged environment would be difficult.

It's a place where Mother Nature occasionally expresses her rage, with freezing winds and torrential rains. In between such storms, Lake Doo feels like Ireland condensed into a single location: a pristine, salmon-rich lake tucked between steep, green mountains where ancient people previously farmed but where only tough sheep now roam. Lake Doo is wild and stunning whether it is covered in snow, whipped by gales, or lighted by a sunny day. Visitors have plenty of time to take in its beauty while hiking the 5mi (8km) round around the lake.

Lough Key Forest Park (Roscommon County)

I glimpse a majestic old castle while stranded in a pristine lake surrounded by dense forest. Its mirror in the quiet lake appears flawless until it is pierced by a swarm of swans gliding by beneath a cloudless sky. This appears to be a scene created by CGI artists charged with creating a heavenly setting for a children's film.

Everything appears almost too flawless to be genuine, but this is how Lough Key Forest Park appears every time the sun shines brightly in County Roscommon. That's also the greatest time to swim in the lake, picnic on the park's wide waterside lawns, trek the park's more than 10mi (16km) of forest trails, or row a hiring boat out to visit McDermott's Castle, an 800-year-old castle.

Keem Bay (Mayo County)

Growing up in Perth, Australia, which is known for its beautiful coastline, I'm not often taken aback by a beach. Despite this, every time I drive around the mountainous bend to receive my first glimpse of Keem Bay, it happens.

The blue sea water laps against a 1,600ft (488m) expanse of beautiful white sand on Achill, Ireland's largest island. The massive cliffs that guard the bay and seem like a gigantic green horseshoe from above are what make this beach on Ireland's western coast so remarkable.

Because to its fortunate geography, Keem Bay is delightfully peaceful for much of the year. Many of Ireland's most beautiful beaches are hampered by strong winds and turbulent surf. Keem, not so. In every sense of the term, it's a haven.

Glencar (Leitrim County)

Tabletop mountains with heavily forested slopes tower above magnificent waterfalls, broad green plains, and transparent lakes. Nonetheless, the picturesque valleys of County Leitrim are rarely visited, either by people or tourists. With barely 32,000 residents, Leitrim is Ireland's smallest county and is sometimes neglected by visitors. Despite this, it is the most picturesque county in the country. I've yet to come across an unattractive area of Leitrim.

"I stood enchanted at the scene of grandeur and light," sang Larry Cunningham in his song Lovely Leitrim, an homage to the county's underrated charms. Glencar, where a waterfall cascades down the beautiful slope into a stream that feeds the nearby lake, epitomizes the county's magnificence. There's a 4-mile (6.4-kilometer) hiking track through the hills above the lake, or a 0.7-mile (1.1-kilometer) walk from the lakefront parking lot to the waterfall and back.

Gougane Barra (Cork County)

"Go where the monasteries are." When I asked an elderly Irish cousin where to discover the country's most serene areas, he given me half-joking but fully practical advise. It makes natural that Ireland's monks would congregate in regions of great peace and beauty in a country abounding with lonely spots.

Kerry and Cork are widely regarded as Ireland's two most gorgeous counties, therefore anywhere spanning their borders must be similarly beautiful. That's what I reasoned as my Cork-born brother drove me to one of his favorite spots, Gougane Barra, a hill-hemmed lake where St Finbar established a monastery 1,500 years ago.

It is still a Catholic pilgrimage site, with some people walking the old St Finbar's Path. This hiking trek begins in the Cork town of Drimoleague and travels through mountains, rivers, and lakes before arriving at Gougane Barra.

Itinerary for a road trip

Renting a car is by far the most convenient method to tour Ireland. After landing in Dublin, drive northwest for 4 hours to County Donegal. From the magnificent Slieve League cliffs, take the well-marked Wild Atlantic Way south, a breathtaking 1,550mi (2,494km) driving route along Ireland's west coast.

Take a little detour inland to County Leitrim, and you'll arrive to Glencar after 1 hour and 40 minutes of driving. It's only a 20-minute journey into County Sligo to reach my particular hideaway, Dooney Rock Forest. Then, drive 1 hour south to the lush Lough Key Forest Park. After that, it's a three-hour drive west to quiet Keem Bay on Achill Island, which is connected to the mainland by a small road bridge, and a 90-minute drive south via some of Ireland's most pristine coastal scenery to the rocky Doo Lough.

The final stage of the voyage is the most difficult, a 4.5-hour ride through counties Galway, Clare, and Limerick until you reach the breathtaking Gougane Barra in County Cork. This road journey should take at least a week to accomplish.

Chapter 29: Unforgettable Culinary Adventures in Ireland: Nine Must-Try Food Experiences

Food in Ireland is more than just fine-dining quality in the city's best restaurants. It's about eating seafood on a beach, eating apple pie in a remote spot, and dining on the very freshest fish you've just pulled from the water.

1. Moran's Oyster Cottage in County Galway for lunch

Moran's Oyster Cottage is the place to go if you want a unique dining experience. This 250-year-old home on the cliffs of the Atlantic Ocean in County Galway has fed everyone from Julia Roberts to Roger Moore. Sit inside in a quiet nook in the old structure, or outside at a table to take in the magnificent surrounding seascapes. Plates of Galway Bay oysters, wild native clams, and steamed Galway Bay mussels are available. What is our recommendation? Finish with a pint of Guinness. It doesn't get much better.

2. Harry's Shack in Portstewart

Nothing beats lying on a beach with your toes in the sand and eating unbelievably fresh seafood, no matter where you are in the globe. There is a site in Northern Ireland where you may do precisely that. Since its inception in 2014, Harry's Shack has developed a cult following. The humble hut here is home to some of the best seafood cookery on the island of Ireland, with a lovely beachfront setting on Portstewart Strand. All you have to do is show up, relax, and have fun.

3. Belfast Food Tour, City of Belfast

Belfast has one of the most inventive restaurant scenes on the island of Ireland, from refined tastes at Ox to fine-tuned seafood at the Mourne Seafood Bar. But, to really get to know this Northern Ireland gourmet hotspot, join the multi-award winning Belfast Food Tour. The tours capture the spirit of Belfast's distinct flavors, producers, and eateries, covering everything from whiskey to bars to delectable snacks with energy, excitement, and insider knowledge.

4. The Happy Pear, Wicklow, Ireland

Greystones, a busy little town in County Wicklow, is a 30-minute DART (train) trip from Dublin, but it feels a million miles away from the city's urban hustle. The Happy Pear, a vegetarian hotspot, anchors the town's cuisine culture. The café, run by twins David and Stephen Flynn, has become a favorite of both vegetarians and carnivores due to its excellent and imaginative take on plant-based dishes. On a bright day, the atmosphere is fantastic, with tables and chairs strewn about outside and a busy throng. If you're feeling brave, join the twins for a dawn swim in Greystones' Ladies' Cove, where they take to the waves with locals and guests every morning. Follow that up with breakfast at the Church Road café, and you've got yourself a fairly memorable start to the day!

5. Dingle, County Kerry Ice Cream

Dingle has the word "feel-good" written all over it. This happy small town in County Kerry has terrific bars, great restaurants, and a laid-back bohemian feel that draws travelers from all over the world. If you go, you'll observe a bustling line that seems to linger outside a blue shop on Strand Street. Murphy's Ice Cream is a magnificent temple to all things dairy. The flavors here are worth driving miles for: Dingle sea salt, caramelised brown bread, and Irish coffee, all produced with the finest fresh farm milk and local cream. It's ice cream with a distinct Irish flavor.

6. Pyke 'N' Pommes, DerryLondonderry

Pyke 'N Pommes in Foyleview may appear to be an unusual location for one of the island of Ireland's best cuisine experiences, but they prefer to do things differently. This informal meal with a gourmet touch and a very local heart is located on the waterfront in the historic city of DerryLondonderry. Tacos, a famed Wagyu burger, slow-roasted pork, and some of the freshest fish in town - it's a gastronomic treasure.

7. Cork's English Market is number seven.

The English Market, which dates back to 1788, is much more than a typical food market. This restaurant, located in the center of Cork's gourmet city, delivers an explosion of flavors, a riot of colors, and time-honored delicacies that you won't find anywhere else. A O'Reilly & Sons serves tripe and drisheen (a form of blood pudding), Tom Durcan's serves traditional spiced beef, and Frank Hederman's serves some of the best smoked salmon in the world. After visiting, travel upstairs to the Farmgate Café for some classic local meals like tripe and onions with drisheen, lamb's liver and bacon, and, of course, sausage and mash!

8. Cupán Tae, Cork County

The stunning wave-lashed peninsula of Sheep's Head in County Cork is a notch above when it comes to coastal wildernesses. Walk out to the top of the lighthouse and you'll be surrounded by the white-tipped Atlantic Ocean and vistas that extend on forever. This strange little place, however, is also home to "the tea shop at the end of the world." Cupán Tae ("cup of tea" in Irish) is run by Bernie Tobin and is the epitome of basic food done well, including salmon sandwiches, light fluffy scones, and famed apple pie. Simple meal, gorgeous scenery, and memories made.

9. Gourmet Fishing Trip, County Kerry

Derrynane in County Kerry is something exceptional - a site of extreme beauty on the Wild Atlantic Way, with butter-colored sands, blue waters filled with islands, and a backdrop of undulating mountains. It's also the location of a memorable culinary adventure: a gourmet fishing expedition with Atlantic Irish Seaweed. Boatman John Fitzgerald takes visitors around the islands of Derrynane Bay to fish and feast on sashimi and ceviche Irish-style. Wild, beautiful, and an unforgettable experience.

Chapter 30: Fourteen Exceptional Irish Food and Drink Experiences

The food and drink culture in Ireland is excellent, with everything from exciting hotspots to artisan trails, foraging lessons to luxury dining. Ireland's rapidly rising culinary reputation can be attributed to its creative and talented chefs, ardent food enthusiasts, and master distillers.

Padraig O'Raighne, Galway, will take you on a tour of Connemara and the Aran Islands.

Padraig O'Raighne takes you on a tour of two prominent Gaeltacht locales, Connemara and Rainn (Aran Islands). Padraig of Connemara Pub Tours, a Gaeltacht man himself, blends his local knowledge with food-industry insider knowledge. Experience the breathtaking landscape of Connemara's Gaeltacht while sipping a drink and listening to people tell stories and sing traditional melodies.

If you want to go any further, take their rain cruise and see life off the shore of the Atlantic Ocean. Take a picturesque flight over the water to Inis Oorr (Inisheer) and see three Irish establishments. There, you may enjoy traditional Irish cuisine and drink before touring the island with your knowledgeable guide.

Catch and cook at Kerry's Dingle Cookery School

Catch and Cook at Dingle Cookery School will take you out on the water to experience the pleasure of catching your own food in the Atlantic and then utilizing fresh ingredients to create a great meal. This is a real supper not to be missed as you head out to the Dingle Bay fishing grounds to catch mackerel, pollock, or cod.

You'll be asked back into the cookery school's kitchen to prepare your catch once you've caught it. This is followed by a culinary course in which you will learn how to make exquisite side dishes for your dish. And what about the prize? From the sea to the plate, you've prepared an incredible seafood dinner.

Dine at the Long Dock Pub and Restaurant.
The Long Dock, which was built in the 1820s, was always a pub, but it also served as a hardware store, grocer, and even a drapery. You'll be captivated by the Carrigaholt pub's old-world charm and comforts from the moment you walk through the door.

When in County Clare, try some traditional Irish pub fare such as wonderful racks of lamb ribs, roasted pork belly, and of course The Long Dock's famed seafood soup with baked brown bread, a local favorite and heavenly experience.

Go on a wild food hike with Wild Kitchen.
On her guided hikes, Oonagh O'Dwyer from Wild Kitchen will share her knowledge and passion for all things related to wild cuisine. Discover a variety of edible seaweeds, plants, flowers, herbs, berries, and fruit, and learn how to forage responsibly and securely with the assistance of an expert.

Plant identification, recipes, seasonal suggestions, and, of course, eating the natural bounty that you harvest are all part of the walk. It's an immersive experience that everyone can enjoy, with your lunch or supper coming directly from nature.

Roe & Co Whiskey Distillery in Dublin offers a drink.
Roe & Co Whiskey Distillery is a top-notch urban distillery and whiskey attraction located in Dublin City's Liberties neighborhood. Step inside the renowned former Guinness Power Station for a journey from conception to completion.

Discover the secrets of Roe's one-of-a-kind blend in Room 106, and learn about the flavor pillars to determine your optimum taste profile. This is an intimate and personal tour that allows you to get up close and personal with modern whiskey at its best.

Sweet treats are available at Highbank Organic Orchards in Kilkenny.
Enjoy a drink of cider or apple crystal gin from 'pip to sip' at Highbank Organic Orchards in Kilkenny. The Calder-Potts family first built these orchards in the 17th century.

Here you'll find pleasant apple juice, cider, and mulled apple juice, as well as their own orchard syrup, which many people enjoy. These orchards and organic farm shop are part of the Taste of Kilkenny Food Trail and are well worth a visit.

Drink at the Franciscan Well Brewery in Cork.
Learn about the enigmatic art of brewing at Cork City's award-winning Franciscan Well Brewery. This brewery was founded in 1998 on the site of a historic Franciscan convent dating back to 1219. Today, the brewery combines modern technology with age-old tradition to produce flavorful beers such as lager, ale, stout, and wheat beers.

Carlow, go foraging with Blackstairs Eco Trails.
With Blackstairs Eco Trails in Carlow, spend a day foraging for wild edibles and exploring wildlife in the hedgerows. Discover the Blackstairs Mountains' bounty of wild edibles on a fully guided hike suitable for all ages. As you enjoy a rustic day in the countryside, meander through gorgeous alleys, lowlands, and bogs.

Goatsbridge Trout Farm in Kilkenny serves smoked fish.
Goatsbridge Trout Farm is a local family company that was founded in 1961. Take a farm tour and observe the trout at various phases of development, from ova in the hatchery to maturity at 20 months in the earthen pond. During your stay, try their fresh, smoked, and barbecued fish, as well as their amazing trout caviar.

Macalla Farm on Clare Island, Mayo, offers a wellness resort.
Set sail for Clare Island and get ready for an outstanding gourmet experience in a lovely location at Macalla Farm. Explore the organic farm, see sheep graze on the open boglands, and take a lovely walk through the

woods. After you've worked up an appetite, head to the Stone Barn Café for a meal crafted with farm-fresh ingredients. This is genuinely farm to fork dining, with the ingredients for their soups, salads, and desserts growing just steps from your table.

Mungo Murphy's Seaweed Co in Galway serves fishy delights.
Visit the Connemara coast for one of Ireland's most unusual and wonderful seafood dishes: abalone. This sea snail flourishes in Irish waters, and Mungo Murphy's Seaweed Co. offers an abalone tasting trip where you can learn more about this fascinating critter.

Abalone is a luxury ingredient that tastes like a cross between scallops and foie gras. Mungo's gastronomic tours don't end there; take a seaweed tasting trip and let the professionals identify components for your next dish, or buy some pre-packaged jars from the shop.

Carlow, enjoy a day out on the Carlow Food Trail.
With GAA teams like The Scallion Eaters, it's no surprise that Carlow residents enjoy their cuisine, and there's no better place to do so than on the Carlow cuisine Trail. Set out on a self-guided culinary tour through picturesque towns and villages in Ireland.

Relax in a modern setting at the art gallery VISUAL, and then head to Lennon's for a meal created with sustainable and locally produced food. After that, stop by Carlow Brewing Company to learn more about these excellent, small batch beers. Desserts are essential on any cuisine trip, so stop by The Chocolate Garden of Ireland for some sweet treats.

Enjoy the scenery at Caffe Banba in Donegal.
Caffe Banba, located at the top of Ireland's most northerly point, Malin Head, is one of those Donegal attractions that you simply must see for yourself. It is known locally as the "café on wheels" and serves some of the best coffee in Ireland, as well as beautiful views of the Atlantic Ocean and the neighboring Donegal mountains. In the neighboring Banba Malin Head Bakery, you may find a variety of delicious baked goods that the Banba

staff makes from scratch every day and enjoy a wonderful treat in a magnificent setting.

After you've had your fill of tea and coffee, tour the mountainous region around the coffee cart to discover where some of the iconic scenes from Star Wars: The Last Jedi were shot.

Visit The Happy Pear in Wicklow for a coffee and a dip.
As you travel along Church Road in Greystones, Wicklow, you can't miss this vividly colored wholefood store and restaurant. The Happy Pear, with its eye-catching shopfront, has become a landmark location to visit in this tiny seaside town.

You can enjoy a delicious meal in the restaurant upstairs, at one of the outdoor tables on the street below, or order it to go. It is open seven days a week and serves a range of hot and cold vegetarian meals.

Chapter 31: Embracing the Irish Experience

Ireland has over 3,000 kilometers of coastline, over 40 mountain ranges, 37 rivers, 6 national parks, and innumerable beautiful beaches to explore. There is plenty to do in Ireland, especially if you don't mind getting your feet wet.

Watersports

Kayaking and canoeing are popular activities in Ireland's oceans, rivers, and lakes. Explore the sea caves, islets, and secret coves off the coast of Co. Waterford, or go midnight kayaking through Co. Kerry's Gold Tier International Dark-Sky Reserve for some of the best stargazing in the Northern Hemisphere. Canoe.ie has further information on centres and clubs.

Ireland's abundance of shoreline and wind provide for some fantastic surfing, and the sport has gained in popularity over the last decade. Surf sites may be found all along our coast, but the most famous are in the west of the island, such as Lahinch in Co. Clare and Bundoran in Co. Donegal. Mullaghmore, Co. Sligo, is one of the top large wave surfing places in the world for the more advanced surfer. You'll also have access to a variety of other water sports in Ireland, including windsurfing, kitesurfing, and wakeboarding.

Of course, as an island, Ireland is ideal for diving, with around 40 dive sites throughout the Atlantic and Irish Sea shores. Check out Diving Ireland for additional information if you want to experience snorkeling for the first time, become a dive teacher, or join an underwater hockey team (yes, really).

Hiking, running, biking, and horseback riding

There are virtually an unlimited number of paths for walking, running, hiking, and bicycling throughout Ireland, and the majority of them may be found on Irish Trails, which lists over 4,000km of National Waymarked Trails. Explore the land by following trails across hills, mountains, woods, and glens.

Would you rather travel on two wheels? There are numerous options. Whether your notion of a good time is a leisurely ride along the beach, a tough circuit around the Ring of Kerry, or crashing down a muddy mountain at breakneck speed. Join a local group or ride your bike alone. For information about day tours, classes, bike rentals, and events, see Biking.ie.

Alternatively, what better way to experience Ireland than on horseback? Whether you're looking for a riding school or just want to attempt a one-day trek, equestrian centers cater to all levels around the country. Take a scenic ride through the Burren or a stroll along the beaches of Co. Wicklow. More information can be found at Irish Horse Riding.

Mountaineering, rock climbing, and cave exploration

If you're tired of being on the ground, there's plenty to do above (or below) sea level. If you want to stay high and dry, Ireland has a plethora of mountains to choose from. Carrauntoohil (1,028m) in Co. Kerry is Ireland's tallest peak for those searching for a challenge. Or make the yearly pilgrimage to Croagh Patrick in Co. Mayo, where thousands Irish people ascend to the summit in their bare feet each July. Rock climbing and bouldering have grown in popularity, so there are now many indoor facilities where you can practice before taking your talents outdoors to rockfaces and cliffs throughout the country - check Mountaineering Ireland for more information.

If you're searching for something a little deeper and darker, go caving (also known as potholing) underground. There are some amazing caves to explore in Ireland, particularly in the midlands of Co. Cavan, Co. Fermanagh, and Co. Clare, where the peculiar limestone environment is home to tunnels with incredible rock formations.

Golf

There's always golf for those who want to keep their shoes clean and feel a little more civilized. Ireland is, in truth, a golfer's heaven. Our small island is home to one-quarter of the world's true links courses, including the Royal County Down, which was recently rated the world's best golf course by Golf Digest. Ireland has hosted numerous golf championships, and the world's best golfers return time and again to tee off on our greens, many of which offer breathtaking coastal views.

Chapter 32: Ireland's Top Seven Hiking Trails

The treks detailed below are among the best in Ireland. Some of these hikes may take you a day, while others will take you a week. Everything will give you a terrific sense of the country.

Don't let the fact that Ireland is known for its rain deter you from trekking here. It rarely poured all day, in my experience. I thought it exhilarating to have survived the harsh weather on the occasions when it did rain all day.

Remember that there is no such thing as bad weather - only lousy clothing. (While hiking the Dingle Way, I learnt to pack my wet hiking boots with newspaper to speed up the drying process.) If you come prepared, you'll have a great time on this sampling of Ireland's top treks.

Mweelrea Mountain as a day climb and the Dingle Way as a multi-day hike are two of my favorite hikes in Ireland. Whatever trek you do, be prepared with the ten hiking essentials and let someone know where you are going and when you intend to return.

1. Croagh Patrick

Croagh Patrick is a sacred mountain in County Mayo, not far from Westport. On Reek Sunday, the last Sunday of July, up to 15,000 pilgrims trek the mountain, some barefoot. While it is not a particularly challenging peak to scale, appearances can be deceiving.

When I first tried it, I was completely blown off. John and I called it a day after hiking for 90 minutes bending over at the waist. My recent Wilderness Ireland vacation included a visit to the peak. Although we could have hiked it in principle, it was pouring rain and it would have been a dismal day with no views - one of the main reasons to trek it.

Croagh Patrick stands only 764 meters (2,507 feet) tall. For the first half of the walk, the trail is wide and the grade is moderate. The path then steepens significantly and becomes a rock-strewn path with uneven footing.

A chapel has been built on the peak. Patrick is said to have spent 40 days and 40 nights fasting and praying on the top in 441 AD.

2. Cliff Walk on the Cliffs of Moher

While most visitors walk from the parking lot to the Cliffs of Moher (Aill Na Searrach), skilled hikers can take a 20-kilometer coastal trek from Doolin in the north to Liscannor in the south.

On a clear day, enjoy spectacular views of the cliffs, Galway Bay, and the Aran Islands. If you are limited on time and/or energy, there are other options.

The Cliffs of Moher Visitor Centre is 5 kilometers from Hags Head, 12 kilometers from Liscannor, and 8 kilometers from Doolin. Extreme caution should be exercised near the cliffs, and be aware that fog, winds, and rain can blow in and up at any time. Even though this is one of the nicest walks in Ireland, it is a difficult one with steep ascents and tiny steps.

3. The Wicklow Route

The Wicklow Way is one of Ireland's top walks and the country's oldest way-marked long distance hiking track. It begins in Dublin and proceeds southwest for 127 kilometers through the highlands of County Wicklow, ending in Clonegal.

Most usually allot 8 to 10 days to complete the entire path. The Wicklow Way trail traverses a variety of terrains, including parkland, forest, undulating countryside, and even mountains. Self-guided (pre-order a hiking guide with thorough route finding directions) or tour company.

4. The Kerry Way - one of Ireland's most spectacular walks

The Kerry Way is Ireland's longest and most well-known sign-posted walking trail, stretching 203 kilometers (122 miles). The Kerry Way is a driving version of the Ring of Kerry, however it rarely reaches the sea.

It is mostly an inland route that begins in the southwest Irish town of Killarney. Most people climb it in a counterclockwise orientation over a period of 8-10 days. In general, towns are well-spaced and offer a variety of lodging and dining options, though the selection is restricted on the first few days out.

Enjoy a variety of scenery, including MacGillycuddy's Reeks, lonely valleys, magnificent lakes, untamed moorlands, and some spectacular coastal vistas. That is what makes the Kerry Way one of Ireland's best walks.

The trail is generally adequately marked, and attempts are being made to correct any ambiguities. If time allows, a day trip to the Skellig Islands from Cahirciveen could be the highlight of your trip. It was intended for me.

5. The Dingle Way - one of Ireland's best multi-day walks

The Dingle Way is one of Ireland's greatest long-distance walking pathways, offering some of the loveliest scenery in the country. The 179-kilometer (112-mile) trail alternates between quiet farmland and wild coastal panoramas, cliff-tops, and small towns.

The town of Tralee in County Kerry serves as the starting point. From here, one travels to Camp and then the rest of the Dingle Peninsula in a clockwise direction, with some retracing of steps on the last day as one returns to Tralee from Camp.

The hike is best completed over seven or eight days to really appreciate the experience. Expect to walk between 17 and 29 kilometers per day.

The trek over Mount Brandon's slope contains the only significant height rise (650 m), however there are other little ups and downs along the way. The signage is excellent.

6. Mweelrea Mountain is the highest peak in western Ireland.

Mweelrea Mountain is located near the community of Leenane. With a peak elevation of 814 m (2,700 ft), there is no risk of altitude sickness, and thunderstorms are not as common in this part of the world as they are in the Rocky Mountains.

Nonetheless, this mountain must be regarded seriously, particularly when the fog sets in. When you're surrounded by a cloud of white, it's easy to become bewildered.

The tremendous drop-offs near the summit of Mweelrea Mountain make it extremely risky. Even though the mountain appears to be innocuous in the images, people have perished on it. And, with the absence of a defined route to follow in any direction, navigating can be difficult at any time.

7. The Twelve Bens

While dedicated hikers attempt to trek all Twelve Bens, quartzite peaks in the Connemara province of western Ireland, mere mortals can easily knock off two or three Bens in a day. That's exactly what our Wilderness Ireland group accomplished in late April.

We parked a little distance from Kylemore Abbey and followed a path that led us past an ancient lime kiln. From there, it was a couple of hours to the first Ben, Benbaun - if my map reading abilities are correct after my phone chose to eat my notes.

From there, it was an easy downhill to Benbrack, then a slight rise up Cnoc Breac before descending to the N59 and a short walk back to the car.

Expect no well-marked paths with maps pointing to them. You have arrived at the walk's markers. In case of fog, a comprehensive topographic map is essential. However, these mountains should be on every peak-bagging enthusiast's bucket list.

Other trekking options in Ireland

The Ring of Beara is another region that should be on your radar - it is now on mine. You can trek it and possibly combine it with the Kerry Way, but you can also drive it. Paula from Contented Traveler said she preferred it to the Dingle Way and the Kerry Way.

You'll need to eat as well, right? Check out Irish Food Reinterpreted for alternatives to Guinness and dishes to replace Irish stew.

If you enjoy trekking, Ireland is a fantastic destination. There are tours available, but there are also numerous self-guided possibilities. After my good experience with Wilderness Ireland, I would highly recommend them.

Chapter 33: Navigating Scotland: Transport and Travel Options

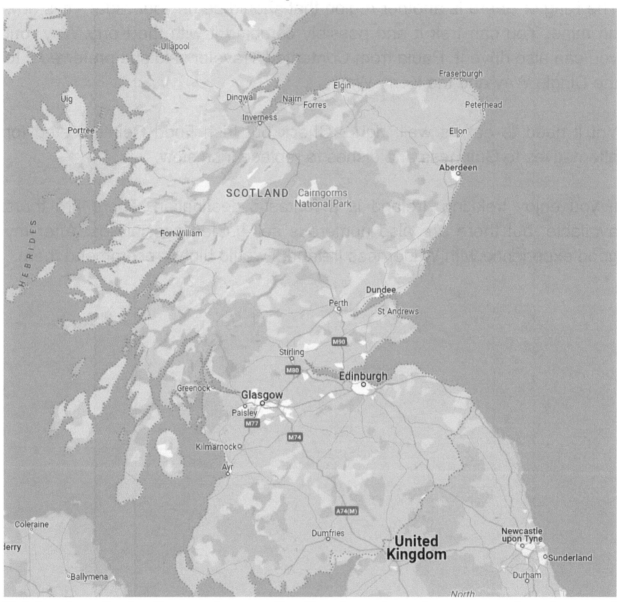

Driving is a fantastic way to see Scotland, and we have an extensive road network that makes it simple to travel around. However, if you intend to drive while in Scotland, there are a few things you should be aware of in order to keep yourself and others safe!

First and foremost, Scotland, like the rest of the United Kingdom, drives on the left side of the road!

We understand how vital it is to arrive at your destination on time, but we take road safety extremely seriously and have rigorous speed limits in place. These speeds will vary based on the sort of road you're on, but the relevant speed will be clearly marked.

We have 12 National Tourist Routes and the North Coast 500, which may be explored with VisitScotland's Road Trips book, in addition to major motorways that make inter-city travel quick and easy. These alternate driving routes may take a little longer to reach to your destination, but they will take you through some of Scotland's most breathtaking landscapes.

AIR Scotland is served by multiple international airports, making it easier than ever to enter and exit Scotland. With connections to the majority of significant destinations worldwide, we are able to welcome tens of millions of travelers each year.

We also have regular services in and out of key corporate centers such as London and Frankfurt. With London only an hour away and Frankfurt only 90 minutes away, it is now easier than ever to attend that crucial meeting.

Flying is also an excellent alternative if you have limited time or are visiting islands such as the Outer Hebrides, Orkney, or Shetland. If you wish to see Scotland from above, scenic flights are also available.

TRAIN
We have a large and well-developed rail network that not only provides cross-country connections within Scotland, but also regular connections to the rest of the UK. Most of our trains also have Wi-Fi, so whether you're commuting for work and need to check emails, or you're on vacation and want to post your photos online, we've got you covered.

Scotland also has some of the most gorgeous railway lines in the world, so taking the train is more than just a mode of transportation; it's an experience in and of itself! Purchase your desired ticket type, board the ship, and take in the scenery.

COACH AND BUS

It is believed that 95% of Scotland's population lives within a five-minute walk of a bus stop, making it simple to get where you need to go quickly and affordably.

Because of a network of dedicated bus lanes, many of our inner-city bus services can get you around town faster than any other mode of transportation. In addition, we have various cross-country coach companies that can take the stress out of traveling across the country. Allow someone else to drive while you sit back, relax, and plan your journey.

Nothing beats seeing your destination on the horizon and arriving the magnificent island or tucked-away peninsula via ferry. In Scotland, both passenger and car ferries operate, and larger islands are frequently served by many routes.

Chapter 34: Exploring Scotland: Transportation and Mobility

The central belt, which stretches from Glasgow in the west to Edinburgh on the east coast, is home to the vast majority of Scots. The public transportation system in this city is efficient, and places are easily accessible by rail and bus. Off the main routes, public transportation may be more limited, especially in more distant areas of the Highlands and Islands.

Everything is accessible with good planning, and you will have no issue getting to the key tourist spots. The low level of traffic in most parts of Scotland, particularly on picturesque backroads, makes driving gloriously stress-free.

Edinburgh, Glasgow, Glasgow Prestwick, Aberdeen, and Inverness all have international airports. Scotland also has a number of tiny airports that are handy for reaching remote islands.

Airports in Edinburgh and Glasgow
There are numerous connecting flights between each of them and the major hubs. Internal flight fares may appear pricey when compared to budget carrier prices, but the time savings compared to other modes of transportation may make it beneficial.

Flybe operates the majority of flights. Loganair is the only way to book inter-island flights in Shetland (except Fair Isle). Eastern Airways operates additional trips between the mainland and numerous key islands. Also, Loch Lomond Seaplanes offers an unforgettable vacation experience as you fly by seaplane over some of Scotland's most magnificent scenery.

Coach
All of Scotland's major towns and cities are served by long-distance bus services known as coaches throughout the United Kingdom, the bulk of which are operated by the national operator Citylink. There are several discount cards available for individuals with children, those under the age of 26, those over the age of 50, and full-time students: contact Scottish Citylink for more information. Coaches are often less expensive than identical train journeys and so quite popular.

For busy routes and travel during weekends and high season, purchase tickets in advance from the website or any bus stop in the UK, as this will ensure you a seat. Check the baggage allowance limits, as coaches frequently have limited space for larger things like prams, charge for other excess baggage, and have rules about moving items like bicycles.

There are numerous coach companies in Scotland that provide a variety of services - Scottish Citylink can provide further information here. Local bus services within Scotland are provided by the main operators, First, Stagecoach, and National Express, as well as a number of independent operators. Services are more frequent in cities and towns, but less so in rural areas. Visit the TravelineScotland website for information on all services in and around Scotland's towns and cities.

Some rural locations, particularly in the Highlands and Islands, are solely served by the Postbus network, which consists of several minibuses transporting mail and carrying between three and ten fare-paying passengers. The Royal Mail website has information on Postbus routes and timetables.

If you travel frequently in England and Wales, you may benefit from a National Express Brit Xplorer Pass, which allows them unrestricted travel on National Express coaches throughout the United Kingdom.

Cruising
Scotland is unquestionably one of the top cruise destinations in the world. Scotland is the ideal cruise destination due to its breathtaking scenery, gorgeous cities, haunting history, UNESCO World Heritage Sites, and a range of ports large and small.

Scotland's cruise ports are perfectly situated for inclusion in Scotland itineraries, transatlantic repositioning, or combining with voyages to Iceland, the Faroe Islands, or the Norwegian Fjords, as well as Europe.

Driving

To drive in Scotland, non-UK individuals must supplement your national driving license with an international driving permit, which is available for a minimal price from state and national motoring organizations at home.

If they are bringing their own vehicle into the UK, they must have their vehicle registration or ownership paperwork with them at all times. Furthermore, they must be appropriately insured, so they should review their current insurance.

Ferry

Scotland has over sixty inhabited islands, with scheduled ferry connections to over half of them. The vast majority of boats carry automobiles and vans, and the vast majority can and should be booked as long in advance as feasible.

Ferries on the Clyde and to the Outer Hebrides

Caledonian MacBrayne (abbreviated 'CalMac') holds a monopoly on services on the River Clyde and to the Hebrides, sailing to a total of 21 islands. They provide two kinds of reduced-fare passes. If you are taking more than one ferry, the cheap Island Hopscotch tickets are worth considering. If you plan on traveling a lot of ferries, an Island Rover, which enables 8 or 15 consecutive days of unrestricted ferry travel, would be a better option. It does not, however, guarantee a seat on any ferry, therefore booking ahead of time is advised.

Orkney and Shetland ferries

NorthLink Ferries now operates car ferries to Orkney and Shetland from Aberdeen and Scrabster near Thurso. Pentland Ferries operates a car ferry from Gills Bay near John o'Groats to St. Margarets Hope in Orkney, while John o' Groats Ferries operates a passenger ferry from John o'Groats to Burwick in Orkney during the summer. Orkney Ferries operates services that connect the several Orkney islands.

The inter-island ferries in Shetland are operated in collaboration with the local council, and information on routes and timetables may be found on the Shetland Islands Council website.

Train

The rail network in Scotland is most dense in the middle belt, with only a few significant lines in the Highlands connecting with most of the important ferry ports to the west coast islands. The majority of train services are provided by Abellio ScotRail, which connects all major towns on lines that have been designated as among the world's most scenic routes.

Rail Passes

You can buy train tickets at stations, major travel agencies, over the phone, or online using a credit card. If the ticket office at the station is closed, they can normally purchase a ticket from the inspector on board with cash or a credit card. The inspector, on the other hand, is not always able to issue discounted or special-offer tickets.

Fares, Passes, and Apps at a Discount

ScotRail trains provide a wide range of ticketing options, with savings offered across a wide range of categories, including age, number of passengers traveling, advance booking, time of departure, and combining train travel with other modes of transportation.

Visit the National train Enquiries website for information on all of the several discounted national train passes that run to, from, and around Scotland.

Chapter 35: Exploring Scotland via Public Transport: Tips and Recommendations

Taking public transportation is a terrific way to see Scotland. It is a sensible and environmentally friendly method to experience the nation at a slower pace. But where can you go in Scotland by train and bus? How do you use the public transportation system? Is it possible to see the Islands and Highlands without a car? This guide to public transportation in Scotland will teach you everything you need to know.

From hefty travel expenditures, particularly when traveling alone, to the dread of driving on the opposite side of the road. Renting a car and driving in Scotland might be difficult.

When I travel throughout Scotland, I normally drive, but I am frequently asked, "What do you do if you don't (want to) drive?" Is public transportation available in the country? Is it possible to travel there by rail and bus?

If you've ever considered visiting Scotland without renting a car, you'll be relieved to know that the short answer is yes. You may easily travel around Scotland by public transportation.

You may simply need to adjust your plan and travel pace accordingly.

I recently went on a trip to Glencoe and Fort William and had to leave my car behind. I relied on buses and trains to tour the Scottish Highlands for five days and quickly realized that I needed to change my plans to fit everything in.

The Advantages of Taking Public Transportation in Scotland
First, consider the benefits of touring Scotland by bus, train, or boat.

Save yourself the hassle of driving. If you can't drive or are concerned about driving on the left side of the road, in a manual car, or on narrow mountain roads, taking public transportation eliminates the need to drive. There's no need to be concerned about driving, traffic, or the roads.

Take in the scenery. Driving down gorgeous roads in Scotland is wonderful, but the driver rarely gets to appreciate it as much as their passengers do. After all, they must concentrate on the actual road. Traveling by public transportation allows everyone to take in the sights and appreciate the scenery.

Be more environmentally conscious. Taking public transportation, whether by bus or train, is healthier for the environment than renting a car. If your carbon footprint when traveling is important to you, public transportation may be the way to go.

Save some cash. Traveling via public transportation can be far less expensive than renting a car and paying for gas.

Excellent for lone travelers. All of the preceding is especially true if you travel alone. You'll save yourself the stress of driving and navigating on your own, you'll be able to focus on the scenery, you'll be able to travel more responsibly, and you'll save some money along the way.

However, there are certain drawbacks, such as being tied to timetables, needing to modify your pace accordingly, and not being able to follow your nose down odd routes. However, with proper planning and thinking, you can travel almost anyplace using public transportation.

Before I tell you how to do it, let me guide you through the numerous public transportation options in Scotland, travel cards, and how to buy tickets.

Explaining Public Transportation
Train
In Scotland, there are numerous scenic train rides, and it is perhaps one of the most beautiful and soothing ways to experience the countryside.

Train companies in Scotland

ScotRail is the principal train operator in Scotland. They operate services throughout the country, including the West Highland Line, which connects Glasgow with Oban and Mallaig through the southern and central Highlands, the Kyle Line, which connects Inverness to Kyle of Lochalsh, and the Highland Main Line, which connects Glasgow and Edinburgh to Inverness via Perthshire. Trains stop in the majority of Scotland's major towns and cities, including Dunfermline, Perth, Dundee, Aviemore, Thurso, and Dumfries.

Other train companies that provide services between Scotland and England include CrossCountry, Avanti West Coast, and others. Many passengers take the Caledonian Sleeper Train from London to Fort William or Inverness, leaving the south in the evening and waking up in the Highlands.

Where can I find train schedules?

The most dependable source for train times is the ScotRail app or website. You can also use Google Maps, however it does not always show cancellations, substitute rail services, or delays. Rome2Rio is another excellent app to utilize.

How to Purchase Train Tickets

rail tickets can be purchased at rail stations or through the ScotRail app or website. I strongly advise purchasing tickets in advance to ensure you receive the lowest pricing. If you go from Scotland to England with a different operator than ScotRail, you can still purchase tickets through ScotRail.

There are peak-time trains (weekdays before 9.15 a.m. and between 4.42 and 6.11 p.m. - more information here) and off-peak trains, which are less expensive and less crowded.

If you purchase your tickets online, you must pick them up from a ticket desk or machine at a station. Remember to bring the confirmation email's ticket code as well as the payment card. Both are required to pick up your tickets.

Train Travel Tickets

ScotRail provides four main types of travel passes:

- Spirit of Scotland Pass: Includes unlimited travel throughout Scotland on trains, buses, coaches, and Calmac & Argyll ferries, as well as discounts on Northlink Ferries, city tour buses, loch cruises, and more. You can pick between 4 consecutive days of travel (£149) or 8 consecutive days of travel (£189).
- Central Scotland Rover: A three-day travel pass for trains in Scotland's Central Belt as well as the Glasgow Subway (£55). The main lines connect Glasgow and Edinburgh, as well as Stirling, Falkirk, North Berwick, and Tweedbank.
- Highland Rover: A travel card that permits you to travel across the Highlands on four consecutive days for the price of £95. Trains from Glasgow to Oban, Mallaig, Inverness, Ullapool, Thurso, and Aberdeen are included, as are ferries to Skye and Mull, select bus routes in the west Highlands, and discounted tickets for Northlink boats to Orkney and Shetland.
- Train travel on the West Highland Line (Glasgow to Mallaig), Kyle Line (Kyle of Lochalsh to Inverness), and Highland Main Line (Inverness to Glasgow or Edinburgh), boat travel to Skye, and bus travel from Armadale to Kyle of Lochalsh comprise the Scottish Grand Tour. The pass is usable for four travel days during an eight-day period, but only in one direction (£89).

Tickets for the PlusBus

If you're visiting a Scottish town or city, you can book your train ticket and a day pass for local buses in one transaction by adding PlusBus to your train ticket through the ScotRail website. On the day of your train journey, you can use local public buses with the PlusBus ticket.

Edinburgh, Glasgow, Dundee, Aberdeen, Stirling, Dunfermline, and more cities are served by PlusBus.

Bus

The majority of Scotland is served by bus networks, thus you can go practically anywhere by bus. However, buses are frequently slower than trains and, of course, are more dependent on road traffic.

They tend to stop more regularly, and many drivers will make an unscheduled stop to let you off between stations if you ask respectfully. It's better not to rely on that, as they may be on a tight schedule, unable to find a safe place to stop, or the bus is too crowded to accommodate particular requirements.

On islands, buses are also the only means of public transportation. It should be noted that some islands, such as Coll and Colonsay, do not have public transportation. Walking, riding, and hailing cabs will be your only alternatives.

Scotland's bus companies

In Scotland, there are several bus companies that provide local, intercity, and regional buses (or coaches). Citylink and Stagecoach are two of the largest operators. National Express and Megabus both operate intercity services. Both are also excellent for inexpensive travel between English and Scottish cities.

Individual tickets and multi-day passes for their networks are available. The Citylink Explorer Pass grants you access to the whole Citylink network for three travel days spread over five days, five days spread over ten days, or eight days spread over sixteen days (£49/79/97). Stagecoach's MegaRider pass (from £7.50) is good for 7 or 28 days and includes all services in certain cities and areas.

Where can I find bus schedules?

Google Maps and Rome2Rio are excellent at displaying bus routes. However, to be absolutely certain, I recommend double-checking bus timetables on the operator's website or on Traveline - especially on the islands.

How to Purchase Bus Tickets
Tickets for intercity connections and popular routes should be purchased in advance. You can buy your ticket on the bus for shorter travels or on regional buses. Most accept contactless card payments, but have adequate cash on hand as a backup.

Ferries
Unless you visit the Isles of Skye or Seil, you will have to take a ferry to explore the Scottish isles if you wish to go island hopping.

Ferry companies in Scotland
The bulk of ferry routes in Scotland are operated by two significant ferry companies. Calmac operates the majority of the ferries to the west coast islands, from Arran to Lewis. Northlink Ferries operates vessels from Scrabster (Thurso) and Aberdeen to Orkney and Shetland.

The majority of these ferries transport passengers and automobiles, but on other islands (such as Rum and Eigg), cars may only be transported by residents or with a license. Ferries must usually be reserved in advance when traveling by automobile. As a passenger without a vehicle, you normally do not need to reserve tickets in advance; but, due to Covid's restricted capacity, you should book all ferry tickets before you travel.

Western Ferries, Corran Ferry, and John o Groats Ferries are among the smaller local ferry operators that sail short routes.

Where can I find ferry schedules and buy tickets?
You can check ferry schedules and purchase tickets directly from each ferry operator's website. Some ferries require advance reservations, while others operate on a first-come, first-served basis.

Rail and Sail Tickets

Rail & Sail tickets, as the name implies, allow you to travel by train and boat on the same ticket. There's no need to wait in line at the ferry terminal; simply board with your Rail & Sail ticket.

This type of ticket will take you to Orkney, Shetland, Mull, Skye, the Outer Hebrides, Bute, Arran, and other destinations.

10 Public Transport Travel Tips for Scotland
Now that you know why you should use public transportation and what your options are, let's make the most of your stay in Scotland.

Here are some public transportation travel suggestions for Scotland.

Take it slowly.
When you are reliant on rail and bus schedules, you may have to adjust your itinerary. You won't be able to make as many stops in a day as you would if you were traveling by automobile.

If you wish to jump on and off throughout the day, keep in mind that trains and buses can be pretty far apart, so you may only be able to spend a few hours in each site.

Instead than hurrying through each night, try spending numerous nights in the same location to explore an area more thoroughly.

Be adaptable.
There is little you can do if a bus or train is cancelled. That's why it's critical to have a plan B (and possibly even a plan C) in place to ensure you don't lose out on a day of exploration.

Prepare to think quickly on your feet. If times don't work out as planned, have a couple alternate solutions in mind and go with the flow.

Get ready to walk a lot.

You will walk from rail or bus stations to your lodging, sights, restaurants, and so on. Traveling via public transportation requires you to walk farther than if you were driving.

Walking shoes must be comfortable!

Budget for taxi journeys or private transportation instead.
Only in Glasgow and Edinburgh is Uber available. Local taxi firms can be found in various places. In towns, they are usually near the train stations; in villages, they may come from further afield, so it is essential to reserve ahead of time.

Make a list of local taxi numbers and make sure you have a working phone to call.

Check scheduled departures twice and three times.
Check the correct timetable and take note of any differences between weekday and weekend schedules.

If feasible, double-check at the station (ideally) or online to ensure that a service hasn't been abruptly canceled. Twitter is a fantastic place to find the most up-to-date scheduling information. Refer to advice 2 ("Be Flexible") if a service is canceled.

Pack lightly.
The fewer and lighter your bags, the easier it will be to maneuver buses, trains, and strolling with your luggage.

I recommend one large bag, such as a backpack or wheelie suitcase, for use on luggage racks or down below in buses, and one small bag to carry with you at all times.

Consider purchasing a Railcard.

If you are under 30, over 65, or traveling with a partner or family, getting a Railcard may be worthwhile. A Railcard costs £30 for a year and offers up to a third off ordinary ticket pricing.

Railcards are also offered to visitors, however they cannot be shipped outside of the country. You must purchase a digital Railcard to use on your mobile device if you do not have a UK address.

On congested routes, plan ahead of time.
I recommend purchasing advance tickets to popular places, such as the train to Oban or Fort William, the bus to Glencoe or Portree (Skye), or the train to Inverness.

Services that connect with ferry services, such as the bus from Ullapool to Inverness from the Stornoway ferry, should also be reserved in advance. Weekends and peak season are especially busy.

Book lodging near train stations.
It makes things so much easier if you plan accommodations that are within easy walking distance of bus and rail stations. You can also request to drop off your bags before checking in, saving you time trekking back and forth.

Alternatively, for longer journeys, budget for taxis or private transfers.

Bring a battery pack.
When you travel by public transportation, you may find yourself spending more time on your phone, taking photos, listening to podcasts or audiobooks, taking pictures out the window, and so on. While some buses and trains include outlets or USB ports for charging your electronics, I wouldn't rely on them all the time.

Bring a portable charger to keep your phone charged while on the run.

Get handy travel apps.

Here are some of my favorite apps for navigating Scotland's public transportation:

- ScotRail - for train schedules and ticket purchases.
- Google Maps is my go-to for researching possible routes.
- First Bus - to purchase tickets and view FirstBus schedules in Glasgow
- Lothian Buses - purchase tickets and view Lothian bus/tram schedules in Edinburgh.
- To book taxis in Glasgow and Edinburgh, use Uber.
- Traveline - to look for public transportation schedules in Scotland.
- Rome2Rio is also useful for checking public transportation schedules.

With these considerations in mind, I have successfully traveled around Scotland on public transportation. From visiting Outlander places in Fife to island hopping to Bute or the Outer Hebrides, to discovering the Scottish Highlands in Glencoe, Fort William, and Arisaig, there is something for everyone.

Chapter 36: Exceptional and Unique Accommodations in Scotland

Scotland has many unique places to stay, including castles, country houses, and centuries-old buildings that have been converted into stunning holiday accommodations. Explore Scotland's most unusual lodging to uncover extraordinary locations to stay that will transport you back in time. Enjoy one-of-a-kind accommodations that you won't find anywhere else.

Isle of Lewis, Gearrannan Blackhouse Village

If the prospect of staying in a home with strong stone walls and deep Scottish links makes your heart skip a beat, there is no more distinctive place to stay in Scotland than a traditional blackhouse (a stone constructed building with a thatched roof).

Gearrannan Blackhouse Village, located on the Isle of Lewis in the Outer Hebrides, dates from the 1800s and features three historic blackhouse dwellings and one huge bunkhouse.

Similarly, with their exposed stone walls, modern 'broch' residences draw inspiration from medieval broch defenses (such as Mousa Broch on Shetland) while adding a slew of modern conveniences.

Loch Lomond's The Drovers Inn
If you prefer comfortable log fireplaces, hearty meals, and an on-site pub, a stay at a traditional Scottish inn will be ideal.

Inns are rich in history, dating back to the days when people traveled across the country in horse-drawn stagecoaches. These medieval drinking holes were popular stopping points for travelers as they made their way throughout the nation, and you can still find inns in some of Scotland's most picturesque locations to this day.

The Drovers Inn in Inverarnan, just north of Loch Lomond, dates back over 300 years and serves as an excellent base for exploring the National Park and surrounding area.

Wester Ross, Torridon
Looking for a rural retreat? A country house or ancient lodge will provide you with lots of space to spread out, as well as easy access to outdoor activities amid Scotland's stunning scenery.

The Torridon in Wester Ross was erected in 1887 as a shooting lodge. Nowadays, you can anticipate luxury hotel accommodations and a plethora of thrilling outdoor activities, such as guided walks and sea kayaking.

Ferry Cottage in the Highlands
A stay in a quirky cottage will be your ideal vacation hideaway if you enjoy making meals from local foods and relaxing in your own holiday accommodation.

There are many unique Scotland stays to select from, ranging from contemporary residences in lovely locations to historic structures that have been turned into pleasant places to stay.

Ferry Cottage on the Balmacara Estate in the west Highlands is a fascinating lodging option. It was previously the waiting area for boat and steamer passengers traveling to and from Balmacara. Traditional elements such as antique wall lamps and doors now blend seamlessly with its modern decor.

Angus Newton Farm Holidays
A stay on a working farm in Scotland will give you a flavor of true rural life.

Farming has profound cultural origins in Scotland. Generations of farming families have built their lives on their farms, producing exquisite meat, hearty crops, and fresh food for millennia. Some farms now also provide comfortable lodging where you can immerse yourself in farming life.

At Newton Farm Holidays in Angus, near Dundee, you can enjoy a farm tour and visit the animals, which include sheep, cows, goats, and gentle alpacas.

Chapter 37: Scotland's Quirkiest Accommodations

If you're searching for a place to get away from it all, Scotland is the place to go. Scotland has something for everyone, with jaw-dropping views of craggy highlands, vast coastlines, and stunning beaches. You can see why we adore Scotland immediately!

During my travels, I've had the opportunity to stay in some fairly unique accommodations. I've always been intrigued to offbeat hotels and accommodations, from sleeping in converted railway stations in England to cave hotels in Morocco.

I'm always looking for areas that have that "wow" element, places that are unique to the world. I mean, aren't they the ones you always want to tell your friends and family about?

These are some of Scotland's most unique places to stay.

That's why I wanted to highlight some of Scotland's most odd locations to stay. There are so many unique Scottish retreats to choose from, from camping on remote islands to off-the-grid homes.

Keeping this in mind, here are 12 unique lodging alternatives that will show you the finest of Scotland. Stay in one of these for a romantic weekend away or a family excursion, and it will undoubtedly be memorable.

Unusual Scotland Accommodation
Nest Glamping Pod
Look no further than the Nest Glamping Pod for an isolated hideaway cut off from the rest of the world.

You'll be hard pressed to find a more gorgeous site in the Scottish Highlands than Ardteatle. This lovely tiny cabin, which opened in 2019, allows you to unwind, reconnect with nature, and take in the breathtaking views. When the weather is beautiful, there's even a grill outdoors.

There is no light pollution in the area, making it an excellent location for stargazing. The entire aim of the Nest is to enjoy a digital detox and reconnect with nature. The cottage is cozy for two people, which means additional cuddling in the mornings. There's also an en-suite bathroom, so it's a big step up from camping.

The Nest is located in a peaceful location 2 miles from Dalmally, 15 miles from Tyndrum, and 40 minutes from Oban. For those of you who enjoy the great outdoors, there are some good walks in the neighborhood.

Four Sisters Boatel
Obviously, hotels and AirBnBs are two for the price of one in Edinburgh. However, if you're looking for unique accomodation in Scotland, the Four Sisters Boatel is a must-see.

This is a 4-star self-catering houseboat in the heart of Edinburgh. This Edinburgh Quay location is within a 10-minute walk from Edinburgh Castle and Princess Street. There are also some fantastic restaurants within walking distance.

A fully equipped kitchen with a breakfast bar is located inside the Four Sisters. The two separate cabin bedrooms are nicely designed, and there are two double bedrooms and one for youngsters, making this ideal for a large family. It goes without saying that there is a strong nautical element throughout this lodging.

This, to me, is what fun and eccentric lodging is all about. You couldn't ask for a nicer location, and you get to stay on a houseboat. How awesome is that?

AirShip 002.
If you're seeking for a romantic distant Scottish retreat, this is the place to go.

The AirShip 002 is a modern cabin in the Scottish Highlands that has been dubbed the most unconventional lodging in Scotland.

The AirShip is really spectacular, with breathtaking views of the Sound of Mull. It resembles a James Bond lair crossed with a futuristic space capsule. The structure includes curving glass windows on both ends that provide views of the Isle of Mull. There are a few portholes strewn about that provide views of the environment. This is especially lovely at night when you can stargaze. Yes, you can sleep directly beneath the stars.

The kitchen is modest, but it has all you need for a self-catering stay, such as an induction ring, combination oven/microwave, fridge, toaster, and Nespresso coffee maker. You can't beat those vistas with a cup of coffee in the morning.

The AirShip is located on a 4-acre property, so there are some wonderful treks around. As I previously stated, this is the ideal location for a romantic weekend in Scotland.

Mull of Galloway Lighthouse

Have you ever longed to spend the night in a lighthouse and watch the boats go by? At the Mull of Galloway lighthouse, you can!

The Mull of Galloway Lighthouse is one of the most popular destinations to visit in South West Scotland. It's Scotland's most southerly point, and it's well worth a visit if you're driving the South West Coastal 300.

Many people come to the lighthouse to climb to the top. On a clear day, you can see England, Ireland, and the Isle of Man all from this vantage position. If you're lucky, you might also spot porpoises and dolphins, so keep a watch out.

There are, however, a few rooms available for rent in the former lighthouse keeper's cabin. This means you can stay right on the cliffs in a functional lighthouse. The views of the coastline are breathtaking, and these are what make this section of Scotland so unique. Because this is the only place for miles around, you truly have the place to yourself.

There's also a wonderful café on the cliffs near the lighthouse, so this is a fantastic place to stop for breakfast or lunch. The Mull of Galloway Lighthouse seems to have a little bit of everything.

Five Turrets

The Five Turrets is a grade II-listed property with a fairy-tale facade and its own medieval turrets. However, once inside, you'll be greeted by a bright, contemporary, and modern decor that appears straight out of a design magazine.

This fantastic site to explore Scotland is located near Selkirk, on the outskirts of the Scottish Borders. One of the best treks in the area is Eildon Hill, or you may read more about Sir Walter Scott, who lived in Selkirk. Edinburgh is also only one hour away.

The open-plan living room within the townhouse is framed by high vaulted ceilings and contains a variety of comfortable chill-out areas and vast communal spaces. A few of the apartments also have their own turrets, making this one of Scotland's most distinctive locations to stay.

The Five Turrets accommodation has four bedrooms and two bathrooms, sleeping up to eight people. This makes it ideal for a large family or two smaller families searching for a memorable Scottish vacation.

Iona Pods

Iona is a little island off the southwest coast of Mull in the Inner Hebrides that is regarded as one of Scotland's most beautiful sites.

The island is about 1.5 miles broad and 3 miles long, so I truly mean it when I say it's tiny! It also has only 120 permanent residents. If you're seeking for a distant location in Scotland to get away from it all, you've come to the right place! Not to mention the breathtaking vistas from Iona.

Check out the Iona Pods for something a little different. This is a campground where you may spend the night in these lovely glamping pods. Each pod has a huge open area with a double bed or two/three single beds. Each pod also has power outlets, a microwave, fridge, electric cooktop, kettle, kitchenware, and utensils, so you'll have everything you need.

The finest parts about this location are the mountain views and the fact that it is only a 10-minute walk from the beach. If you enjoy being in the middle of nature, you will adore this location.

Tree Howf

This is a unique distant treehouse. The Tree Howf, near Dunblane, is erected in the branches of an ancient ash tree and provides unbroken views of the surrounding Perthshire countryside.

However, the best parts are found therein. There is a handmade rustic king size bed inside, as well as a large star / tree gazing window over the bed. This is the ideal location for turning off all the lights and gazing at the sky without getting too cold outside.

The entire space is kept warm by a wood-burning stove and oven, as well as an old Belfast sink. There is also a nice hot shower and an Eco-friendly composting toilet outside.

Guests can also use the Wash Howf, which has additional cooking and washing facilities as well as a small honesty shop selling wood, charcoal, and other products.

The View

This lovely cottage is located on the Sleat Peninsula and is an excellent base for exploring the area.

The vacation home itself is an architectural dream, spread across two stories, with two en-suite bedrooms, two lovely lounge areas, and a vaulted ceiling with floor to ceiling windows in the living room.

This location is also well-known for its animal viewing options. Otters, dolphins, pine martens, and a variety of other creatures have been seen from the residence!

There are beautiful walking and cycling trails nearby, and Armadale Castle and the Armadale ferry terminal are only a 15-minute drive away. A short drive away, there are also some excellent restaurants. This is without a doubt one of the most sophisticated and beautiful Scottish vacation homes in Scotland.

Castle Snug

This is, without a doubt, one of the most odd locations to stay in Scotland. It's like to having your own micro-castle within an inner-city apartment. It may seem strange, but maybe the photographs will give you a better notion.

The Castle Snug, located in the center of Edinburgh and approximately 200 meters from Edinburgh Castle, was formerly home to writer James Boswell. What distinguishes this location is that it was constructed to resemble a castle. The coolest part is a hidden pull-out double bed hidden in a bookcase!

A beautiful wrought iron balcony, stained glass window, and hanging tapestry round off the castle scene. There's even a small courtyard outside where you may take your morning coffee.

You can't top this place's position for discovering everything Edinburgh has to offer, so if you're looking for something a little different, I can't suggest it enough.

Lochend Chalets
Lochend Chalets in Port Menteith are a hybrid of luxury glamping and a self-catering vacation resort. There are a selection of cabins, chalets, cottages, and lodges to choose from on a calm area of Lake Menteith with amazing views across the water to Ben Lomond. All have amazing views and provide a calm countryside vacation.

Lochend also features a tennis court and games room, a bike park and rowing boats, and the Nick Nairn Cook School for individuals who want to improve their culinary skills.

This accommodation is only an hour from Glasgow and Edinburgh, making it an ideal location for seeing the beautiful Scottish countryside, with the Highlands and Islands, St Andrew's, and the Cairngorms all within a day's drive.

Still, lingering by the lake and taking in the scenery is extremely easy. Given the variety of chalets available, I believe this is an excellent choice for families seeking to embark on a Scottish trip.

Beach Houses

Two modern holiday cottages are available in this lovely location near Kentallen Pier, just a short drive from Glencoe. They offer stylish décor, all the amenities you could want for a self-catering vacation in Scotland, and even a hot tub on the terrace.

The vista, on the other hand, will entice you. The Beach Houses are in an excellent location, with wraparound balconies to enjoy the view over the lake. Most rooms have floor-to-ceiling windows to take advantage of the environment.

It's also in a terrific location for a family vacation. It's close to a lot of significant sights, events, and fantastic trails, yet far enough away from them to feel like you're going away from it all.

Laggan Outdoors

Laggan Outdoors is a destination in South West Scotland that is jam-packed with adventure activities. Archery, clay pigeon shooting, and off-road segwaying (which sounds like a lot of fun) are all available here. However, when I went, it was for a very other reason.

The longest zipline in Scotland may be found at Laggan Outdoors. This is 820m of high-speed, adrenaline-pumping action. There's nothing quite like flinging yourself off the top of a hill to get the heart racing!

Laggan Outdoors also has its own Sea View Snugs. There are a total of 16 cabins, all of which overlook the Irish Sea.

I slept in the Heather Hut, a charming cabin ideal for lone travelers or couples. If you want to go all out, a number of the snugs have their own hot tubs. With that view and a bottle of wine, you've got the makings of a fantastic night in.

Each cabin is uniquely furnished and has conveniences such as towels, toiletries, and tea and coffee making facilities. Once again, it's all about the opinions.

Chapter 38: Scotland's Breathtaking Scenic Drives

Scotland, oh Scotland! It's no secret that this country is full of breathtaking vistas and extraordinary beauty that doesn't seem genuine until you see it for yourself.

If you want to visit some of the most beautiful spots in Scotland, we've put up a list just for you! These routes pass through Aberdeen, Inverness, Stirling, and other cities.

Dunee to Aberdeen Coastal Route

This drive will take you around the east coast of Scotland, connecting Dundee and Aberdeen, and will provide breathtaking scenery filled with fascinating small communities, brilliant natural vistas, and more. The Grampian Mountains to the west provide breathtaking views and photo opportunities. As you drive north, you'll pass past the North Sea, which sparkles in the sunlight. Along the journey, you should stop and tour the Dundee Science Center, Broughty Ferry Castle, and Barry Mill.

Aberdeen to Inverness Highland Tourist Route

If you've followed the Angus Coastal Route and arrived in Aberdeen, why not get back in the car and explore more of Scotland's natural beauty? The Highland Tourist Route will take you through the picturesque Scottish Highlands from Aberdeen to Inverness. Along the route, take in the breathtaking beauty of Cairngorms National Park, old castles, and the Culloden Battlefield. Take a break from driving by visiting one of the museums along the way, such as the Gordon Highlanders Museum or the Grantown Museum.

The Forth Valley Tourist Route connects Edinburgh with Stirling.

The Forth Valley Tourist Route will take you past some of Scotland's most popular sites as well as historic villages. The Forth Bridge and the Antonine Wall are both World Heritage Sites. Stop by Linlithgow Palace or Blackness Castle for a look.

Argyll and Bute Coastal Route

This picturesque route will take you from Loch Lomond's stunning blue shoreline to the Western Highlands. You'll be able to see the iconic fairytale-like castle at Inveraray and marvel at the natural beauty of the coast. This will take you all the way to the little town of Oban, popularly regarded as Scotland's seafood capital. Park your car and enjoy some of the most wonderful, fresh fish you've ever had!

The North Coast 500

This trek is regarded as "Scotland's Route 66" and should be at the top of your European bucket list. You'll see many spectacular vistas along the way, including breathtaking mountains and stunning castles. You'll pass through Inverness, Ross, Cromarty, Sutherland, and Caithness on your way. If you want to take a break from driving and see some sights, consider stopping by Dunrobin Castle, The Whaligoe Steps, or Achmelvich Bay, all of which have gorgeous sandy beaches.

Glasgow to Inveraray.

Begin your journey from Glasgow to Inveraray at Loch Lomond's magnificent shorelines. Soon before reaching the Rest and Be Thankful Pass, you'll witness beautiful mountains like the Arrochar Alps. Take a break from driving and stop at a viewpoint to photograph the stunning nature that surrounds you. Are you hungry? Loch Fyne Oyster Bar has enough of delights to keep you going before you hit the road again!

Chapter 39: Scottish Highlights: Must-See Attractions

Are you thinking about visiting Scotland? You've come to the right place! Scotland has some of the most beautiful and attractive cities in the world, not to mention world-renowned landscape, and this is a brief guide to just a few of the highlights.

From the capital city of Edinburgh to Glasgow, Aberdeen, and Inverness, there is something for everyone to enjoy on their journey.

Edinburgh and Glasgow

If you want to visit a city with history, culture, and plenty of things to see and do, Edinburgh is the place to go. Edinburgh, Scotland's capital city, is home to some of the country's most recognizable landmarks. Explore Edinburgh Castle, the Royal Mile, or one of the numerous museums and art galleries.

Don't miss the Grassmarket, which is packed with boutique stores, cafes, and restaurants. For a dose of nature, visit one of the city's many parks or climb Arthur's Seat, an extinct volcano with spectacular views of the city. Whatever you choose to do, there is much to see and do in this beautiful city.

Glasgow, Scotland's largest city, is located on the west coast of the country and is recognized for its friendly residents, busy nightlife, and rich history. Beautiful Victorian architecture may be seen throughout the city center, while trendy clubs and restaurants can be found in the West End. Glasgow truly has something for everyone, with a plethora of festivals, art galleries, and museums.

Glasgow is also a fantastic shopping destination, having both high-street and independent boutiques to visit. So, whether you wish to visit the famous Glengoyne Distillery or stroll around the lovely Kelvingrove Park, Glasgow will not disappoint.

Highlands of Scotland
The Scottish Highlands are without a doubt some of the most stunning regions in Scotland. It's easy to see why this region is so popular with travelers, from the undulating hills and gleaming lochs to the charming settlements. Inverness, the Highlands' capital, is a good starting point for exploring the surrounding area.

If you're searching for a more outdoor-focused vacation, the Highlands are ideal. There are numerous hiking and bike paths, as well as fishing, kayaking, and climbing options. If you prefer to take in the landscape, you can drive up the North Coast 500, which is regarded as one of the world's most magnificent routes.

Urquhart Castle is located on Loch Ness.
This body of water, which runs for almost 20 miles, is maybe Scotland's most famous loch. Its coastlines are adorned with picturesque villages, mountains, and the ruins of Urquhart Castle. Loch Ness, famous for

perhaps being home to Nessie, our beloved monster, is a great place for boat cruises to try to glimpse her.

Saint Andrews

St. Andrews is a small town on Scotland's east coast. It is regarded as one of the top golfing venues in the world. It's simple to see why when you can visit the Par-72 Old Course, the world's oldest golf course.

But St. Andrews is more than simply a golf town; it also has magnificent beaches, castles, and a plethora of small shops and cafes. Visit St. Andrews Castle or the Cathedral ruins for a dose of history. And for some retail therapy, visit one of the town's many independent stores. With so many possibilities in St. Andrews, this is an ideal stop for anyone who enjoys a round of golf or admiring the natural beauty of the area.

Stirling

Stirling is the last but surely not least. This city, located in Scotland's middle belt, is an excellent starting point for your vacation around the country. Stirling is conveniently placed between the big cities of Edinburgh and Glasgow, making it the ideal spot to stay if you wish to explore both.

Stirling is also home to some of the country's most significant historical landmarks. Visit Stirling Castle, one of Scotland's largest castles, or stroll through the old town to view plenty of attractive medieval architecture. The Bannockburn Heritage Centre, which is crammed with many exhibits and displays that recreate the story of this historic conflict, is the place to go for a recounting of the renowned conflict of Bannockburn. After you've finished, take a well-deserved break at one of Stirling's great cafes or restaurants.

Whether you're seeking for history, culture, outdoor experiences, or just a nice escape, one of these cities is guaranteed to meet your needs. Of course, with so many amazing sites to visit in Scotland, it's difficult to choose just a handful. That is why a Private Driver/Guided Tour with

Inspiring Travel Scotland is the perfect way to make the most of your time in Scotland.

Chapter 40: Edinburgh, Scotland: 21 Highlighted Activities

There is so much to do in Edinburgh, Scotland!

A first-time tourist is understandably interested in seeing some of the highlights of this beautiful city, which has two UNESCO designations for its higgledy-piggledy medieval Old Town and its well-planned Georgian New Town. However, you may want to look into a few additional possibilities.

Visit the city's iconic medieval castle, climb an extinct volcano, see the world's largest writer's monument, see Scotland's crown jewels, sip whisky, go underground to explore some of the city's medieval past, view world-class art, and pay homage to a famous little dog. If you have the ability to organize your vacation around one of the city's world-famous festivals, you should do so.

These 21 things to do in Edinburgh are intended to serve as a guide to help you plan your trip, whether it's a quick one-day visit or a week-long vacation.

What is the location of Edinburgh?

Edinburgh is located in Scotland, which is located in the northern region of the United Kingdom. It is located in southeast Scotland, approximately 60 miles north of the Scotland-England border and around 50 miles east of Glasgow, Scotland's largest city.

What are the best ways to get to Edinburgh?

There are numerous ways to visit Edinburgh. To begin, you can travel into Edinburgh Airport, which has flights from Europe, the United States, the United Kingdom, and the Middle East. If no direct route is available, connecting flights from London or Dublin are frequent. Because the airport is only a short bus, cab, or tram trip from town, this is a highly convenient choice. You can pre-book the airport bus here.

If you don't want to fly, there's a quick train from London to Edinburgh that takes about 4.5 hours. You can also travel trains from locations throughout the UK or take the EuroTunnel from Europe to get here via France. By purchasing rail tickets in advance, you can save a significant amount of money on fares.

If you are traveling within the United Kingdom, you can look up fares and order tickets on Trainline and London North Eastern Railway.

If you prefer to travel by bus, there are daily coach connections to Edinburgh from a variety of places that take longer but may save you money compared to train rates. Coach connections and pricing are available via National Express.

Finally, you can drive to Edinburgh, but keep in mind that most hotels, especially those in the city center, do not provide free parking.

When is the best time to visit Edinburgh?
Edinburgh is a city that can be visited all year round since there is always something going on. If you want milder, drier weather, the months of May to September are your best chance; but, the weather in Scotland is temperamental, so pack clothes and be prepared for at least a little rain.

If you're interested in the Edinburgh festivals, you should go during August, when some of the biggest ones take place. Christmas and the Scottish New Year's celebration, Hogmanay, are also popular times to visit Edinburgh. However, keep in mind that the city is much busier than usual at this period, and lodging is both expensive and difficult to find, so plan ahead of time.

If you do not want to attend the August festivals or Hogmanay, we recommend avoiding Edinburgh at these seasons to save money and avoid crowds.

What is the best method to get about Edinburgh?

The majority of Edinburgh's attractions are within walking distance of the city center. Some attractions (for example, the zoo, botanic garden, Royal Yacht Britannia, and Leith ports) are a little further away, in which case we recommend either local buses, which are quite reasonably priced, or local taxi services.

There are also a few other firms in Edinburgh that provide hop-on, hop-off bus services with commentary and sightseeing. This HOHO bus service is recommended because it has three bus routes that stop at the majority of the attractions covered in this chapter.

You don't need a car to get around Edinburgh because public transportation can take you almost anyplace in and around the city, so we'd only recommend renting a car if you plan to visit the countryside or smaller villages.

The majority of Scotland's cities and towns are well connected by train and bus. Even many of the tiny communities outside of Edinburgh, including our own, are well served by public transportation, so we rarely drive into the city to avoid paying for parking.

What about accessibility in Edinburgh?
Despite the fact that most public transportation alternatives are wheelchair accessible and many attractions can accept wheelchairs, Edinburgh can be difficult for persons with limited mobility and those in wheelchairs due to the many hills, cobblestone streets of the Old Town, and historical structures.

If you or a travel partner has limited mobility or is using a wheelchair or mobility scooter, see the Marketing Edinburgh website's accessibility page. It gives information on accessible public transportation, accessible public bathroom sites, disability parking spots, and so forth.

For individual attractions, I'd go directly to their website to learn about accessibility and, if necessary, contact them. For example, due to the historical architecture of the structures, many portions of Edinburgh Castle are inaccessible to wheelchair users.

How long should I stay in Edinburgh?
This, of course, depends on how much you want to do and how much time you have to vacation, but I would strongly recommend spending at least three days in Edinburgh for touring. There are so many fantastic sites, museums, restaurants, parks, and so on to see here that most visitors who spend a rushed day or two in the city regret it. In Edinburgh, you could easily spend a week and not run out of things to do.

What about day trips from Edinburgh?
You can also use Edinburgh as a base to explore some of Scotland's surrounding areas and regions. You can take day trips from Edinburgh to castles, whisky distilleries, Outlander filming locations, Harry Potter movie locations, St. Andrews, Loch Ness, golf courses, the Scottish Borders, and Glasgow. Day travels from Edinburgh can be taken by vehicle, bus, train, or by organizing a day tour.

What are the best ways to save money on Edinburgh attractions?
The Royal Edinburgh Ticket is the main discount pass, and it is excellent value if you want to visit the three main royal sights in Edinburgh (Edinburgh Castle, Holyrood Palace, and Royal Yacht Britannia). It also comes with a two-day hop-on hop-off tour bus pass. If you visit all three attractions and take the bus, you will save roughly 25%. You may read about it and buy it here.

There are no big city passes in Edinburgh; nevertheless, many of the major museums and parks are free to access! Discount vouchers are also likely to be found on Edinburgh city maps and brochures available at the tourist center, and a few attractions offer combo ticket reductions if you plan to visit partner sites.

If you don't want to pick up the pass above, you can typically save money by purchasing your ticket online rather than at the venue for those locations that are not free to visit. For example, if you purchase your Edinburgh Castle ticket online here, you will save approximately £1.50 on the entry fee and will be able to skip the ticket wait.

If you want to spend longer time in Scotland and see historical places, consider the Scottish Heritage Pass (available from April to October) and Historic Scotland Explorer Pass. Despite the fact that both of these passes only cover a few locations in Edinburgh, they each cover over 120 sites throughout Scotland, including Edinburgh Castle, Stirling Castle, and Culloden Battlefield.

Where Should You Stay in Edinburgh?
If you are looking for lodging in Edinburgh, we recommend looking for a central location, especially if you have limited time in the city. You may stroll to many of the key sights this way. Anything within walking distance of Waverley train station is a good central location, allowing you to quickly explore the Old and New Town neighborhoods on foot or via short bus excursions.

Budget Hotels in Edinburgh
- Royal Mile Backpackers - Located along the Royal Mile, this centrally located hostel provides dormitory accommodations.
- Castle Rock Hostel - A popular hostel with a castle theme that offers both dorm and individual rooms. Only adults are permitted. Located near Victoria Street in the Grassmarket neighborhood.
- Stay Central Hotel - A decent budget hotel that is ideal for groups traveling together. The hotel has rooms that sleep from 2 to 9 people, so it might be a wonderful value if you have a group of friends to split the cost of the stay.
- Apartments on Vrbo - If you're looking for a place to live, check out the local Vrbo listings.

Options for Mid-Range Accommodation in Edinburgh
- Motel One is a popular modern affordable design motel in Edinburgh's Old Town.

- The Travelodge Edinburgh Central is a 3-star chain hotel just a few minutes' walk from the Royal Mile.
- The Grassmarket Hotel - Located in the Grassmarket neighborhood, this 3-star hotel is just a 10-minute walk from the Christmas market. The hotel's decor is eccentric and vibrant.
- Holiday Inn Express - This 3-star hotel in the Old Town offers reasonably priced rooms near the Royal Mile.
- Plum Guide is a fantastic alternative that provides a variety of excellent apartment rental possibilities.

Edinburgh's High-End Hotels
- The Balmoral - This 5-star hotel, which began as a classic railway hotel in 1902, has long been a landmark in Edinburgh. This hotel boasts magnificent suites and a blend of traditional and modern decor. It is just near to the Waverley train station and is about as central as it gets.
- The Caledonian, a 5-star luxury hotel, was initially established in 1903 as part of the Edinburgh train station. It is now one of the top luxury properties in the world, including a sophisticated leisure club, spa, restaurants, and bars.
- Klimpton Charlotte Square - Located in the heart of Edinburgh's New Town, this 5-star hotel is made up of seven interconnected townhouses. A nicely furnished hotel that combines modern and traditional travel touches. Across the street from Charlotte Square.
- The Witchery - Named after witches burned at Castlehill in the 16th and 17th centuries, this popular boutique luxury hotel and restaurant. The hotel includes nine themed suites, each of which is beautifully adorned with Gothic accents, enormous four-poster oak beds, antiques, and flashy décor. Edinburgh Castle is a 5-minute walk away.

Where can I obtain additional information?
The Edinburgh city tourism website is a fantastic place to start for more Edinburgh trip planning tips. If you've already explored the attractions

described in this page, take a look at this list of lesser-known things to do in Edinburgh.

If your travels in Scotland take you beyond Edinburgh, visit the Visit Scotland tourism website to organize the rest of your trip around the country. You can also look through my other UK travel entries as well as Laurence's dozens of UK postings.

Edinburgh Highlights: 21 Things to Do in Edinburgh, Scotland

There are many things to do in Edinburgh, but we have limited it down to 21 highlights that we believe any first-time tourist should be aware of and consider when planning their stay. We chose a mix of sites that would appeal to a wide range of travelers, including a spectacular castle, a palace, a famous ship, gardens, whisky tasting, family-friendly attractions, treks, and multiple museums.

This is not in any specific order!

1. The Edinburgh Castle

This would most likely be our choice if this piece was named "top things to do in Edinburgh." The most iconic feature in the city is Edinburgh Castle, which lies atop a volcanic peak and dominates the metropolitan skyline. The castle was the site of a number of significant historical events in Scotland, and many renowned persons, including Mary, Queen of Scots, once visited or lived within its walls.

Inside the castle, you'll find a plethora of historical Scottish items, such as swords, clothing, and even the "Scottish Crown Jewels," also known as the Honours of Scotland. The castle also houses the Scottish National War Memorial and the National War Museum of Scotland (both of which are free with castle admission).

The Great Hall and the 12th century St. Margaret's Chapel, the oldest surviving edifice in the castle and in Edinburgh, were other highlights for us.

From the castle terrace and towers, you may get a bird's-eye perspective of the city.

The firing of the gun, which occurs on most days of the year to mark 1pm (excluding Sundays and holidays), is a popular time to visit the castle. This custom began in 1861, when a muzzle-loading cannon was fired every day to serve as a vital timekeeper for ships in the harbor.

Today, the gun is fired solely for ceremonial purposes. If you want to observe the gunfire, get to the Mill's Mount battery inside the castle long before 1:00 to guarantee a good viewing point.

It should be noted that the castle is one of the most famous sights in Edinburgh and can get very crowded, so try to visit early in the morning if possible.

To avoid long ticket lineups, we recommend purchasing a ticket with fast track entrance in advance. You will also save money over the walk-up entry fee if you purchase your ticket in advance, and you will not have to wait in line for your ticket. On the same day, tickets can be purchased in advance.

If you are going during a busy season (e.g., summer, festivals, holidays), these advance tickets will save you time, but we recommend purchasing them in advance regardless to save money.

The trip is self-directed, however if you want to learn more about the castle, you may hire an audioguide or take one of the free on-site guided tours.

Edinburgh Castle is one of the attractions included in the Royal Edinburgh Ticket (which can be purchased online here), and it is also free for those who have a Historic Scotland Explorer Pass.

2. Take a stroll down the Royal Mile.

The next natural step after leaving Edinburgh Castle is to walk down the Royal Mile. This is the major thoroughfare of the medieval city, and it is still highly busy today.

It runs over a mile from the castle at the top of the hill to Holyrood Palace at the foot. It consists of five streets, none of which are known as the Royal Mile.

This is a busy boulevard with plenty to see along the way, including many of the sights listed below as well as numerous restaurants, cafes, museums, and stores. During your visit, you'll most likely find yourself on and off this street several times!

3. The World of Illusions and Camera Obscura

The Camera Obscura and World of Illusions are located on the Royal Mile near Edinburgh Castle. This attraction has two primary features: first, it contains multiple floors with optical illusions, light tricks, old-fashioned games, and magic shows that we enjoyed playing with.

The "main attraction" on the roof is the Camera Obscura. A camera obscura is a traditional projection technique that sends visible light from the outside world onto a viewing surface in a darkened environment. These have been known about for hundreds, if not thousands, of years and were a popular attraction throughout the Victorian era. In reality, Edinburgh's Camera Obscura dates from the nineteenth century, making it one of the city's oldest visitor attractions.

The rooftop of the tower offers stunning views of the castle and the city of Edinburgh. We had a terrific time here, and it's a great place for families.

We have heard from some visitors that it can be less enjoyable when it is crowded, so we recommend coming outside of the busier summer months or visiting this site shortly after it opens in the morning for the greatest experience.

4. Scotch Whisky Experience

The Scotch Whisky Experience, located across from the Camera Obscura, is a popular stop on the Royal Mile. At their restaurant, you can attend tours, masterclasses, training courses, or simply enjoy some food and whisky. We took the Silver Tour, which is their shortest and least priced whisky tour, and we both had a great day. Tickets can be purchased online here.

It starts with a fun and instructive whisky barrel ride, followed by a self-guided tour of the origin, history, and production of whisky. Then you participate in a guided tasting session and learn about Scotland's many whisky districts. Finally, you take a look around a massive whisky collection, the world's largest of its kind!

Laurence adores whisky and has visited this attraction several times, always having a good time. Even though I don't like the taste of whisky, I enjoyed my visit because I learnt a lot, and I'd recommend the hot chocolate with whisky drink in the restaurant to non-whisky enthusiasts!

If you're very interested in whisky, you could take a more in-depth tour that includes additional samples and tasting instructions, or you may register ahead for a masterclass or one-day training course.

Whisky fans will find shops selling whisky all across the city, and those who are particularly fond of Scottish whisky can visit the Scotch Malt Whisky Society. If you wish to pause and explore the city, there are various whisky walking tours available.

5. Mary King's Close

Did you realize there's a hidden Edinburgh beneath the city streets? There is, after all. The Real Mary King's Close tour is one of the greatest ways to learn more about and see this secret corner of the city.

Mary King's Close, which was covered over by construction in the nineteenth century, was formerly one of the busiest lanes in the medieval city, located right off the Royal Mile. Mary King, a businesswoman who resided in the vicinity in the 1630s, inspired the name.

The one-hour guided tour of Real Mary King's Close is designed to present facts and examples of life in Edinburgh between the 16th and 19th centuries. The trip takes you through a maze of what used to be bustling streets, businesses, animal enclosures, and homes that are now just below street level.

At the time of writing, photography was not permitted on the tour. It's best to book ahead of time to ensure you get the time you desire.

6. St. Giles Cathedral

The majestic St. Giles Cathedral with its crown-shaped steeple is near Mary King's Close and a feature in Edinburgh's skyline. If you only have time to visit one church in Edinburgh, we recommend this one. St. Giles, commonly known as the High Kirk of Edinburgh, is the building of Scotland's primary venue of worship, and the building itself dates from the 14th century.

The Thistle Chapel, built in 1911 for The Most Ancient and Most Noble Order of the Thistle, Scotland's most prominent Order of Chivalry, is our favorite aspect of the church interior. The Queen ruled over this order, which was formed in 1687. The Thistle Chapel is modest, but the roof, as well as the sixteen stalls, one for each Knight of the Order, are incredibly stunning.

On select days, guided cathedral walking tours and rooftop excursions are also available for a price. The guided walking tours can be reserved in advance, however the rooftop excursions can only be reserved on the same day. It should be noted that the rooftop excursions provide a wonderful perspective of the city but do not take you to the top of the skyscraper.

The cathedral is free to enter, although a gift is suggested. The church holds monthly worship services as well as choral concerts and holiday activities on a regular basis. In the back of the church, there is a small gift shop as well as a cafe.

Interior photography is not permitted without a £2.00 photography permit, which may be obtained from the Information Desk. Purchasing a permit is, in our opinion, a worthwhile investment and a wonderful opportunity to contribute to the care of this lovely church.

7. The Palace of Holyrood

The Palace of Holyrood House, often known as Holyrood Palace, is located at the other end of the Royal Mile from Edinburgh Castle. Holyrood Palace is the British monarch's official residence in Scotland. Since the 16th century, it has served as the primary residence of the rulers of Scotland.

The name derives from the 12th century Augustinian Holyrood Abbey, the ruins of which may still be visited today. Mary Queen of Scots and other historical personalities have lived here over the centuries. Self-guided audiotours feature both ancient rooms and those utilized for contemporary state visits, such as Mary, Queen of Scots' royal apartments in the palace's north-west tower.

The historic Royal Apartments and State Apartments of Holyrood Palace, as well as the gardens and grounds, are open to the public most of the year (when not in use for state functions). It should be noted that photography is not permitted within the palace, although it is permitted to capture the outside, gardens, and abbey.

There is also a cafe and a sizable gift shop. The Palace Café serves food and drinks, and you may schedule a wonderful afternoon tea service here (prior reservations required). The gift shop and cafe are both located outside the palace and are free to visit.

Visitors may also choose to pay a visit to the Queen's Gallery, which is located in front of Holyrood Palace and houses a changing display of art and historical objects from the Royal Collection. There are combination tickets available.

The Royal Edinburgh Ticket includes admission to Holyrood Palace. The Royal Edinburgh Ticket does not include access to the Queen's Gallery unless the palace is closed.

8. Scottish National Museum

After exploring the attractions of the Royal Mile, we recommend spending some time visiting the National Museum of Scotland. This great free museum contains exhibits on a wide range of topics linked to both Scotland and the rest of the world, including Scottish history and culture, art and fashion, science and technology, and so on.

Among the highlights for me were Mary, Queen of Scots-related things such as jewelry, money, letters, and furniture. Laurence enjoys the science and technology sections, which include several interactive exhibits.

The museum's vast collection is spread across two main buildings: a more modern structure built in 1998 and a Victorian era part from the nineteenth century. The Victorian part includes a magnificent cast iron grand gallery that is a museum piece in and of itself!

The museum is continuously adding new items and bringing in new exhibits, so if you haven't gone in a while, it's a terrific spot to go back to. We always find new things to see here, and there are often unique activities going on.

There is also a gift shop, a cafe, a casual restaurant, and a fine dining restaurant at the museum. The James Thomson-run Tower Restaurant is located on the museum's roof. On a clear day, there's a wonderful view across Edinburgh's roofs to Edinburgh Castle, which you may enjoy while sipping a cup of tea or a cocktail. The eating selections are also fantastic, and we've enjoyed several delicious dinners there.

9. Try some traditional Scottish cuisine.

During your visit to Edinburgh, you should eat some traditional Scottish meals in addition to visiting all of the wonderful attractions and museums. Haggis is Scotland's national dish and a must-try for all visitors. Haggis is usually produced with sheep components (heart, liver, lungs) that are blended with onion, spices, fat, oats, stock, and spices before being inserted into the stomach of a sheep. It was a poor man's diet, and comparable cuisines have been consumed since ancient times.

Although most restaurants pander to modern palates, and locating a truly traditional haggis (especially those contained in a sheep's stomach) is rare, most visitors agree that the more modern haggis varieties are more palatable. Haggis is traditionally eaten with "neeps and tatties," or mashed turnips and potatoes, as well as a side of whisky sauce. You can even get "vegetarian haggis" at a lot of places, though we're not sure it's still called haggis!

Other delicacies to try in Scotland include local Scottish Salmon, black pudding (Stornoway is famed for its black pudding), cullen skink (smoked haddock, potato, and onion soup), stovies (potato dish), sausage, beef, and lamb dishes, and stovies (potato dish). In restaurants, we frequently request what is local and fresh.

Fish and chips, huge breakfasts (try a full Scottish breakfast and you won't need to eat lunch!), meat pies, and traditional Sunday roast dinners are popular throughout Scotland. Scottish sweets and desserts include cranachan, fried Mars Bars (the Scots appear to be able to fry anything!), tablet, shortbread, and Dundee cake.

There is whisky, of course, but black tea is arguably the most popular beverage. Try the well-known Irn Bru (an orange carbonated soda). Many of the local bars also serve a variety of Scottish gins (Rock Rose,

Pickering's, and Edinburgh Gin, to name a few brands) and beers (Tennent's, Stewart Brewing, and Cairngorm Brewery Company, to name a few Scottish breweries).

There are several gin distilleries in Edinburgh to select from, including Pickering's, the Holyrood Distillery, and 56 North.

If you like food excursions, Edinburgh has a number, including this renowned 3 hour secret strolling food tour. This tour includes six tasting stops, and the instructor explains the history of various traditional Scottish dishes and drinks, including as haggis, tablet, and whisky.

Looking for something a little sweeter? Consider taking a chocolate tour at the Chocolatarium to learn more about chocolate manufacturing and to sample a variety of chocolate (including many Scottish-made chocolates).

10. Princes Street Gardens and the Scott Monument

Sir Walter Scott is the most famous Scottish writer, and Edinburgh is a UNESCO City of Literature. He composed poems, dramas, and novels and is credited with establishing the genre of historical fiction. His works include Ivanhoe, Waverley, The Lady of the Lake, and Rob Roy. He is a well-known and well-loved person in Scotland, and Edinburgh's principal train station is named Waverley after his first novel.

As a result, there are several memorials to him, the most notable of which is the massive Scott Monument (the largest monument to a writer in the world!) on Princes Street, right above the Princes Street Gardens.

Close inspection of the monument reveals figures from Scott's novels, as well as other prominent Scottish writers, poets, and figures. This renowned monument is open to the public, and for a little price, you may climb to the top for a good view of Edinburgh. Just keep in mind that there are many steps and a small spiral staircase! On the first level of your journey, there's also a tiny museum room where you may learn about Sir Walter Scott's life and works.

If you want to learn more about Scott and other notable Scottish writers, we recommend paying a visit to The Writers' Museum (just off the Royal Mile). If you're a big fan of Sir Walter Scott, we recommend taking a trip to the picturesque Scottish Borders, where he got a lot of inspiration and where he constructed his home and is buried.

The Princes Street Gardens are located just below the monument. Once a wetland, the region was eventually transformed into the Nor Loch, an artificial lake that served as a protective barrier to Edinburgh Castle as well as a dumping ground for medieval Edinburgh's sewage and waste.

Beginning in the 1760s, the Nor Loch was drained and turned into gardens, with two gardens built - Princes Street Gardens East and Princes Street Gardens West, divided by a man-made mound known as "The Mound" formed from the excavation of the New Town.

Today, the public gardens are a popular destination for both visitors and tourists, and there are frequently outdoor events held in this area. It's a great spot for seeing Edinburgh Castle and enjoying a sunny Edinburgh afternoon (they happen, I swear!).

11. Ascend Arthur's Seat

One of the nicest aspects of Edinburgh is the availability of large open green spaces close outside the city core. Not far from Holyrood Palace are the towering relics of an extinct volcano known as Arthur's Seat; the term is thought to have arisen from King Arthur's legendary tales.

Calton Hill and Nelson's Monument, among other spots, provide excellent views of Arthur's Seat. Arthur's Seat is the highest point in Holyrood Park, and you can climb it to burn off some calories from all the Scottish food and get a great view of Edinburgh and the Lothians. It's a tough climb to the top (wear climbing shoes and bring water), but the vistas are well worth it, with views stretching for kilometers in every direction on a clear day.

If you have a car and want the quickest and easiest trek, park at Dunsapie Loch and take the significantly shorter hiking path to the summit. Visit the 15th century St Anthony's Chapel, get close to the Salisbury Crags, and observe the birdlife at Duddingston Loch while in the park.

12. The Edinburgh Zoo

Families who want to get up close and personal with over 1,000 animals flock to Edinburgh Zoo. The penguin treks and seeing the resident giant pandas are two of the most popular attractions (note that you normally get a specific viewing time window because they are so popular!). We've also liked seeing tigers, lions, wallabies, chimps, red pandas, and monkeys here.

Many people are upset that they cannot see the pandas (or other animals), but they are frequently in areas of the enclosure where they cannot be seen or sleeping; this is actually a very positive thing because animals are not always forced to be on display to the public.

Check out the zoo's website for live video feeds to see what the Giant Pandas, penguins, tigers, and squirrel monkeys are up to! Throughout the year, the zoo also hosts a variety of educational programs, events, and activities. A food court, casual restaurant, coffee shop, picnic area, and gift store are also available.

For individuals with limited mobility, Edinburgh Zoo includes several steps and steep hills in some locations, but it also features an accessible route, free manual wheelchair rentals (first come, first served), and a mobility vehicle.

The Edinburgh Zoo is located a little outside of the city center. The zoo has its own parking area, although there is a cost and parking places are limited. A bus from the city center is also easily accessible. Two bus stops are located near the zoo and are currently served by Lothian busses 12, 26, and 31, as well as some CityLink routes.

13. National Gallery of Scotland

If you enjoy art, set aside at least an hour or two to visit the Scottish National Gallery, one of Edinburgh's many superb free museums. Scotland's National Art Gallery, located on The Mound near Princes Street Gardens and the Scott Monument, holds a huge collection of paintings and other art from the Renaissance to the turn of the twentieth century, with both Scottish and international artists represented.

The collection is housed in a neoclassical structure erected by William Henry Playfair in 1859. If you prefer modern art, you should go visit the Scottish National Gallery of Modern Art instead.

Laurence is drawn to landscape paintings, whereas I am drawn to 18th century Italian and Impressionist works. We never had enough time in our two brief visits to see the entire collection, and there are constantly fresh temporary exhibits to see (excellent Impressionism display over the summer!).

There is a coffee shop and restaurant if you need a break from looking at all the art. If you need some shopping therapy, there is also a gift shop.

The museum is free to visit, however donations are greatly welcomed.

14. The Scottish National Portrait Gallery

If you enjoy portraiture, the Scottish National Portrait Gallery has something for you. The gallery, which is housed in the world's first structure purpose-built as a portrait gallery (in 1889), only contains portraits of Scottish people, however not all of the artists are Scottish.

Portraits of Stuart kings and family members, including portraits by Dutch painter Arnold Bronckorst, are among the highlights. The "Scots in Italy" collection is one of my favorite galleries. The museum also has a collection of prints, pictures, and statues in addition to portrait paintings.

The Gothic-style structure itself is pretty lovely, and the entrance hall is definitely worth exploring. As you walk in, you'll see a monument of Robert Burns, stunning paintings of famous Scots, stained glass windows, and various busts.

We were here for a Sky TV filming project and spent a lot of time looking at the Scottish Royal portrait paintings. We are not portrait specialists or enthusiasts, but after spending several hours here over two days, we learned to appreciate the collection and the lovely architecture.

On the ground level, there is also a pleasant cafe that is ideal for lunch or a coffee break. The museum is free to visit, however donations are greatly welcomed.

15. Visit Harry Potter websites

Harry Potter enthusiasts like Edinburgh, and we've even dedicated a whole section to Harry Potter attractions in the city. J. K. Rowling wrote in Edinburgh cafes while working on the Harry Potter book series.

Nicolson's Café was a first-floor diner on the junction of Nicolson and Drummond Street, where J. K. Rowling is alleged to have written a substantial portion of her first Harry Potter novel as a newly single mother. Since then, the location has been transformed into a Chinese buffet and, most recently, into Spoon, a restaurant.

The Elephant House, where she wrote subsequent Potter novels, is possibly the most well-known Harry Potter site. If you wish to look inside The Elephant House, you must order food or drinks or pay a nominal fee for photographs.

If Harry Potter writing places are of great interest to you and you are not going on a budget, you can consider staying in the J. K. Rowling suite at the popular and historic Balmoral Hotel. Rowling finished the final book in the Harry Potter series in apartment 552. In honor of this, she autographed (graffitied?) a marble bust, which is still on display in the room today.

Other Edinburgh locations that are thought to have inspired the books include Greyfriar's Kirkyard (an old cemetery that contains graves that may have inspired the names of some Harry Potter characters, such as Thomas Riddell's Grave), George Heriot's School, which is similar to Hogwarts, and Victoria Street, which is similar to Diagon Alley.

You can create your own self-guided tour or join other Harry Potter enthusiasts on a fun trip, such as this free tour (tips are strongly requested) or this lengthier 2 hour walking tour.

Those visiting in August should also plan to attend the Edinburgh International Book Festival, which was one of the first venues where an unknown J. K. Rowling (listed as Joanne Rowling) read from her first Harry Potter book to a small group of children in 1997, and where she would return years later to massive crowds in 2004.

16. Attend an Edinburgh Festival

Speaking of festivals, if you enjoy them, Edinburgh is the place to be. To be honest, even if you don't generally appreciate festivals, chances are Edinburgh will have one that you will enjoy. Edinburgh is regarded as the "World's Festival City," and it has 11 major festivals throughout the year that celebrate art, music, movies, theater, storytelling, books, military tattoos, science, and even the entrance of the New Year.

Hogmanay, the Edinburgh International Festival, the Edinburgh Festival Fringe, and the Royal Edinburgh Military Tattoo are undoubtedly the four most well-known festivals, but we have come to appreciate the lesser-known festivals throughout the year.

The festival atmosphere ranges from very low-key (e.g., Edinburgh Science Festival, Film Festival, Storytelling Festival) to a heightened festival frenzy as thousands of visitors flock to the city during August. At the height of the festival season, in mid-August, over 1,000 performances are projected to take place in over 100 sites per day!

If you want to discover more about all of the Edinburgh events and decide which one is appropriate for you, go to the official Edinburgh Festival website, which has up-to-date information on all of the major events.

17. The Edinburgh Dungeon.

The Edinburgh Dungeon, a 2-minute walk from Waverley train station, offers an 80-minute journey of Scottish history, with 11 live actor-led plays and two short underground rides. It focuses on the darker and more grisly aspects of Scottish history (e.g., plague, murder, cannibals, witches) and employs a slew of special effects and scare tactics to keep you on the edge of your seat.

The Edinburgh Dungeon is frequently rated and regarded as one of Edinburgh's top city attractions, and it appears to be especially popular with families with older children (recommended age is 8 years or older). We recently went on a special evening tour when they debuted a new show (The Witch Hunt), which was a lot of frightening fun. The Witch Hunt, The Green Lady, and the drop ride were our favorites.

It should be noted that those who are easily afraid or startled may not enjoy the tour, and that some adult material in the presentations may not be appropriate for young children (trips are normally not recommended for children under the age of 8). Those with impairments or health difficulties should visit this useful accessibility website.

Waiting times can be long during peak months (e.g., July and August, as well as around holidays), so you may want to pre-book tour times online in advance to avoid long lines during those months. Those looking for the greatest costs should book online in advance, as you will almost always get a cheaper deal online.

18. Greyfriars Bobby.

A small dog known as Greyfriars Bobby is one of Edinburgh's most famous historical figures. According to legend, Bobby was a Skye Terrier who belonged to an Edinburgh night watchman named John Gray. When John Gray died and was buried in Greyfriars Kirkyard, it is said that loyal Bobby sat for fourteen years by his master's grave before being buried beside him.

This narrative has been made popular through novels and the 1961 Disney film. Several people have questioned the story's veracity, but it remains a popular, enduring, and heartwarming tale, and it is likely that the story is at least partially based on truth.

You can see Bobby's small statue across the road from the National Museum of Scotland, as well as the graves of Bobby and his owner in the graveyard. The statue is a popular photo location, and it is well worth your time to learn the heartwarming story behind this little dog.

If you want to learn more about Greyfriars Bobby, we recommend paying a visit to the informative (and free) Museum of Edinburgh, which has a Greyfriars Bobby exhibit.

19. Ascend Calton Hill

If the thought of Arthur's Seat makes you nervous, but you still want a good view of Edinburgh, Calton Hill is an excellent alternative. You'll probably notice this hill soon after arriving in Edinburgh, and visitors are often surprised to see a hill that resembles Athens' Acropolis.

Calton Hill is located just east of Princes Street and can be reached via a steep but relatively short set of stairs. A visually interesting but architecturally odd collection of buildings and monuments greets you atop the hill. Many of the structures, such as the National Monument and the Dugald Stewart Monument, appear to be more at home in Athens, Greece.

Calton Hill has housed prisons, residences, government buildings, and the city observatory, among other things. On the hill, there are occasionally events, such as the popular Beltane Fire Festival in April. Take your time exploring the various monuments and taking in the fantastic views of the city skyline; these are probably our favorite views of Edinburgh!

William Henry Playfair designed the City Observatory, the tallest structure on Calton Hill, in 1818. Long closed as an observatory, the space reopened to the public in November 2018 as a contemporary art exhibition center. The original Transit Telescope from 1831 is also on display.

The Observatory also has a restaurant, gift shop, and a rooftop viewing terrace with stunning views of Edinburgh. The City Observatory is open to the public for free. Reservations are strongly advised if you want to eat at the Lookout Restaurant.

Consider visiting the small museum in the Nelson Monument and then climbing the 143 steps to the viewing platform on top (small fee) of the 105 foot (32 meter) high monument, which offers wide vistas over Edinburgh, to learn more about Calton Hill's history and for a particularly excellent view of Edinburgh. The small museum tells the story of the monument and the man who inspired it, Admiral Horatio Nelson, who led the British navy to victory during the Napoleonic Wars at the Battle of Trafalgar.

The Nelson Monument has a time ball that was dropped at 1 o'clock every day (except Sundays) to coincide with the firing of the guns at Edinburgh Castle, which were once used to alert ships of the time. On most days, the guns at Edinburgh Castle are still fired.

20. The Royal Botanic Garden

If you want to stretch your legs, get away from the hustle and bustle of the Royal Mile and Princes Street, and learn a little botany along the way, the Royal Botanic Garden in Edinburgh is the place to go. The garden has been in its current location since 1820 (though it was originally planted in Holyrood Park in 1670).

The garden is free to enter and a lovely place to spend a couple of hours in Edinburgh if the weather is nice! You'll never run out of things to look at with 70 acres of gardens and over 273,000 plants! The Victorian Temperate Palm House, Rock Garden, Poppy Meadow, and Queen Mother's Memorial Garden were among the free highlights.

The gardens are free to enter, but we recommend paying the small entry fee to gain access to the glasshouses, where you can see some of the more exotic plants in the collection, such as a Victoria amazonica (a giant waterlily) and Amorphophallus titanum (which smells like rotten flesh when in bloom!).

Check out what's in bloom before you go to make the most of your time at the garden; spring and early summer will have the most variety, but you'll find plants of interest here all year.

The gardens are about a half-hour walk or a short bus ride from the city center. They are easily accessible by public transportation from the city center or on some routes of the hop-on hop-off sightseeing buses.

21. Royal Yacht Britannia

The Royal Yacht Britannia, officially known as Her Majesty's Yacht Britannia, was home to Her Majesty The Queen and the Royal family for over 40 years and was consistently voted Scotland's Best Attraction by VisitScotland.

The yacht sailed over 1 million miles around the world on hundreds of state visits from 1954 to 1997! It is now docked at Edinburgh's historic Port of Leith and can be toured by the public using the included self-guided audioguide.

The Queen Elizabeth II's bedroom, the room where Charles and Diana spent their honeymoon in 1981, the Bridge, the state dining room, drawing rooms, and the crew quarters and workspaces are all open for tours. During our visit, we also saw the Royal Barge, a retired Rolls-Royce Phantom V state car, and a racing yacht owned by the royal family on display.

Onboard the ship, you can also have afternoon tea or lunch at the Royal Deck Tea Room. The Ocean Terminal shopping mall, which is directly in front of the Britannia, also has food and shopping options (as well as a cinema).

This is a popular attraction that can get crowded, especially during the summer and around holidays. So keep this in mind when you go. Tickets can be purchased in advance or at the attraction. Admission to Royal Yacht Britannia is included on the Royal Edinburgh Ticket.

The yacht is docked about 15 minutes from the city center, and you can get here by car (free parking), local public bus, hop-on hop-off bus, or taxi.

We would recommend taking some time to walk around Leith before heading back to the city center; head towards Shore Street which is a short 15-minute walk away. There are plenty of shops and dining opportunities in Leith and it is quite scenic on a sunny day. There is also the Trinity House Maritime Museum (check opening hours in advance).

The above should give you a great list of places to consider if you are going to be in the city for one day or one week. Even if you are on a tight budget, a large number of our recommended things to do in Edinburgh are free (e.g., most of the city's museums, Calton Hill, and the Royal Botanic Garden) or low cost (e.g., a plate of haggis, many festival events, or a view from Nelson Monument).

As you plan your trip, just remember that part of the allure of the city is just wandering around and soaking up the historical and lively charm so be sure to leave a bit of free time in your schedule. We discover new things to do each time we visit which is often!

Chapter 41: Essential Scottish Destinations: Five Must-Visit Places

Scotland's must-see sites provide something for everyone, whether you're looking for the echoes of old tales, the embrace of nature's grandeur, or the lively energy of metropolitan life.

Scotland is a senior-friendly destination because to its intelligently constructed activities and lodgings. Its magnificent surroundings, which range from the rocky Highlands to the tranquil Lowlands, provide a slow pace and ease of access for elders to explore. Historic monuments such as Edinburgh Castle and Stirling Castle have accessible elements that allow seniors to immerse themselves in the country's rich history. Seniors are drawn to lovely streets, such as Edinburgh's Royal Mile, with their charming shops, cozy pubs, and street performances that allow for a leisurely stroll. The breathtaking magnificence of the island landscapes, such as the mystical Isle of Skye and the calm Isles of Lewis and Harris, is accessible by well-maintained trails.

Edinburgh

Edinburgh, the capital of Scotland, is a city rich in history. Edinburgh Castle, with its medieval and Georgian design, stands majestically atop the famed Castle Rock, affording panoramic views of the city below. The Royal Mile, which connects the castle to the Palace of Holyroodhouse, is a treasure trove of quaint stores, traditional Scottish bars, and enthralling street acts.

A visit to the National Museum of Scotland and the Scottish National Gallery is a must for history buffs. The legendary Edinburgh Festival, where art, music, and theater take center stage, brings the cultural landscape to life. Edinburgh is an ideal location for the mature, discerning tourist, whether wandering through the tranquil Princes Street Gardens or ascending up Arthur's Seat, an extinct volcano.

Skye Island

The Isle of Skye is a veritable fantasy for those looking for an unearthly encounter. This island is known for its ethereal scenery, which include majestic cliffs, intriguing fairy lakes, and captivating old-world castles. The Quiraing, a landslide feature, provides stunning views and excellent hiking options.

The Trotternish Peninsula is a photographer's dream, with renowned landmarks like the Old Man of Storr, a dramatic rock pinnacle tower rising above the valley. If you enjoy history, you can visit Dunvegan Castle, Scotland's oldest continually inhabited castle, and learn about the interesting folklore of the island. Skye is a lovely destination for families, couples, and elders.

Stirling

Stirling transports you to the heart of Scotland's medieval heritage. This historic city was crucial in the country's battles for independence, and the renowned Stirling Castle stands as a testament to those turbulent times. The National Wallace Monument, which offers panoramic views of the surrounding area, commemorates William Wallace's victory at Stirling Bridge.

A visit to Loch Lomond & The Trossachs National Park, which is only a short drive away, is a must for nature lovers. The park's varied environment varies from beautiful lochs to craggy highlands, providing excellent chances for hiking, boating, and animal viewing. Stirling's history and natural beauty combine to make it an ideal destination for history fans and outdoor enthusiasts of all ages.

Glasgow

Glasgow, Scotland's largest city, is a thriving metropolis. The Kelvingrove Art Gallery and Museum, known for its art scene, holds a broad collection, while the Riverside Museum highlights the city's transportation heritage. The massive Victorian buildings that dominate the city center will delight architecture buffs.

The music culture in Glasgow is legendary, and tourists can enjoy live performances in a variety of locations, creating an electrifying environment. Families may spend time together at the Glasgow Science Centre, where interactive exhibits pique the interest of visitors of all ages. As a result, Glasgow is a great city for seniors to explore at their leisure.

Isle of Lewis and Harris

The wild beauty of the Isles of Lewis and Harris off the northwest coast of Scotland beckons. The island of Callanish, famous for its ancient standing stones, creates a tale of mystery and enchantment via its rocky terrain. The ivory beaches of Luskentyre and Scarista conjure up images of tropical paradises, with routes appropriate for senior exploration, and the clean seas attract visitors of all ages to relax and unwind. Outdoor enthusiasts can explore the untamed coastline and quiet coves, while senior birdwatchers can marvel at the diverse species.

Chapter 42: Sampling Scotland: Ten Traditional Scottish Dishes

Scotland, known for its rich history and unique cuisine culture, has a lot to offer in terms of traditional and tasty meals. From delicious Scottish oatmeal to the iconic national dish of Haggis, Scotland provides a gourmet cuisine unlike any other in Europe. With ingredients such as fresh veggies and high-quality meats, here are 10 different types of traditional Scottish dishes to taste during your holiday.

Scottish Pies

Scotch pies are small yet excellent double-crusted meat pies that originated in Scotland. These savory pies, filled with minced mutton or other types of meat, can be served hot or cold and are cooked fresh at Scottish takeaway restaurants or bakeries across the country. Every year since 1999, the Scottish Bakers trade group has organized a World Scotch Pie Championship, where people from all over the world compete for the renowned Scotch pie trophy.

Scottish Oatmeal

This popular breakfast meal dates back to the early days of Scotland. Unlike most people outside of Scotland, Scottish porridge is cooked with salt rather than sugar, making it a savory breakfast rather than a sweet one. This classic Scottish dish, made with fresh porridge oats boiled in milk, is the ideal dish to start your day before heading out touring in the Highlands.

Cullen Skink

This creamy smoked fish soup is another traditional Scottish meal that originated in the northeastern area of Scotland in a little community called Cullen. Cullen skink is made with smoked haddock, cream, potatoes, and onions and is traditionally eaten with toasted bread. While it originated as a Cullen delicacy, this delicious soup may now be found on Scottish menus across the country.

Deep-fried Mars Bars

Deep-fried Mars bars are a tasty and distinctive dessert concept established in 1992 by a guy named John Davie in Stonehaven, near Aberdeen, at the Haven Chip Bar. The iconic European chocolate bar is battered with flour, eggs, and milk before being deep fried, resulting in melted chocolate encased in crispy batter. This delectable delicacy is available in fish and chip establishments (also known as chippers) throughout Scotland.

Haggis

Haggis, Scotland's iconic national food, is made of sausage meat produced from sheep innards blended with onions, oats, suet, stock, dried herbs, and other seasonings. These components are blended and then boiled within the stomach lining of a sheep. While this may not sound appetizing, if you're feeling brave during your journey to Scotland, the tasty Haggis will fill you up and leave you satisfied.

Tatties and Neeps

Neeps and tatties are two excellent side dishes that are frequently served alongside the national dish of haggis. They are produced from root vegetables that have been boiled and mashed into two delicious side dishes. The dish is known as a "Burns supper" when served with Haggis. Healthy and delicious, neeps and tatties are simply another term for potatoes and turnips and may be found in a variety of Scottish cuisines.

Traditional Scottish Tablet

This little, sweet snack is produced of sugar, condensed milk, and butter, which is crystallized to form small pieces of delectable semi-hard candy. This scrumptious dessert is commonly flavored with vanilla or whisky and can be found in shops all around Scotland. It is as sweet as fudge but not as soft. If you have a sweet tooth, traditional Scottish tablet will quench your appetite.

Cranachan

Cranachan is a traditional Scottish dessert that is frequently served at Christmas and other special occasions. This sweet delicacy served in a tall glass with ingredients such as whipped cream, scotch whisky, honey, oats, and fresh raspberries may commonly be found on many restaurant dessert menus. Traditionally, it is presented by bringing out a dish of each component and allowing each individual to build their own dessert.

Stovies

Stovies is a beef and potato-based meal that is commonly served as an appetizer or as an accompanying dish in many restaurants and pubs in Scotland. Stovies is the perfect traditional Scottish cuisine to try during the harsh winter months, made by blending potatoes, sausages, roast and minced beef, and spices, and boiling everything in one pot.

Soup Cock-a-Leekie

Cock-a-leekie soup is considered as Scotland's national soup because of its nice mild flavor and great scent. This classic dish is created with peppered chicken stock, leeks, and occasionally prunes, and it can be thickened with rice or barley. This Scottish take on classic chicken soup dates back to the 16th century and is the ideal dish for a chilly day in Scotland's changeable weather.

Chapter 43: Scotch Cuisine and Drink

To say that food and drink are central to Scottish culture is an understatement. Scottish cuisine and drink is more than just a night out; it is the very lifeblood of Scotland's culture and economy.

Scotland produces some of the best and most sought-after natural produce in the world, thanks to its rolling, rural hillsides, pure coastal waters, and lush, rich fields.

From succulent Aberdeen Angus steaks to world-class seafood like wild trout, salmon, oysters, and langoustines, not to mention our lifeblood, whisky, the 'Made in Scotland' stamp has become synonymous with flavor and excellence. Even our cheese can compete with the best in France!

PRODUCE

Scotland's breathtaking landscapes are more than simply beauty; they are also where our high-quality produce is raised, harvested, and grown. Hand-dived scallops, Aberdeen Angus meat, Ayrshire potatoes, and Fife soft fruits are just a few of the items available to Scottish chefs. Local butchers and fishmongers, as well as farm shops, food festivals, and farmers markets, are excellent places to stock up on fresh ingredients for your own recipes.

Some Scottish produce is sufficiently distinctive that the European Union has recognized it as a Protected Geographical Indication (PGI). To be eligible to use the regional label, these high-quality commodities must be produced in a consistent manner and inside a defined geographical area. So when you sample Stornoway Black Pudding, Traditional Ayrshire Dunlop cheese, Orkney Scottish Island Cheddar, and Scottish Wild Salmon, you know you're getting the real stuff. And there's nothing like eating them in their own region!

FOOD AND DRINK TRADITIONAL
Haggis

Haggis, a savory pork pudding, is Scotland's national meal, often served with mashed potatoes, turnips (known as 'neeps,' and a whisky sauce. This brings us to the national beverage, whiskey. This amber-colored beverage is produced by over 100 distilleries in Scotland, several of which may be visited on a tour. There are five Scottish whisky districts, each with its own particular flavor, and it's said that if you don't think you like whisky, it's just because you haven't found the right one yet!

Desserts like Cranachan, sweet delicacies like shortbread and tablet, and savory dishes like Scotch broth and black pudding are also typical. Throughout the country, you may get a variety of regional sweets and nibbles, such as Aberdeenshire butteries, a type of bread roll, Dundee Cake, and Cullen Skink, a wonderfully creamy crab soup.

SCOTISH BEVERAGES

We must begin with our most important export, whisky, which is, for good cause, our national drink. A distillery tour or a taste is a terrific opportunity to learn about this complex and diverse drink.

Scotland has a long history of beer production and an increasing number of small brewers. Many may be visited and host sampling events and beer festivals; use Scotland's Craft Beer Map to find out more.

There's also gin. Scotland produces more than half of the gin in the UK, with over 50 producers producing about 100 different gins – explore them with Scotland's Gin Map.

Do you want something a little softer? IRN BRU, known as 'Scotland's other national drink,' should be your first port of call while visiting Scotland.

RESTAURANT OPTIONS

It's time to eat - there are many possibilities for dining out in Scotland. Throughout the country, there are a variety of restaurants, historic pubs, pleasant cafés, beautiful tearooms, and down-to-earth takeaways. Dine in one of Scotland's Michelin-starred restaurants. To savor a variety of excellent gastronomic experiences, join a foodie walking tour in Edinburgh or Glasgow. In Scotland's seaside towns, enjoy fresh seafood meals, a classic afternoon tea, or take a food and drink trail for a culinary road trip. If you can't decide what to eat, look for businesses that have Taste Our Best accreditation, which ensures that they serve high-quality Scottish fare. Glasgow was named the 18th most vegan-friendly city in the world in 2021, demonstrating that Scotland truly has something for everyone.

EXPERIENCES IN FOOD
Food festivals, pop-up restaurants, street food, and cooking workshops are just a few of the food-related activities available in Scotland.

FUN FACT
Each second, 40 bottles of Scotch Whisky are exported worldwide (yep, you read it correctly!).

In France, more Scotch Whisky is sold in one month than cognac in a year. Scotland supplies more than two-thirds of the world's langoustines.

Scottish salmon was the first foreign product to be awarded France's prized 'Label Rouge' quality label.

Scottish lobsters can be found on the menus of more than 20 Michelin-starred restaurants in Tokyo alone.

In 1970, there were just 11 breweries in Scotland; today, there are over 100 craft brewers in Scotland creating a diverse range of specialty beers.

Some Scottish items, such as Scotch Beef and Lamb, Scotch Whisky, and Orkney Cheddar, have Protected Geographical Indication (PGI) status.

WHISKY
Scottish whisky - often known as 'Scotch' - has a history dating back to the 11th century and is a vital component of our Scottish identity. The story of whisky-making in Scotland is as intriguing and complex as the drink itself.

Chapter 43: Essential Scottish Food and Drink Experiences

Scottish food and drink are unrivaled. As a result, when visiting, make the most of your time by being adventurous and trying everything this region has to offer. Scotland is a must-see destination for any foodie, with world-renowned seafood, sweet desserts, and even the birthplace of Scotch whisky.

So take a deep breath and prepare to delve into the greatest Scottish food and drink collection we have to offer.

1. The Arbroath Smokies
These haddock fish are made in Arbroath using a historic procedure that dates back to the 1800s. They're salted overnight to preserve them, then roasted for about an hour over a very hot, humid, and smokey fire.

It is critical to utilize high heat and heavy smoke to avoid burning the fish. This also gives the distinct smokey flavor and aroma that customers anticipate from Arbroath Smokies.

2. Fish Dinner

This fried fish in batter with a side of deep-fried chips, often known as Fish &' Chips, has become a staple lunch in the United Kingdom. Which flavor to add to this Scottish dish is a hotly debated question. Salt and vinegar are commonly used in Glasgow. Whereas in Edinburgh, the most popular alternative is a combination of brown sauce and malt vinegar, simply called as 'sauce' or 'chippy sauce'. Try them both and you're bound to have a favorite.

In Scotland, there are numerous famous Chippies (Fish and Chip businesses) where people come considerable distances to eat their favorite greasy comfort meal. Along the Fife coast, we recommend the Anstruther Fish Bar. On our St Andrews day tour, you can sample one of their famous chippies.

3. West Coast Scallops

West coast scallops are the second Scottish food on our list. But this isn't your average fish dish. Hand-dived scallops can cost twice as much as dredged scallops. However, as customers become more conscious of the need of sourcing food in a more ethical and ecological manner, they are prepared to pay a premium for an artisan hand-dived scallop.

4. Smoked Salmon

Scotland is known for producing some of the best salmon in the world. Because of the abundance of shoreline and lochs, you're never far from a fresh mouthful of delicious Scottish cuisine. Take our day tour to Oban to experience the greatest smoked salmon and shellfish.

5. Aberdeen Angus Beef

Aberdeen Angus beef is a Scottish food dish that is popular throughout the United Kingdom. This is a hornless cattle breed that originated in Aberdeenshire, in the north-east of Scotland. The majority are black or crimson in color and can currently be found all over the world. Superior beef is distinguished by its marbling, which improves flavor, softness, and keeps the meat moist when cooking.

6. Porridge

Porridge is a hot cereal meal produced by soaking a grain in water or milk and then cooking it. It has become a popular Scottish morning item for many Scots as well as those from other countries. For flavor, sugar, honey, fruit, or syrup are frequently used. Our North American friends could call this oatmeal. It's not only a healthy dinner, but it's also high in fiber, which keeps you satisfied for a long time.

7. Haggis

This is the most well-known Scottish dish, and it is made from sheep's heart, liver, and lungs, as well as oatmeal, spices, salt, and stock. It was originally cooked in the stomach of an animal. Nowadays, it's more likely to be cooked in an artificial casing. Some people adore it, while others despise it. You must make your own decision. If you're celebrating Burns Night in Scotland, you'll almost certainly be served haggis as your main course. After all, Robert Burns wrote a sonnet to Scottish food called 'Address to a Haggis'.

8. Blackberries Pudding

Another breakfast time companion is the following Scottish food. Black pudding is cooked with pork blood, pork fat or beef suet, and a grain, most commonly oatmeal, oat groats, or barley groats. The large quantity of grain, as well as the inclusion of specific herbs such as pennyroyal, distinguishes black pudding from blood sausages consumed elsewhere in the world.

Many people believe that Stornoway has the best tasting black pudding. If you're courageous enough, you can remain there overnight on our Isle of Lewis tour.

9. Breakfast in Scotland

A full breakfast in Scotland contains the same items as a full English meal:
- eggs,
- bacon, back
- sausage link,
- baked beans, etc.
- toasted buttered bread
- A cup of tea or coffee.

It can, however, incorporate traditional Scottish fare such as black pudding, Lorne sausage, and a tattie scone (potato scone).

10. Oatcakes

Oats are one of the few grains that grow well in the north of Scotland and were the staple grain used in many Scottish dishes until the twentieth century. Oatcakes are made with oatmeal and baked on a girdle or baking tray. They're high in slow-digesting, low-GI carbs that will keep you satisfied for hours and are healthier than bread.

Nairn's, Paterson's, and Walkers are popular commercial brands.

11. Cheddar Cheese, Mull

The cows in this area eat fermented grain from the adjacent Tobermory whisky distillery (may be the happiest cows in Scotland). This results in a pale ivory-colored cheese with a very strong, fruity flavor. It's an artisan cheese prepared on the farm of Sgriob-ruadh utilizing traditional processes and unpasteurized milk (which is slightly alcoholic). Intrigued? We're not surprised.

12. Scottish Pie

Scotch Pie is a double-crust meat pie filled with mutton or another type of meat. This Scottish dish is also known as "football pie" since it is frequently sold among other hot dishes at football stadiums. Many takeaway eateries, bakeries, and outdoor events sell Scotch pies. Aside from being delicious, they're also useful because the hard crust of the pie allows you to enjoy it without wrapping.

13. 'Bangers and Mash'
Sausage and mash is a popular British dish consisting of mashed potatoes and sausages. Cumberland pork sausages and onion gravy are commonly used, and lavishly dribbled on top. This dish is simple and quick to create in large quantities, which helps to establish it in our memories as classic pub fare.

In a survey commissioned by TV channel Good Food in 2009, the meal was named Britain's most popular comfort food.

14. Leek and Tattie Soup
Leek and tattie (potato) soup is a creamy classic that will keep you toasty during the winter months. This Scottish cuisine is available in many restaurants, but it is also simple to prepare at home. This leek and tattie recipe is delicious when served with melba bread.

15. Cullen Skink
Cullen Skink is a thick, hearty Scottish soup made with smoked haddock, potatoes, and onions. It is traditionally eaten with bread in the Moray region of Scotland. This Scottish dish has been described as'smokier and more aggressive than American chowder, yet heartier than classical French bisque' by others.

16. Bacon Butty
In the United Kingdom, a bacon butty, sometimes known as a bacon sandwich, is a guilty pleasure. This simple mix of buttered bread and bacon with ketchup is hailed as the best hangover treatment, and it will console you throughout that difficult morning.

17. Stovies
Stovies are a hearty Scottish dish that focuses heavily on potatoes. While the recipes and ingredients differ, the main ingredients are large chunks of

potato, carrots, onions, lard, and occasionally meat. Slow-stewing the potatoes in a closed saucepan with fat (lard or butter) cooks them.

Oatcakes are frequently served as a side dish and are used to scoop up some stovies for a nice mouthful.

Sweet Scottish Food to Try

Scotland is obsessed with confectionery. Sugar consumption is much higher than in the rest of the United Kingdom. But how did Scotland become so fascinated with sugar?

The British empire is responsible for a big portion of it. During imperial expansion, a large amount of raw cane sugar was carried from the Caribbean to the United Kingdom. Much of it ended up in refineries near Glasgow to go through the granulation process.

Because of the abundance of inexpensive sugar in the Glasgow area, a cottage industry of candy-making developed. Sweetie Wives were ladies who bought bulk sugar and cooked it into homemade sweets to sell at local markets.

This fact, combined with the colder weather in Scotland, which causes the human body to seek sugary foods in order to increase blood sugar levels, contributed to the creation of a culture of sugar-hungry Scots.

18. Tunnock's Tea Cakes

These teacakes are a Scottish specialty that are typically served with a cup of tea or coffee. They are made up of a little round shortbread biscuit that has been topped with hand-piped Italian meringue and covered in milk chocolate. Since their introduction in 1956, these teacakes have become popular treats in the United Kingdom and an excellent choice for entertaining visitors for a cup of tea.

19. Caramel Logs

Tunnock's is a Scottish food brand whose famed Caramel Logs deserve a second mention. These were invented in Scotland in 1955 and are made of wafer and caramel wrapped in flavorful chocolate and gorgeous golden roasted coconut. It's like a caramelized Kit Kat, but better.

Surprisingly, this product proved extremely popular in the Middle East as well.

20. Stoats Bars
Stoats Porridge Bars, manufactured by an Edinburgh-based company that produces simple and on-the-go oat snack bars, are the second Scottish dish on the list.

21. Berries
In Scotland, the districts of Fife, Angus, and Perthshire are known for their abundance of red fruits. Raspberries, in particular. They enjoy excellent temperatures and moisture in this area, which does not become as hot as southern England or as much rain or frost as the west of Scotland.

This sweet spot of weather and rain allows farmers to produce these high-quality berries, which can then be used in delectable Scottish delicacies.

22. Dundee Marmalade
Dundee Marmalade was invented in the Scottish city of Dundee in 1797. This preserve, created by James Keiller and his wife, was distinguished by large chunks of bitter Seville orange rind.

According to a Scottish tale, orange marmalade was accidentally developed in Britain. The story goes that a boat transporting oranges broke down at Dundee harbor. As a result, some resourceful locals turned the shipment into marmalade. And we are grateful that they did so so that we can eat this delicious Scottish food on a regular basis.

23. Durness' chocolates

Durness is a town in Scotland's northwestern Highlands. Visit Cocoa Mountain and sample some of the greatest gourmet chocolate in Scotland. Chocolate may not be the first thing that comes to mind when thinking of Scottish food, but after sampling this, you'll want to bring boxes home.

24. Ice cream with a whisky flavor

On a rare sunny day in Scotland, the combo of scotch whisky and ice cream is unbeatable. You can enjoy the chilly feeling of the ice cream followed by the distinctive and uplifting notes of a high-quality whisky by using locally-sourced double cream and a generous dosage of single malt scotch whisky.

If you're interested, go to Scotch Corner in Pitlochry or Balvenie St Ice Cream in Dufftown.

25. Tablet

If you enjoy sugar, you'll enjoy this. Tablet is a medium-hard Scottish confection. A sugar, condensed milk, and butter-based version on the well-known fudge tablet. It is heated before being allowed to crystallize. The result is a more brittle and gritty texture than fudge, but it's still wonderful.

26. Sticky Toffee Pudding

This dessert is considered a modern British classic. Sticky Toffee Pudding is a moist sponge cake topped with a toffee sauce and typically served with vanilla custard or ice cream on the side. If you have a sweet craving, this wonderful Scottish cuisine will not disappoint.

27. Shortbread

Shortbread is a classic Scottish dessert that was initially made from leftover biscuit bread dough. You may make a more sweeter biscuit by gradually removing the yeast and substituting it with butter. Mary Queen of Scots is said to have been a major fan and helped extend its popularity. It's the ideal snack for an afternoon tea break.

28. Edinburgh Rock Candy

Edinburgh Rock is a unique dessert that differs from traditional rock candy. It is made up of sugar, water, cream of tartar, colorings, and flavors. This Scottish dish has a soft and crumbly texture and is typically sold in sticks. Alexander Ferguson is the mind behind it, and he brought his experience from working in the Glasgow candy trade to Edinburgh during the nineteenth century. If you visit Edinburgh, you must have this delectable treat.

29. Scones

A scone is a famous British baked good made of wheat or oatmeal and leavened with baking powder. They're a staple of cream tea and are frequently served with jam or clotted cream. Plain, fruit, and cheese scones are the most common. The only decision is whether to start with jam or cream.

30. Buttery

A buttery, also known as an Aberdeen roll, is a savory bread roll that originated in Aberdeen, Scotland. This Scottish dish has a flaky texture and buttery flavor that is comparable to a croissant but slightly saltier. It is customary to smear jam or butter on them and eat them with a cup of tea. When toasted, the significant fat content within causes them to become incredibly hot.

According to folklore, butteries were first made for fisherman traveling from Aberdeen harbor. This was due to the fact that they required a food source that would not go stale during their weeks at sea. The substantial fat content supplied an additional source of energy.

31. Deep-fried Mars Bar

Without include the king of unhealthy snacks, the deep-fried Mars bar, no sweet tooth Scottish food list would be complete. This famed snack was established as a novelty item in chip shops in the Scottish town of Stonehaven. Simply cook a regular Mars bar in the batter used for deep-frying fish.

However, its popularity has surged when it was taken up by various mass media outlets. It is currently available at many chip shops in the UK and abroad, as well as select restaurants.

Mars Inc. has not publicly backed this practice because it contradicts the company's goal to encouraging healthy and active lifestyles. We don't hold it against them.

32. Irn-Bru

Irn-Bru is Scotland's national hangover remedy. So it would be wrong not to include it on our list of Scottish foods and drinks. A.G. produces this ginger-colored carbonated soft drink in Glasgow. Barr. It's famous for its vivid orange color and unusually sweet flavor. Irn-Bru has a devoted fan base who drink their favorite beverage on a regular basis. It's so popular that 20 cans of Irn Bru are sold every second in Scotland, according to reports.

33. Whisky

Scotch, also known as whisky in Scotland, is derived from the Gaelic 'uisge beatha,' or "water of life." That should give you a notion of the historical significance of this amber liquid in Scotland.

Scotch malt whiskies are classified into five categories:
- Highland
- Highland,
- Islay,
- Speyside, Scotland
- The town of Campbeltown

Because of the native water and varied methods, each place has its own distinct flavor. A single malt whisky is made in one of these regions, but a blended Scotch whisky is made out of single malts from various distilleries. Blended Scotch whisky accounts for 90% of all whisky produced in Scotland.

To choose your favorite sort of whisky, go on a whisky tasting tour in one of Scotland's cities. Then, on one of our whiskey tours, you can learn about the history, how it's manufactured, and sample a variety of drams. Don't be concerned; we'll drive you home.

34. Hot Toddy

On a cold winter evening, there are few things better than a Hot Toddy. A alcohol (typically whiskey), hot water, and honey or sugar are combined to make this Scottish drink. This is not only delicious, but some people feel it might help with cold and flu symptoms. According to Victoria Moore, the drink contains "vitamin C for health, honey to soothe, and alcohol to numb."

35. Beer

Scots may have scotch in their veins, but they also know how to enjoy an ice-cold pint of beer. Scotland's beers range from pub classics like Tennent's Lager and Caledonia Best to craft beer agitators like Brewdog.

Brewdog originated in Aberdeenshire but is now available as far afield as Australia. Caledonian and Innis & Gunn are well-known Edinburgh breweries, while Tennent's is produced nearby Glasgow.

36. Edinburgh Gin

If you prefer a Gin & Tonic to a dram or pint, Edinburgh Gin is for you. This award-winning small-batch distillery makes some of the world's best gin. Visit their visitor center in Scotland's capital for a guided tasting and to try your hand at producing your own.

So you're ready to sample your way through Scotland. The western islands have Mull Cheddar, the Highlands have Scotch, Aberdeen has butteries, and Edinburgh has rock candy. A broad choice of food and drink may be found in every area of Scotland. Treat your taste buds to something different the next time you visit Scotland. Consume Scottish food and drink with the natives to connect with a flavorful and welcoming culture.

Chapter 44: Scotland's Premier Hiking Routes

Scotland's walking routes are distinctly waymarked, generally off-road and traffic-free, and feature a variety of visitor services along the way, making them ideal for a multi-day walk or overnight stay.

10 Must-Do Walking Routes

Long distance walking routes in Scotland allow you to discover the best of Scotland's environment and landscapes while also learning about its history and culture.

Are you looking for a thrilling path for your first challenge? Discover beginner-friendly long-distance walking routes.

Trails Along the Coast

With this collection of beautiful coastal trails, you may breathe in crisp salty air, immerse yourself in dramatic seascapes, explore secluded coves and bays, and view some spectacular marine species.

THE JOHN MUIR WAY

Begin at Helensburgh, Argyll.
End at Dunbar in East Lothian

Length: 134 miles (215 kilometers)
Timeframe: 7 to 10 days

From coast to coast The John Muir Way honors John Muir as the father of national parks and global conservation.

THE MULL OF GALLOWAY TRAIL
Begin at the Mull of Galloway.
Ends at Glenapp
Distance: 35 miles (56 kilometers).
Duration: 2 to 3 days

The Mull of Galloway Trail connects the Ayrshire Coastal Path with Scotland's most south-westerly tip via Stranraer and Glenapp.

WEST ISLAND WAY
Start location: Kilchattan Bay, Isle of Bute
Final destination: Kames Bay, Isle of Bute
30 miles (48 kilometers)
Duration: 2 to 3 days

Explore the West Island Way on the Isle of Bute in the Forth of Clyde, which features lovely beaches, moorland, forest, and agriculture.

COASTAL BERWICKSHIRE PATH
Cockburnspath, Scottish Borders, as a starting point
Berwick-upon-Tweed, Northumberland, is the destination.
28.5 miles (45 kilometers)
Duration: 2 to 4 days

The beautiful Berwickshire Coastal Path in southern Scotland takes in some of the most breathtaking cliff and coastal scenery in the UK.

THE MORAY COAST TRAIL
Begin: Findhorn

End: Cullen
Distance: 50 miles (80 kilometers).
Duration: 3 to 5 days

The Moray Coast Trail follows the Moray Coast, offering views of the Moray Firth and North Sea from coves, beaches, and skerries.

ARRAN COASTAL WAY
Begin with Brodick.
End at Brodick
Distance: 65 miles (105 kilometers).
Duration: 4 to 6 days

The Arran Coastal Way circles the lovely Isle of Arran off the coast of Ayrshire.

AYRSHIRE COASTAL PATHWAY
Begin: Glenapp
End: Skelmorlie
Distance: 100 miles (160 kilometers).
Six to eight days

The Ayrshire Coastal Path provides breathtaking views of the Ayrshire coast and the Firth of Clyde.

FIFE COASTAL PATH
Kincardine Bridge is the starting point.
Finally, Newburgh.
Distance: 117 miles (187 kilometers).
Duration: 7 to 9 days

The Fife Coastal Path connects the Firths of Forth and Tay, passing through historic settlements, award-winning beaches, and wildlife reserves.

THE KINTYRE WAY

Begin: Tarbert, Argyll
End: Kintyre, Machrihanish
Distance: 100 miles (160 kilometers).
Timeframe: 7 to 10 days

Along the Kintyre Way on Scotland's south-west coast, explore the stunning countryside, coast, and beaches of the Kintyre peninsula.

TRAIL OF JOHN O'GROATS

Begin in Inverness.
John O'Groats is the last destination.
Distance: 147 miles (237 kilometers).
Timing: The complete trail takes 9-14 days, however there are various shorter or longer routes that are part of the trail.

The John O'Groats Trail runs along the coast from Inverness to John O'Groats and can be completed in portions, as a long-distance route, or even from the beginning or conclusion of the journey to/from Lands conclusion!

Mountain ranges and lochs

If you're looking for something wild and amazing, these routes have enough of it. Pack your rucksack (or, if you're doing the Great Glen Canoe Trail, your canoe!) and enjoy some of Europe's best and most stunning mountain and loch views.

WEST HIGHLAND WAY

Begin: Milngavie, near Glasgow
End: Fort William.
Distance: 96 miles (153 kilometers).
Six to eight days

The West Highland Way, Scotland's most popular long distance trail, passes through some of the country's most renowned scenery.

THE GREAT GLEN WAY

Begin: Fort William.
End: Inverness
Distance: 79 miles (127 kilometers).
Timeframe: 5 to 6 days

The Great Glen Way, the walking/biking equivalent of the Canoe Trail, winds through spectacular mountain and lake landscapes.

THE THE THREE LOCHS WAY

Begin: Balloch, Loch Lomond.
End: Inveruglas, Loch Lomond
34 miles (54 kilometers)
Duration: 2 to 3 days

The Three Lochs Way, which includes Loch Lomond, The Gareloch, and Loch Long, is the ideal way to immerse yourself in breathtaking scenery.

LOCH LOMOND & THE COWAL WAY

Begin: Portavadie, Cowal
End: Inveruglas, Loch Lomond
Distance: 57 miles (91 kilometers).
Duration: 3 to 5 days

The Loch Lomond & Cowal Way follows waymarked forest and hill tracks, quiet roads, and serene shorelines through stunning Argyll scenery.

THE SOUTHERN UPLAND WAY

Begin in Portpatrick, Dumfries and Galloway.
Cockburnspath in the Scottish Borders
Distance: 212 miles (339 km)
Duration: 12 to 16 days

Our longest Great Trail is the epic coast-to-coast Southern Upland Way across the south of Scotland.

THE GREAT TROSSACHS PATH
Begin in Inversnaid, Loch Lomond.
End in Callander, Trossachs.
30 miles (48 kilometers)
Duration: 2 to 3 days

Along the Great Trossachs Path, you can discover the treasures of Loch Lomond and The Trossachs National Park.

THE GREAT GLEN CANOE TRAIL
Begin at the Caledonian Canal near Fort William.
Ends ay Inverness
Distance: 60 miles (96 kilometers).
Timeframe: 5 days

The Great Glen Canoe Trail, which follows the Caledonian Canal and includes Loch Ness, is a fantastic adventure for experienced canoeists.

Source to Sea Routes
Follow these routes from their source to coastal end, stopping along the way at some remarkable visitor attractions. Keep an eye out for shy riverside wildlife, or simply enjoy a picnic on a peaceful river bank.

SPEYSIDE WAY
Start: Aviemore
End: Newtonmore
Length: 100.6 miles (162 km)
Timeframe: 5 to 6 days

Linking the Moray Coast with the Cairngorms National Park, the Speyside Way passes through whisky country and leads into the UK's largest National Park.

CLYDE WALKWAY

Start: Partick, Glasgow's West End
End: New Lanark World Heritage Site
Length: 40 miles (64 km)
Duration: 2 to 3 days

Connecting Scotland's biggest city with a UNESCO World Heritage and the Falls of Clyde, the Clyde Walkway takes in history and wildlife along the way.

RIVER AYR WAY

Start: Glenbuck Loch, East Ayrshire
End: Ayr, South Ayrshire
Length: 44 miles (70 km)
Timing: 3 – 4 days

Passing through historic landscapes and areas rich in wildlife, explore tranquil East Ayrshire before reaching the seaside town of Ayr along the River Ayr Way.

ANNANDALE WAY

Start: Devil's Beef Tub, near Moffat
End: Annan, Dumfries & Galloway
Length: 55 miles (88 km)
Timing: 4 – 5 days

Heading through delightful Dumfries & Galloway countryside, with steep climbs and rough ground at times, the Annandale Way is a long distance route to savour.

Historical Trails

Step back in time with these fascinating historical trails. Follow in the footsteps of pious monks and a saint or learn how less saintly Roman invaders, marauding cattle-rustlers and the notorious Rob Roy MacGregor left their indelible marks on today's landscapes.

CROSS BORDERS DROVE ROAD
Start: Harperrig, Pentland Hills Regional Park
End: Hawick, Scottish Borders
Length: 52 miles (83 km)
Timing: 4 – 5 days

The Cross Borders Drove Road follows ancient routes once used for moving livestock to the old markets at Falkirk and Crieff.

ROMANS AND REIVERS ROUTE
Start: Ae Forest, near Dumfries
End: Hawick, Scottish Borders
Length: 52 miles (83 km)
Timing: 4 – 5 days

Step back in time along the Romans and Reivers Route and discover old Roman roads and trails used by the notorious Border Reivers (raiders).

BORDERS ABBEYS WAY
Start: Jedburgh
End: Jedburgh – though you could start and end at any of the towns along the route
Length: 68 miles (109 km)
Timeframe: 5 days

The circular Borders Abbeys Way links the four great ruined Borders abbeys at Jedburgh, Melrose, Kelso and Dryburgh.

ST CUTHBERT'S WAY
Start: Melrose, Scottish Borders
End: Lindisfarne/Holy Island, Northumberland
Length: 62.5 miles (100 km)
Timeframe: 5 days

Dedicated to St Cuthbert, a seventh century monk, bishop and hermit, the St Cuthbert's Way is a great route for revitalising body and spirit.

ROB ROY WAY

Start: Drymen, Loch Lomond & The Trossachs National Park
End: Pitlochry, Perthshire
Length: 77 miles or 94 miles (123 or 150 km)
Timing: 7 days

Follow in the footsteps of one of our most celebrated outlaws (or folk heroes!) through outstanding Trossachs, Stirlingshire and Highland Perthshire scenery along the Rob Roy Way.

ST MAGNUS WAY

Start: Egilsay
End: St Magnus' Cathedral
Length: 58 miles Timing: 4-5 days

Immerse yourself in Orkney's rich history and heritage by taking on St Magnus Way. The route is inspired by the life and death of Magnus, Orkney's patron saint.

CATERAN TRAIL
Start/End: Route can be joined/end at any stage, but perhaps start and end in Alyth or Blairgowrie
Length: 64 miles (103 km)
Timeframe: 5 days

Follow the Cateran Trail and discover ancient tracks that were once used by cattle rustlers (Caterans) who plundered nearby glens from the middle ages to the 17th century.

Towpaths, old trainlines and two wheels

Explore easy-going long distance routes that lie along some of our former railway lines, canal towpaths and quiet country roads, where the attractions and scenery will take your breath away.

CALEDONIAN CANAL
Begin in Fort William.
End at Inverness.
Distance: 60 miles (96 kilometers).
Timeframe: 5 days

An engineering marvel, built by Thomas Telford, the Caledonian Canal runs through Neptune's Staircase and past lochs Lochy, Oich, Ness and Dochfour, before meeting the Moray Firth at Inverness.

DAVA WAY
Start: Forres End: Grantown-on-Spey
Length: 24 miles (38 km)
Timing: 2 days
The Dava Way, through Speyside and the Cairngorms National Park, follows the old Highland Railway line, climbing from sea level to 1050 feet at Dava summit.

FORMARTINE & BUCHAN WAY
Start: Dyce, near Aberdeen
End: Fraserburgh, Aberdeenshire
Length: 40 miles (64km) - with 13-mile (21 km) spur option from Maud to Peterhead
Timing: 3 - 4 days

Passing through some lovely Aberdeenshire countryside, this route runs along the old Formartine & Buchan railway line.

UNION AND FORTH & CLYDE CANAL TOWPATHS
Start: Bowling, West Dunbartonshire
End: Edinburgh

Length: 62 miles (100 km)
Timing: 4 - 5 days

Cutting Scotland in half between the Firth of Forth and the Firth of Clyde, the Union and Forth & Clyde Canal Towpath route follows marvellously engineered and flat towpaths.

THE LOCHS & GLENS WAY
Start: Glasgow
End: Inverness
Length: 215 miles (346 km)
Timing: 5 - 12 days

The Lochs and Glens Way long distance cycling route runs through some of the finest central belt and Highlands scenery and crosses through Scotland's two national parks.

CRINAN CANAL
Start: Crinan
End: Ardrishaig
Length: 9 miles (14 km)
Timing: 1 day

Set amidst breathtaking Argyll scenery, cross the Mull of Kintyre on the short but rewarding Crinan Canal towpath.

THE HEBRIDEAN WAY
Start: Isle of Vatersay, Outer Hebrides
End: Butt of Lewis, Outer Hebrides
Length: 150 miles (240 km)
Timing: 6 days

Enjoy a two-wheeled island odyssey like no other exploring the Outer Hebrides archipelago along the awesome Hebridean Way. This epic route, on the very edge of Europe, uses causeways and ferries to hop between islands.

THE CALEDONIA WAY
Start: Campbeltown, Kintyre
End: Inverness
Length: 237 miles (379 km)
Timing: 6 - 11 days

Experience Scotland's magical west coast by bike along the Caledonia Way. From the quiet roads and captivating coastline of Kintyre, to the lochs and mountains of Argyll and The Highlands, this is a route to savour.

Chapter 45: Scottish Highlands Outdoor Adventure Guide

Scotland is separated into two parts: the Highlands and the Lowlands. The Lowlands cover the south and southeast of the country, while the Highlands cover the north and northwest. While the entire country begs to be explored, the Scottish Highlands are genuinely unique.

Towering mountains, island chains, jagged shoreline, and hundreds of lakes entice adventure enthusiasts to visit. Because of the low population and broad region, there is plenty of space to explore without having to navigate people.

For those who wish to spend each day doing something different, Fort William and Glencoe are ideal stopovers. From trail running and mountain biking to water activities and long distance hikes, the Scottish Highlands have something for everyone.

Outdoor Activities in Scotland's Highlands

Mountain riding Fort William and Glencoe are world-renowned mountain riding destinations, with trails suitable for both adrenaline junkies and total beginners. Since 2002, Fort William has hosted the UCI Mountain Bike World Cup, which attracts some of the world's most talented riders as well as thousands of fans each June.

The endless trails, forest roads, and rugged mountain terrain should place this country at the top of any serious mountain biker's bucket list. Glencoe Mountain Resort is an excellent starting point because you can take the gondola to the summit and then explore the trails of the Nevis Range from there. With the tourism board's trail map, you may drool over all the paths while planning your trip.

Running on Trails

Thousands of miles of trails wind through the glens (or valleys) and up and over the slopes of the Nevis Range, providing trail runners with a wonderfully isolated and rocky playground. In reality, the region claims that the first mountain race ever held on Ben Nevis took place in 1895.

Following in their footsteps, choose from many pathways that top Ben Nevis, the UK's tallest peak, or plan a run-cation along the 154km (96-mile) West Highland Way. If you think you have what it takes, you may always try the Ring of Steall SkyRace or "the Scottish Vertigo," a 29 km (18 mile) race with an elevation increase of 2,382 meters (9,291 feet) that is part of the difficult Golden Trail Race Series.

Kayaking and paddle boarding

With over 31,000 lochs in Scotland, as well as various sea, canal, and river choices throughout the Highlands, seeing the region by water offers a completely different perspective of the mountainous scenery.

There are numerous waterways to explore, ranging from day outings to multi-day paddle camping adventures. Tours and boat rentals are available from a variety of operators across the Highlands. Look for Rugged Paddle Board in Fort William. After paddling across the world, owners Rob Kingslad and Keren Smail realized there was no better site for the sport than the United Kingdom.

Rugged Paddle provides instruction, short expeditions of 1-2 hours, and a longer full day tour touring the region by SUP, depending on your level of skill. You can also rent your own board and go wherever you want.

Hiking There's a reason the Scottish Highlands are recognized as the UK's Outdoor Capital. Thousands of kilometers of routes connect over the Nevis Range, crossing rivers and plunging into valleys.

Hikers can pick from a number of long-distance hikes, including the 117 km Great Glen Way (72 miles), the Cape Wrath Trail (378 km/234 mi), and the East Highland Way (128 km/80 km).

For day trips, you can "bag a munro" (one of Scotland's 282 summits that climb beyond 3,000 feet, including Ben Nevis) or go waterfall hunting at Steall Falls or Eas Chia-aig Waterfall.

Cairngorms National Park, the largest in the UK, is an hour and a half drive from Fort William. The park encompasses 4,500 square kilometers (2,800 miles) of untouched scenery, including five of the country's six largest mountains and 42 munros.

Beachcombing

The coastline in the Scottish Highlands is truly breathtaking. Despite being quickly swamped by tourists, there are still some undiscovered beaches. From Fort William, take the Road to the Isles to the beaches of Arisaig and Mallaig.

Water laps over the golden beach, and rocks jut out. Sand dunes rise over the coastline, begging to be climbed and then dashed down. Visitors can take a variety of boats to surrounding islands for even more isolated beaches.

How to Dress

Expect rain and cold weather in Scotland at any time of year. Bring plenty of layers, and waterproof clothing is a necessary. We recommend the following KÜHL products:

- On wet walks, the Jetstream Rain Pant will keep you dry and comfy.
- The Virtue Short Sleeve dries fast and provides UPF 30 sun protection.
- On hot days, the Aspira Tank will get you through any trail runs or lengthy excursions.
- The Deflektr Hybrid Shell keeps you dry in heavy weather or unexpected storms in the highlands.
- Stay toasty at night or on cooler days with the Sora Hoody, a great midlayer long sleeve.
- Relax at camp or at the bar in the Traverse women's legging, which moves from trail to city and can withstand long days outside.

- The Sloane Hoody is a nice lightweight zipped layer that you can add or subtract depending on the weather.

Chapter 46: Scotland's 27 Unique Accommodations: Favorite Hotels, B&Bs, Hostels & Self-Catering Cottages

This is a list of my favorite places to stay in Scotland, ranging from modest hotels and superb B&Bs to quirky hostels and exceptional self-catering cottages located around the country. Every recommendation on this list has been hand-picked by me and is based on my personal experience - each is so unique that you'll want to schedule your trip to stay at as many as possible!

Booking lodging may not be the first step in planning a trip to Scotland. There are plenty additional questions you may want to consider first. You may even put accommodation last because all you need is a place to sleep. That is entirely OK. This topic may not be for you, but you might like my "Best of Scotland" itinerary!

However, if you are the type of person who would travel to a location simply to stay in an extraordinary hotel, meet an exceptional host, or wake up to a breathtaking view, this chapter is a must-read!

I've developed a refined taste for lodging. I can still get by in most locations as long as they are clean, but I really adore indulging in a beautiful hotel or bed and breakfast. I'm also a big fan of unique hostels (sorry, no party hostels) and lovely self-catering accomodation.

If this sounds familiar, selecting the best locations to stay in Scotland is an important part of planning your vacation. After all, you don't want to "just" see Scotland; you want to stay somewhere lovely, restful, and indulgent!

This chapter offers four categories of my favorite Scotland accommodations:
- Small Inns
- Bed and Breakfast
- Self-Catering Lodges and Hostels

As a result, I'm sure there are many more places to add to my list, which will grow as I stay in additional motels across the country. If you stayed somewhere you enjoyed, please let me know in the comments and I will add it to my list!

Without further ado, here are my top picks for places to stay in Scotland.

Scotland's Favorite Hotels
The Coll Hotel on Coll Island
The Isle of Coll is one of my favorite Scottish west coast island vacations. Apart from the gorgeous scenery, there isn't much to do or see on Coll, yet that is entirely the appeal.

There are only a few lodging options on the island, including one hotel. But it's a fantastic one!

The Coll Hotel is located in the middle of Arinagour, the island's major village. Their rooms have breathtaking sea views, and in 2019, they rebuilt and inaugurated a new restaurant and bar annexe to the old main part of the hotel.

The hotel is privately owned and operated by a family. Guests will be treated as members of the family.

Hotel Loch Melfort in Argyll
Argyll has the longest coastline of any Scottish region, and this hotel offers one of the nicest views of it I've ever seen. The photo below was taken FROM MY BED following a lazy lie-in.

The Loch Melfort Hotel, despite its proximity to Loch Melfort, offers spectacular views of Loch Shuna, the Isle of Shuna, and other adjacent islands. Oban, the lively west coast town, is about an hour north of here, and many other Argyll attractions (such as the Isle of Seil, Loch Awe, and Kilmartin Glen) are also close!

The hotel was constructed in the nineteenth century as the principal house of Arduaine Estate, which also houses Arduaine Garden. The house was finally sold by the family who owned it in the 1960s and converted into a hotel. The National Trust for Scotland (NTS) presently manages the garden, which is located right next to the Loch Melfort Hotel.

NTS members get free admission to Arduaine Garden and all other NTS locations, as well as free parking at their locations with parking costs! You can join NTS by clicking here.

On my 2-week west coast road trip, I stayed here and enjoyed a night in one of the wonderful apartments with views of the loch and gardens. In the morning, I could watch otters and sea birds from my window, and in the evening, I sipped a few drams at the quiet lounge bar. The restaurant is open to the public and serves delicious food; on a bright day, you might even dine on the terrace!

Kingshouse Hotel, Glencoe

The Kingshouse Hotel in Glencoe is one of the Scottish Highlands' most iconic hotels!

Since the 1750s, the Kingshouse Hotel has served as a haven for weary travelers. It has been expanded and restored over the ages, yet it has never lost its warm welcome and Highland friendliness.

The Kingshouse reopened in 2019 with the addition of a new annexe to the old historic edifice. The rooms offer stunning views of the River Etive and the Glencoe mountains, particularly Buachaille Etive Mor.

For family getaways or romantic vacations, the wide bar and restaurant provide plenty of space for groups without seeming impersonal.

You've probably heard about the famous deer that visit Kingshouse Hotel on a daily basis. Many people feed them, however because they are wild creatures, it is advisable to remain your distance and shoot photos rather than feed them.

The Kingshouse makes an excellent home base for a Highland road trip, a day trip to Glencoe, or a sumptuous night on the West Highland Way.

Ardanaiseig Hotel, Loch Awe

I discovered Ardanaiseig Hotel when looking for romantic getaways in the Scottish Highlands, and I spent my birthday here.

The Ardanaiseig Hotel is located on the shores of Loch Awe, one of my favorite lochs in Scotland.

The main house has several rooms, a bar and drawing room, and an intimate restaurant. The entire property is decorated in a traditional way, with roaring fireplaces and odd antiques throughout.

Stay at the restored Boathouse (shown below) for a spectacular escape with unobstructed views of the loch and complete seclusion. It contains a small kitchen, but you may also eat at the main home of the hotel.

The hotel would be a fantastic home base for a few days of exploring Argyll, such as seeing Oban, Kilchurn Castle, and Inveraray. But I recommend spending some time at the hotel, taking in the views and exploring the estate's beautiful grounds.

The Colonsay Hotel, Isle of Colonsay.
The Isle of Colonsay is a small but remarkably adaptable island off Scotland's west coast. Colonsay is easily accessible by ferry from Oban and Islay, making it an ideal weekend escape.

The Colonsay Hotel is located in Scalasaig, the island's principal settlement. It is visible from the ferry, and it is simple to drive, ride, or walk there from the port.

The 1750 hotel is a tranquil haven, stylishly designed with natural materials and bright splashes of color. The restaurant has breathtaking views of the bay and the nearby Isle of Jura. The accommodations have views of the sea, the garden, and the nearby hills.

Colonsay is best explored by automobile or bicycle, while the nicest beaches also necessitate the use of walking boots (Balnahard Bay) or wellies (Oronsay). You can borrow wellies from the hotel instead of bringing your own!

I only stayed on Colonsay for one night, but I'd love to return one day and laze in one of these lounge chairs all day!

Delnashaugh Hotel, Speyside
The Speyside region of Scotland's north-east is famous for its whisky distilleries and stunning mountain landscapes. This hotel allows you to experience both to the utmost!

When I hiked the Speyside Way, a multi-day hike that stretches 65 miles from Aviemore in the heart of the Cairngorms all the way through Speyside to the Moray Coast, I stayed at Delnashaugh Hotel. While we sought to stay in hostels and budget hotels for the majority of the trip, we chose to spend on this hotel after viewing its magnificent views from the sunny balcony and elegantly appointed rooms.

The hotel is a traditional inn that has long given shelter and delicious meals. The motel is family-run and welcomes both weary hikers and whisky enthusiasts.

Delnashaugh Hotel is well located in Speyside, making it easy to travel north to Aberlour, Dufftown, and Craigellachie, or south to Grantown, Glenlivet, and Tomintoul.

Other nearby attractions include the Osprey Centre near Nethy Bridge, trekking in the Cairngorms National Park, castles such as Ballindalloch and Balmoral, and lovely towns such as Elgin and Cullen.

Carradales Luxury Guest House, Campbeltown
Off the usual path is worthwhile, especially when a B&B like this awaiting you at the end of the road.

Carradales Luxury Guest House is literally at the end of the road from Campbeltown to Carradale, a peaceful settlement on the Kintyre peninsula's east coast.

The guest house, which is owned by a hospitable couple from the south, is a delightful respite from daily life, as you can sit back and enjoy everything the guest house has to offer. From magnificent rooms with comfortable mattresses and stunning views to breakfast and dinner prepared by Steve, who used to cook for celebrities in London before moving to Scotland.

The lounge has an impressive bar, so you won't have to leave the house much throughout your stay. However, there are several things to see and do in the surrounding area. Walk down to Carradale Bay and into the hamlet, take a distillery tour at Kintyre Gin down the road, or go a little further to discover Campbeltown, the Mull of Kintyre, or the Isle of Gigha.

Glenegedale House, Isle of Islay
Some places just feel like home, even if they seem a lot nicer than your own.

Glenegedale House on Islay is a true island hospitality haven. Graeme and Emma operate the B&B and welcome you into their magnificent home, which has four well-appointed rooms and two big guest areas. All rooms have views of the moorlands surrounding the house and, in the distance, the sea.

The B&B is located close to Islay's small airport, but don't worry, there aren't many planes that fly by here, and they're so small that you can barely hear them. It was more of a novelty to witness them land or take off - and it's an added benefit for anyone arriving by plane.

Glenegedale House also serves evening meals and has a large selection of whisky and gin. Glenegedale is a fantastic home base for a journey to Islay because Emma offers the best recommendations for places to explore on the island.

Newton Farm Holidays, Forfar
Newton Farm Holidays is a small B&B in rural Angus near Forfarm. They just have one room that can sleep two adults (or two adults and two children at most). This location is unique in that it is located on a working farm!

Farmer Lou is a wonderful host who provides a fantastic breakfast for you every morning.

After that, why not go on a farm trip with her? You may take a tour of the farm and see all of the animals, which range from chickens, ducks, and peacocks to cattle, sheep, and goats. They do, however, have alpacas and Highland cows that you may meet on unique experiences such as walking with alpacas and brushing coos.

You can also plan a customized lamping experience during lambing season in the spring. What a wonderful location to learn about Scottish small-scale agricultural culture and where your food originates from!

PS: Newton Farm Cottage, a 3-bedroom self-catering property adjoining the main farmhouse, is also available!

Ashbank House, Pitlochry.
Did you know that you can book many classic Scottish B&Bs through AirBnB?

I discovered this hidden gem of a B&B while looking for a somewhere to stay in Pitlochry for my trip to The Enchanted Forest event.

Ashbank House B&B is a classic bed and breakfast that provides comfortable rooms, a full Scottish breakfast, and a friendly Highland welcome. The owners moved to Pitlochry from Perth, exchanging a fairly large city for the picturesque countryside of the town.

The B&B is a 10-minute walk from Pitlochry's main street, yet with views of a nearby woodland, it feels like you're in the middle of nowhere.

Pitlochry is an excellent starting point for exploring Perthshire. There is plenty to do in the small town, but it is also close to many other attractions such as Blair Castle, Killiecrankie Castle, Aberfeldy, and The Hermitage.

Thornhill Nithbank Estate

What a charming bed and breakfast! The Nithbank Estate is a stunningly restored Victorian mansion on the fringes of Thornhill, a small community in the Nith valley near Dumfries.

Melanie and Allen, the hosts, poured their hearts into beautifying the beautiful rooms with river views and providing loving hospitality of the greatest caliber. The bathtubs alone are worth mentioning!

The house is surrounded by a gorgeous garden, and the couple even has a few Galloway Belties - the characteristic black and white cows found only in this region - on the premises.

Your visit will undoubtedly be a culinary joy. From the full breakfast served in the magnificent sun room to the afternoon scones and fruit, as many components as possible are acquired from local farmers and producers.

Drumlanrig Castle, Robert Burns' Ellisland Farm, the lochs, glens, and mountains of the Galloway Biosphere and Southern Ayrshire Biosphere, the town of Dumfries, and other attractions are nearby.

Ashfield House in Arrochar is now closed.

Sometimes the best things happen by chance! After a restless night of wild camping on the Isle of Tiree, I was able to stay the night at Ashfield House B&B in Arrochar - it was late March and still very cold, so I couldn't take another night in my tent as planned. This B&B was the answer, and it turned out to be one of my favorite locations to stay that year!

Cristina, an American expat who fell in love with the Scottish Highlands and came up here with her British husband, runs Ashfield House B&B. Who could fault her?

The B&B is quite exquisite, with stunning interior decor, spacious rooms, and subtle touches throughout.

Arrochar is a beautiful settlement in the Southern Highlands. Perfect for exploring Loch Lomond and Argyll, as well as a superb home base for a few days of hiking in the Arrochar Alps.

Parkhead House, South Queensferry.
Are you a fan of Outlander? There is no better place to stay near South Queensferry than Parhead House. This B&B is located on the grounds of Hopetoun House, a popular Outlander filming location.

Several locations on the estate, including Midhope Castle, make regular appearances on the show. Lallybroch. They are within easy walking distance of Parkhead House.

Booking a walking or driving tour with host James is the greatest way to enhance your stay at Parkhead House. He is familiar with all of the sites utilized in the show and has been on set numerous times; he may even reveal some behind-the-scenes secrets along the way!

Parkhead House's rooms are actually huge suites; the ground floor suite sleeps two people while the upper suite sleeps four.

Scotland's Favorite Hostels
Achmelvich Beach Youth Hostel, North Coast 500
The Great Outdoors Magazine awarded us a silver medal for Best Hostel/Bunkhouse of the Year 2019!

I slept in seven hostels along the North Coast 500 route, including five run by Hostelling Scotland (Inverness, Torridon, Gairloch Sands, Ullapool, and Achmelvich Beach) and two run by independent associate hostels (Tongue and Helmsdale). Most have individual accommodations, are family and group friendly, and are ideal for all road trippers!

The Achmelvich Beach Youth Hostel, which is just a few feet away from the beautiful beach, is my favorite hostel on the North Coast 500. The hostel has dorms and a few private rooms (all with shared toilets), as well as a comfortable lounge with a fireplace and a huge outdoor area. On-site, there are entertaining hostel chickens, and the cheerful live-in hostel administrators greet tourists with open arms.

I only stayed one night but could have stayed for several days, watching the sunset over the bay, walking to surrounding beaches, or driving to other towns and places like Lochinver, Arvreck Castle, or Stac Pollaidh.

Please keep in mind that the hostel is only open from April to September.

The LoFT CoDE, Edinburgh

There are several hostels in Edinburgh, many of which are cheaper than this one, while others have more social areas or even a bar, but that is not what I look for in my favorite hostels. I need a hostel that is clean and comfortable, has kind and helpful staff, and, most essential, provides some privacy while being less expensive than a hotel room.

Pod hostels are all of these things and more. CoDE was Edinburgh's first pod hostel, and they now have two locations: The LoFT in New Town and The CoURT in Old Town.

I've been at The LoFT twice now and think it's a terrific alternative for more mature hostel guests. The pods are reasonably spacious and equipped with useful facilities such as plugs, shelves, and hangers. The curtains block out all outside light, and the pod structures are highly robust, so any noise or movement from neighboring pods is kept to a minimum.

As a solitary traveler, the option of pod hostels over party or economy hostels is really appealing! My full review of The LoFT may be found here.

Blackwater Hostel, Kinlochleven

When I hiked the northern half of the West Highland Way, I initially slept at Blackwater Hostel in Kinlochleven. It is an independent walker-friendly hostel with a beautiful kitchen and common room, as well as pleasant little dorms. They also have neighboring glamping pods and a campsite, as well as a B&B and a self-catering lodge for parties.

Kinlochleven is a mountainous settlement in the heart of the Highlands. It's a little off the usual path, but it's only a 15-minute drive from Glencoe or 40 minutes from Fort William, making it an ideal base for hikers.

There are restaurants and shops nearby, as well as a great wild swimming site in the river and the stunning Grey Mare's Tail waterfall, Scotland's third-tallest.

Craignure Bunkhouse, Isle of Mull.
The Isle of Mull is one of my favorite Scottish islands to visit, but finding accommodation may be difficult, especially if more than two people are traveling together.

Our group of four did not want to splurge on last-minute B&B accommodations, but we discovered that most self-catering cottages required a one-week minimum stay - but we only needed three nights.

Instead, we stayed at Craignure Bunkhouse in a modest en-suite dorm, and I'm so glad we did! The hostel features a welcoming common space as well as a fully equipped kitchen. We ate most of our meals on the terrace outside, which overlooked the sea.

Craignure is an excellent island home base. The ferry port is right around the corner, and there are plenty of things to do on Mull: head north towards Tobermory, north-west towards Ben More and the Isle of Ulva, or south-west towards Fionnphort and the Isle of Iona.

A modest hotel with a restaurant, a bar, and a small shop for supplies is located next to the hostel.

Portree Youth Hostel, Isle of Skye

Skye is notoriously congested. During the summer, finding lodging on the island is difficult unless you plan long in advance, and costs are frequently higher than on the mainland due to strong demand.

I've spent twice at Portree Youth Hostel, which is the ideal solution. You must still reserve the hostel in advance, but the price is significantly lower than many surrounding options.

The hostel is located in the heart of Portree, close to restaurants, shops, and the bus stop. There is a huge kitchen and the lounge offers the nicest view of the Cuillin mountains anyone could wish for!

There are dorms, private en-suite rooms, and family rooms, making the hostel suitable for everyone - not just young solitary visitors!

Loch Ossian Youth Hostel

Hikers and outdoor enthusiasts will appreciate Loch Ossian. This remote location in the Scottish Highlands can only be accessed on foot or by train.

The West Highland Line, which runs from Glasgow to Fort William, comes to a halt at Corrour station, which appears to be in the middle of nowhere. If you've watched the film Trainspotting, you might recognize this location! There are no roads in this area, only mountains and the stunning Loch Ossian.

Loch Ossian Youth Hostel, a modest eco-hostel a few minutes' walk from the train station, provides basic accommodation for hikers. There are only two dorms, one for men and one for women, plus a cozy kitchen and lounge space in the center. The hostel manager lives on-site and ensures that the fire is kept burning and that the place is kept clean.

The hostel uses solar and locally sourced energy, compost toilets, and a reed bed soakaway to handle all greywater.

The neighboring Munros provide fantastic days out in the hills, and there is a road that leads all the way around the lake for an easy walk or cycling. The hostel is ideal for a hiking vacation to the Scottish Highlands and a one-of-a-kind experience in Scotland.

Scotland's Best Self-Catering Cottages
Woodlands, Glencoe

Look no further than Woodlands Glencoe for a magnificent hideaway in the Scottish Highlands!

Woodlands' magnificent lodges are a dream come true. Each has a private hot tub with a view of either a tranquil woodland and river or the water and mountains of Loch Leven.

The lodges are wonderfully constructed, offer maximum privacy thanks to clever angles and carefully selected materials, and are outfitted with all the amenities you could want, including a projector and screen for movie nights!

Glencoe is one of my favorite spots in Scotland, with enough to do and see. Inquire with the staff about recommended treks, rent e-bikes from Woodlands, or book one of the estate's other activities. You will have a fantastic time in the Highlands!

Kings Reach Self Catering, Kilmartin Glen

Nothing is more peaceful and reassuring for a vegan tourist than staying in vegan-friendly accommodations with vegan hosts. You may be confident that you will be taken care of without having to ask hundreds of questions. While you may dine vegan in any self-catering cottage in Scotland, and most hotels and B&Bs can prepare plant-based menu selections, vegan accommodation also provides cruelty-free amenities, beds with down-free bedding, and vegan-friendly interior decor. There will be no wool, leather, or hunting trophies.

There is a growing vegan accomodation sector in Scotland, and one of my favorites is Kings Reach Self Catering in one of my favorite places, Kilmartin Glen in Argyll.

Kings Reach includes two 2-bedroom self-catering apartments (one with views of the old Dunadd Fort ruins) that are ideal for longer visits to explore the surrounding area. (3-4 nights required)

The neighborhood is particularly vegan-friendly. Most nearby restaurants have vegan options, and if you explore deeper into the region, you will find some wonderful vegan eateries. There is also enough to do here, making Kings Reach an ideal location for exploring Kilmartin Glen and beyond, including Loch Awe, Slate Islands, Inveraray, Kintyre Peninsula, Oban, and so on.

Storm Pods, Isle of Islay

Islay is a fantastic destination to visit, especially if you enjoy peaty whiskies!

The Storm Pods are located on Islay's whiskey coast, which is a strip of coastline in the island's south-west that is home to three distilleries within walking distance of each other: Ardbeg, Laphroaig, and Lagavulin. The cabins overlook the same bay as the Lagavulin Distillery and provide stunning views of the Dunyvaig Castle ruins.

There are multiple pods of varying sizes, but each is positioned to provide maximum privacy. My pod comprised a large living room with a kitchen, a bedroom, a tiny bathroom, and a deck with a BBQ and breathtaking sea views.

The pods offer an excellent base for exploring the Isle of Islay, visiting the island's nine whisky distilleries, hiking, and discovering historical places.

Creeside Escape Shepherds Hut, Ayrshire

Few places feel more "in the middle of nowhere" than this shepherd cabin at Creeside Escape!

Creeside Escape is an eco-friendly glamping retreat in the Galloway and Southern Ayrshire Biosphere, located on a sheep farm in the south-west of Scotland. The hut has unobstructed views of the Cree River below and the Galloway Hills in the distance.

The hut features one room with a wide, comfortable bed and a cooking area, as well as a tiny bathroom with a composting toilet.* A small, but efficient fireplace heats the location quickly, making it a fantastic hideaway all year. Sheep may surround the hut in the morning, inquisitive if you will serve them a breakfast treat.

Creeside Escape is an excellent choice for eco-conscious travelers. It is easily accessible by bike or public transportation from a nearby village (for example, Barrhill or Newton Stewart). It's a great site to explore the Galloway Forest Park and a great area to just be and enjoy the scenery.

Please keep in mind that there is no shower.

The Bothy, Perthshire
I discovered this small gem on AirBnB when I was looking for a gorgeous mountain getaway that was not far from Glasgow yet felt very remote.

Glenlyon in Perthshire proved to be an excellent decision!

The Bothy at West Cottage and Stables is a rustic wooden cabin with a skylight above the bed and a fantastic kitchen with a woodburning stove.

There is no phone reception for miles and no WiFi at the cabin - it's time for a DIGITAL DETOX! You can, however, check your emails at the main house.

The cabin is located on the outskirts of a wooded area, and with luck, you will be able to see red squirrels and a variety of bird species from the comfort of the cabin. There are numerous walks in Glenlyon and the Lawers Range, and trails to several Munros begin right outside your door.

Aberfeldy is only a short drive away, and Perthshire is right at your doorstep!

House in the Wood, Ballachulish

Ballachulish is a small community near Glencoe that is primarily known for its historic slate quarries and the Ballachulish Bridge, which connects to Fort William to the north. However, it is worthwhile to remain for a few days, such as in a woods cabin at House in the Wood.

There are four cabins scattered around the woods, each with two bedrooms, a comfortable parlor, a modern kitchen, and a bathroom, as well as a smaller cottage for two people nearby.

The chalets are ideal for hiking or skiing in Glencoe or the Nevis Range, water sports on Loch Leven, and day visits to surrounding towns like Oban or Fort William.

Inverlonan, Argyll

Who hasn't fantasized about an off-grid cottage in the woods? This dream can come true in Inverlonan!

Choose from three lovely bothies, each with all you need for a sustainable off-grid retreat: a wood burning stove, solar power, a private composting toilet, and a pure sense of being immersed in nature.

The luxuries available at Inverlonan are not the same as those found at a metropolitan hotel. Staying here allows you to disconnect from everything while yet having access to the minimal necessities.

The bothies are tastefully designed, with many of the furnishings and finishes sourced locally. The bed linen is among the most comfy I've ever slept in - hotel-quality 10 times over!

While you're here, go for a swim in Loch Nell, get a pizza kit to bake in your wood-fired pizza oven, explore the loch with one of the sit-on kayaks or paddle boards available to visitors, or arrange a session in the eco-friendly lochside sauna.

PS: Although there is no shower in the bothies, there is an outside shower bag that you may fill with hot water from the kettle.

Old Paper House, Melrose
This 4-bedroom holiday home may be too large for the usual travel group, but it is ideal for families looking for a trip in the Scottish Borders.

The Old Paper House in Melrose is a wonderful self-catering property with four spacious bedrooms on the ground and first floors, two bathrooms, a huge TV lounge with ample seating, a bright dining space with exposed beams, and a lovely kitchen. The garden is sprawling and teeming with flowers, trees, and wildlife.

Melrose's attractions, restaurants, and stores are only a short drive or 25-minute walk away.

From the house, you can see the Eildon Hills and begin your journey up these iconic hills. Melrose Abbey, Tweedbank's Abbotsford House, and Kelso's Floors Castle are also neighboring attractions.

Most of the time, the destination comes first, followed by the lodging - you pick where you want to go first, then find a place to stay.

I like to travel differently from time to time and let my vacations be guided by the lodgings that appeal to me the most. And I've never been disappointed - fortunately, Scotland is stunning all over!

I hope this list of my favorite places to stay in Scotland inspires you to look for unusual spots to include in your Scotland itinerary!

Chapter 47: Dressing for Ireland: Packing Tips and Irish Outfit Ideas

Do you want to know what to dress in Ireland and what apparel to buy in Ireland? With this helpful guide, we're here to assist you. While Ireland is known for its lush green scenery and severe weather, your clothing choices don't have to reflect this.

All that rain makes for some spectacular scenery. It's difficult not to fall in love with the country's lush rolling hills, crumbling castles, stunning coastlines, friendly residents, and lovely farms.

Don't be put off by the weather; Ireland has no bad weather, only the incorrect attire. We reveal our top picks for a fashionable and comfortable trip to Ireland. This book should include something for everyone, whether you're a first-time visitor or a seasoned traveler.

Packing Tips for Ireland

I would recommend that everyone bring a few essential items on their journey. Because Ireland is notorious for its rain, the weather will influence what you bring in your bag or suitcase. But don't worry; most of Ireland is down-to-earth, and simple wardrobe choices seem well at home. There are always exceptions, such as a trip to the Abbey Theatre in Dublin or a delicious supper in Galway.

We spend the most of our time in Ireland dressed in a sweater, jeans, boots, and a rain jacket. Most visitors, including ourselves, will spend our time outside seeing Ireland's countryside. It's full of historic walking pathways, castles, snug taverns, sheep, and charming towns; it's the ideal spot to get lost.

Packing rain gear such as a rain jacket, umbrella, and weatherproof boots is always a smart idea.

Packing cubes aid in the separation of damp and unclean clothes from clean ones.

You should bring no more than three pairs of shoes—a nice, casual, and athletic shoe/boot.

Ireland is a laid-back country, so unless you're staying at one of the great golf clubs, there's no need to dress up.

Pack your favorite wool sweater or cardigan because it's virtually always sweater season.

If there is a cold in the air, a scarf and hat are excellent ways to keep warm. It's not always freezing outside. Summers can be hot and humid, with beautiful weather. Check the weather forecast ahead of time and pack some warm-season clothing. We've had amazing weather on excursions and awful weather that made us reconsider going to Ireland.

travel-credit-card

The Irish Weather

When deciding what to wear in Ireland, always consider the weather forecast. Ireland has an oceanic climate that is chilly, moist, and rainy throughout the year. Temperatures do not vary significantly throughout the year. A hot day in the summer is as uncommon as snow in the winter. This is great news for packing because you won't have to pack for several climates.

It's a good idea to check the Irish weather a week before your travel to have an idea of what the temperatures will be like.

Ireland's seasons
Spring

In Ireland, spring is an extremely cold time of year. The weather is cold from March to April, but it begins to warm up by May. We enjoy spring since it is the driest season of the year.

Summer

Temperatures range from moderate to cold with periodic rain showers from June to August. The typical daily maximum temperature is around 19/20 degrees Celsius (66/68 degrees Fahrenheit), with cold evenings. There are some bright days with temperatures in the mid-25s Celsius (77 degrees Fahrenheit), if not higher.

Fall

September to November can be the wettest and windiest months of the year. Temperatures have continued to plummet after the milder summer. Daytime highs in the fall range from 10 to 17 degrees Celsius (50 to 63 degrees Fahrenheit).

Winter

Winters can be cold, but temperatures rarely fall below freezing. It is frequently cloudy, and the winds can be strong. Temperatures are a few degrees above freezing at night and around 7-10C (45-50F) during the day.

Documents You Must Pack

- Passport - This should go without saying, but you won't get very far without one.
- Credit Cards - We always utilize a variety of travel credit cards that provide purchase protection, incentives, and no foreign transaction fees.
- Visa - If you require one, be sure you have one.
- Debit Cards - Carrying euros is recommended in Ireland. We never use money exchanges that offer poor exchange rates. Instead, when we arrive, we use the ATM. Foreign transaction costs are low or non-existent at Charles Schwab, Ally, and Capital One. Keep in mind that the Republic of Ireland utilizes the Euro, while Northern Ireland uses the British Pound.
- Driving License - If you intend to rent a car, you will need your driver's license, as well as a second form of identification. If your license is not in English, you may require an IDP translation.

What Should I Bring to Ireland?

I have two suggestions for luggage for a trip to Europe. You can choose between a standard hardshell suitcase on four wheels and a travel backpack.

Suitcases with four wheels are ideal since being able to travel sideways down a train aisle or a sidewalk makes life much easier. We chose hardshell because it provides superior protection and security. The Delsey Helium Aero 25″ is our favorite hardshell suitcase.

Young backpackers, digital nomads, and minimalists will love travel bags! They're also great if you want to avoid paying checked bag fees with your airline.

If paying for taxis or auto rentals makes you nervous, you should stay near public transportation or travel with a backpack. Our favorites are the Peak Design Travel Backpack and the NOMATIC Backpack, but if you want to learn more, read about the best backpacks for Europe.

What Should You Wear in Ireland?
Sweater Made of Wool
The wool sweater is the one piece of apparel developed specifically for travel in Ireland. A sweater is an excellent travel outfit essential. They're cozy, elegant, and toasty. The season is irrelevant because most of Ireland is temperate and pleasant all year. Summer temperatures will be pleasant during the day and cool at night.

My favorite sweaters are made of organic fabrics such as wool or Alpaca. It's become my favorite vacation memento, and I'm especially fond of my Scottish wool and Peruvian Alpaca sweaters.

Ireland has some fantastic wool and sweater producers, although it may take some searching. In recent years, most tourist stores have sold low-cost foreign-made copies. We did some research and found Tasha's in the photo above at Cottage Handcrafts in Connemara.

A raincoat

After you've packed your wool sweater, grab a rain jacket. If we were betting, we'd say you'll see some rain throughout your trip to Ireland. It doesn't become that green unless it rains a lot. The rain in Ireland varies greatly. Some days may simply see an afternoon shower, while others may experience storms that persist for days.

We recommend a packable rain jacket designed for outdoor use/hiking. They are light, strong, compact, waterproof, and windproof. Any rain jacket can suffice, although those meant for the outdoors will be more durable and useful in inclement weather. They also perform an excellent job of blocking the wind, which may be fierce.

The Flannel Shirt

Flannel shirts are great mid-layering pieces for both men and women. Warmth, comfort, and style are all provided by a great flannel. They're very simple to style for a laid-back outdoor vibe. A warm flannel is ideal for travel, sightseeing, or casual walks.

The majority of Ireland is laid-back, and you'll feel well at home with a flannel or sweater. Combine a flannel with a travel vest for a traditional style that is also warm. It is a simple addition to any baggage.

Down Coat

To stay comfortable in the summer, tourists should bring a wool sweater and a rain jacket. Outside of the summer, a down jacket is a great investment. We recommend a packable down jacket for a cool-weather travel because they are adaptable.

A down jacket is an excellent method to stay warm while not taking up too much space in your suitcase when visiting Ireland. A peacoat is a classic wardrobe choice for a more elegant jacket, but it's bulky, so you'll have to wear it on the plane.

T-Shirt

A classic tee will always be in vogue. We recommend sticking to plain hues such as black, white, or grey. Hiking on a bright day can be quite warm, so we frequently remove clothing. If you already have a few technical shirts, a traditional cotton tee shirt would suffice for leisurely treks or walks around the village.

A merino wool shirt, on the other hand, is a worthwhile purchase and one of the best pieces of travel clothing. Wool shirts last longer and are excellent at temperature regulation. I've tried on a bunch of wool shirts, and my current favorite for travel is from Unbound Merino.

When it comes to tees, we recommend keeping things basic. As a foundation layer, no one needs a flashy designer tee. Cameron prefers the grey since the white is so simple to stain. If you're looking for a classic cotton tee, we adore the quality and ease of shopping from Bombas.

Jeans
There are lots of Irish people wearing well-cut jeans, but nothing baggy or tattered. Jeans are a fashion mainstay, but they aren't the finest packing or travel pants. Travelers, on the other hand, have options such as DU/ER jeans. The organic cotton jeans are fashionable, but a slight blend of polyester and spandex allows them to stretch and avoid creases.

The fit is superb, with a slim fit throughout the leg. You may wear the jeans for lengthy periods of time without feeling uncomfortable. Because of the synthetic combination, they're ideal for long excursions because they don't need to be washed.

Pants for Technical Purposes
Chinos or travel pants are ideal for sightseeing in Ireland. Our first option is a dependable pair of "travel pants" made of synthetic materials. These pants are more stain-resistant, dry faster, weigh less, stay fresher for longer, and are more comfortable than regular pants or chinos.

We appreciate how these tough pants, which were originally only designed for hiking, now look like chinos. It's a traditional pant that looks great with a sweater, dress shirt, t-shirt, or blouse. When selecting a hue, attempt to match it to your destination and season. Light tan pants, on the other hand, are the most versatile.

We recommend the Kuhl Freeflex Pants for outdoor experiences and the Everlane Utility Barrel Pants for a more fashionable city/town style for women. For outdoor experiences, men should consider the KUHL Renegade Rock Pants and the Western Rise Evolution 2.0 Pants.

Scarf

A scarf is a must-have travel accessory and an excellent wardrobe choice for both men and women visiting Ireland. They serve as an addition to your dress while also providing warmth. Because Ireland is known for having windy days, the scarf covers your neck.

Scarves are great for travelers since they can dress up an outfit that you've previously worn three days in a row and can be tossed into a bag or purse to pull out when the sun goes down and the weather cools down.

Sneakers

Hitting the sidewalk and watching the city or town unfold around you is one of the best ways to become acquainted with a new location. When packing for Ireland, both men and women should bring a pair of comfortable shoes.

I wouldn't advocate the clumsy hiking boots or sports shoes that many travelers carry. Because most of Ireland's towns and cities are great for walking, we recommend bringing excellent walking shoes. Allbirds Wool Runners are our favorite travel sneakers because they are sustainable, snug, simple, and comfy. You can read our in-depth Allbirds review here.

Boots

Pack a pair of lightweight hiking boots or leather boots to help you deal with the rain. Locals prefer to wear "Wellies" or Wellington Boots, which are large rubber boots. We're always content with good boots since we avoid farms and bogs.

I'm a leather boot connoisseur who adores traditional boots. If you're looking for the best boots for Ireland, consider Clark's or Timberland for leather boots. Check for Chippewa, Danner, or Red Wing boots made in the United States if you want excellent boots that will last a lifetime. The Blundstone, on the other hand, is our go-to travel boot.

Underwear for Travel
It's best to include several pairs of sports/travel underpants. For a regular trip, we'll bring five to seven pairs of underpants. We recommend purchasing multiple pairs of wool or synthetic underwear.

Because these fabrics are antibacterial, they will last longer and will dry faster if hand washed. Women should avoid wearing their normal cheap cotton underpants. When it comes to women's hygiene, antimicrobial undergarments are a lifesaver when you're out and about in the heat.

Socks Made of Wool
With a good pair of socks, we've learnt to cherish our feet. While strolling around, you'll want to keep your feet dry. Most significantly, because wool socks have inherent antibacterial characteristics, they stay fresh for several days. On any vacation, we bring several pairs of wool socks. Darn Tough and Smartwool are our recommendations for socks.

Sunglasses
A trendy pair of sunglasses is a great way to dress up an outfit. Every person has at least one pair of sunglasses. However, for the sake of your eyes' health, make sure they offer UV protection. Because we are somewhat active, we always travel with two pairs of sunglasses. A pair of Smith Optics for trekking and outdoor experiences, as well as a pair of trendy sunglasses for a day at the beach or around town. My Persols are always stylish, and my Smith Lowdowns are constantly active.

Overcoat

If you want to look elegant while staying comfortable, I recommend investing in a peacoat. An overcoat is ideal for keeping warm while still looking fashionable. While we love our down coats for their warmth and convenience, they aren't the most fashionable items, and you'd look ridiculous wearing one with a dress or suit.

Sleeveless Cardigan

In Ireland, one of my favorite things to wear is a cardigan. A cardigan offers a fantastic relaxed style and appeal while also keeping you warm. They're also small enough to take up little space in a luggage. In Ireland, I pack one for any season because it can be worn with a coat in the winter and is rarely too warm in the summer.

Blouse

While individuals in Ireland are casual, they are nevertheless presentable in public. On chilly days, most women wear a good dress shirt, blouse, or sweater. If you get a rare warm summer day, they'll break out the summer dress. Wear a light blouse instead of a graphic tee or a short-sleeved shirt for most ladies. It's ideal for wearing in the summer because the correct blouse is both cool and comfortable.

Merino Wool Unbound

A merino wool shirt is an excellent investment in travel clothing. Despite the cost, I've converted several of my garments to the material. Wool shirts keep their freshness longer and are excellent at temperature management in Ireland.

I prefer them over cotton shirts, which typically feel oily and heavy after only one or two wears, but wool shirts last for days. I've tried on a lot of wool shirts, but my favorite for travel so far is from Unbound Merino. Their shirts are the appropriate weight, and the fabric is comfortable and long-lasting.

Leggings with a Fleece Lining

Ireland may get fairly cold, especially from late October to April. This is when I frequently reach for fleece-lined leggings, which not only look wonderful while wandering around places like Dublin or Galway, but also keep me extra warm. Fleece-lined leggings can be worn as ordinary leggings and go with any sweater or jacket you own!

These are wonderful for warmth and abrasion resistance, and the hem turn-ups feature hidden reflections to keep you visible. These are neatly knitted on the outside to look smart, yet fleece-lined on the inside. The Crash tights come in a variety of colors, but my favorite is the solid black because it goes with everything.

Romper/Jumpsuit
Rompers are one of my favorite travel outfits since they are fashionable, comfortable, and functional. You can't go wrong here, and I'd recommend packing at least one or two rompers for Ireland. They're perfect for a night on the town in Dublin and, unexpectedly, Irish dress. For travel, we love Patagonia's Fleetwith Romper!

Black Flats
A pair of black flats is a must-have in any suitcase. They're fashionable, comfortable, and take up little luggage room. My advice is to avoid wearing heels because many villages have cobblestone streets and you don't want to break an ankle trying to look attractive. Allow the natives to impress you with their ability to walk in heels.

Overcoat
A fashionable overcoat, like a woman's, will keep you warm. While we love our down coats for their warmth and convenience, they aren't the most fashionable items, and you'd look ridiculous wearing one with a dress or suit.

Dress Shirt and Chinos
Wearing a T-shirt or a flannel to a nice supper in Glasgow would look silly. It's a good idea to pack at least one nice clothing that matches your

personal style. Your travel arrangements in Scotland will have a significant impact as well. Western Rise creates wrinkle- and stain-resistant men's dress garments for travel. They also make an excellent present!

Henley

A henley is an excellent choice of clothes for Ireland. It's more suited than a long-sleeved graphic shirt or technical apparel because it's lightweight while yet providing some wind protection.

Accessories

Daypack

When traveling, you'll need somewhere to store your camera equipment, hand sanitizers, papers, phones, and anything else you'll need for a long day out. Over the years, we've put a lot of daypacks and backpacks through their paces.

Bag for Toiletries

It's usually a good idea to keep your toiletries organized and separate from your clothes. It almost seems as if a toiletry bag is required for any vacation. Furthermore, small or cramped restrooms are not uncommon in Ireland.

If you don't have much counter space, a hanging toiletry bag is a terrific solution. This bag style has a superior organization system with several storage areas than the typical alternative. The Peak Design Wash Pouch is fantastic. It has a secret hook for hanging and excellent organizing.

Adapter for Travel

On your packing list for Ireland, include an adaptor for your electronics. We always keep one in our carry-on bags so we may charge electronics when we arrive or at the airport. For the United Kingdom, you'll need the British "Type G" three-prong adaptor. However, the majority of Europe employs Type C, F, and E adaptors. Check out the one I have that is suitable for Europe.

Camera

If you want to take beautiful photos while in Ireland, a high-quality camera is a must-pack item. We travel with a large number of cameras. Still, the RX 100 is the one we always recommend. There are multiple variants available at various price ranges, but it is a simple point-and-shoot camera that anyone can operate. It also produces excellent photographs with a 20mp resolution and all manual controls.

Towel for Travel

When we travel, we always bring a travel towel with us. It's one of the best international travel basics money can buy. They fold up compact, are antibacterial, and lightweight, so you won't have to buy new towels or wash them all the time. Backpackers need a towel because hostels frequently do not provide them. They are, nonetheless, ideal for people on a tight budget looking for excursions and tours.

Paperwhite Kindle

For travelers who enjoy reading, a Kindle is an important travel item. We adore books, but they are too heavy and take up too much space in my suitcase. We recently upgraded to the Kindle Paperwhite and are really pleased with it. It's compact, has touchscreen capabilities, and a backlight for reading at night without glare. It's difficult to beat curling up next to a wood stove with a cup of tea and a good book.

Packing Cube

Packing cubes are fantastic for organizing any backpack or suitcase. They are one of those packing necessities that should be in every backpack because they arrange all of your clothes and toiletries. Cubes also help to keep garments folded and wrinkle-free.

Peak Design presently makes our favorite packing cubes. It's a sleek design with dividers to segregate clean from soiled clothes in each cube. This eliminates the need for additional cubes and simplifies organization.

Passport Holder

I recommend that women travel with an anti-theft black and elegant purse to keep their valuables. Cameron keeps his passport and credit cards in an amazing passport wallet, which he never leaves anywhere.

Travel Insurance
You never know what can happen while you're away, and your home insurance coverage may not cover medical emergencies abroad. Having the assurance that we have a robust backup plan allows us to sleep better at night.

What Should You Not Wear In Ireland?
Now that we've covered what to wear in Ireland, let's move on to what not to wear. First and foremost, a classic fanny pack. Wearing a fanny pack automatically identifies you as a tourist.

Revealing clothing
Although Ireland is gradually becoming one of the most progressive countries in the world, it retains its Catholic roots; Irish Catholicism is still prevalent throughout the country, and people generally dress conservatively outside of major cities.

Athletic Clothing
We touched on this earlier, but sports clothing is intended for use in the gym or while exercising. Unless you are heading to or from the gym, wearing sports shorts, tank tops, or running shoes will make you stand out. Don't get me wrong: you can wear whatever you want while it's hot outside, but it makes you a tourist target.

Shorts
Shorts are rarely, if ever, seen on Irish men, because they aren't typically essential. That said, attitudes are changing, and with global warming, I'm sure they'll warm up to the idea.

Athletic Socks in White

Tall white socks are not typically worn by Europeans. Wear patterned socks with black socks, or match your socks to your clothes.

When Is It Best To Visit Ireland?

I believe the greatest months to visit Ireland are April, May, and September - but it all depends on your preferences! The prime season is June-August, but it is also summer in Ireland, and the cities are bustling with people and tourists alike. It's also Ireland's best chance for bright weather.

However, my favorite time to visit Ireland is in the autumn. September is when you get the last of the summer and the most gorgeous products of the season. The icing on the cake is that tourism is slowing.

What Is the Price of a Pint?

If you visit Ireland, you will most likely want to drink at least one pint of Guinness in a pub. A pint of Guinness should cost no more than €5; if it does, you're most certainly in a tourist trap.

However, we recommend paying a visit to the Guinness Store House. The most expensive Guinness you'll ever pay for is €17 per ticket, but the entire experience and tour is well worth it when visiting Dublin. You can avoid the wait by purchasing priority access tickets here!

Research Your Ancestors!

We were asked at least five times why we decided to visit Ireland. Were we looking for our ancestors? Were there any relations in Ireland? Do we have Irish ancestors? We came for the gorgeous scenery, history, and friendliness of the residents. (I also enjoy PS I Love You).

So we had to always inform our new friends that we weren't Irish and that neither of us had Irish relatives, at least not that we were aware of. We were bombarded with questions because many tourists in Ireland, namely American tourists like us, are looking for their ancestry.

Between 1820 and 1930, 4.5 million Irish people came to the United States. They once made up more than a third of all immigrants in the country. That means there are a lot of Irish Americans out there now, and many of them desire to trace their roots!

You do not require a car.

I've visited Ireland three times now. I went backpacking around Europe the first time and took public buses everywhere. Ireland's bus and train systems are quick, inexpensive, and dependable, with most modes of transportation offering free WiFi. We rented a car to get around the island on our most recent vacation, which was both reasonable and dependable.

A car is always the most comfortable and handy option, but if you are only one person, the rental and fuel costs may exceed your budget. I would recommend checking Ireland's bus schedules to ensure you can get where you need to go by public transportation. If you are traveling in a group of two or more, consider hiring a car.

Just keep in mind that drivers in Ireland and Northern Ireland drive on the left side of the road, and you should know how to drive a manual car because automatics are pricey.

Speed restrictions in Ireland are in kilometers per hour, however in Northern Ireland they are in miles per hour, which might be misleading. We rented a car from Dublin airport for €150 for two weeks and paid €1.20 a liter for fuel. You are free to drive the vehicle in and out of Northern Ireland as often as you please.

Safeguard Your Assets

Ireland is extremely safe, and we've never felt even the slightest bit unsafe when traveling around the country. Dublin is a popular tourist destination in Europe, which attracts pickpockets. These burglars like to operate in congested areas and crowds where they can avoid detection.

We recommend wearing garments that assist safeguard your belongings to protect them. When I'm out and about in cities, I usually wear pants with a wallet in the front pocket. It makes attempting a pickpocket extremely tough. When I wear a jacket, I always keep my phone and valuables in the inner breast pocket, preferably one with a zipper.

When it comes to theft while traveling, it's all about eliminating opportunity - most of the time, you won't have any problems.

When traveling, it's wise not to forget things like medications, toiletries, and other personal necessities. However, pharmacies may be found in every Irish city and town. However, this is a generic Ireland packing list that anyone can use.

Remember, Ireland isn't the end of the world, and if you forget something, you'll most likely be able to find it when you arrive.

Chapter 48: Scotland Road Trip Essentials Packing List (2024)

A road journey is unquestionably one of the best ways to discover Scotland's dramatic landscapes and stunning shoreline panoramas. A road trip across the Scottish Highlands and Islands ensures a one-of-a-kind driving experience no matter which route you take, as well as complete freedom to create your own epic journey.

Hiking, kayaking, castle seeking, wildlife viewing, seafood dining, forest treks, distillery hopping, wild swimming, or a little bit of everything. The choice is yours with a road vacation.

However, ensuring sure you've packed the necessary stuff can make or break a road trip excursion. Because having the correct items in your car can assist ensure that your vacation is both stress-free and unforgettable.

So, here are my Scotland road trip requirements, as well as all of the greatest products to bring on your Scottish excursion.

WHAT TO BRING ON A ROAD TRIP IN SCOTLAND

Following many years of road tripping around Scotland, here's what I pack on a Scotland road trip:

1. THE APPROPRIATE CLOTHES

It's safe to say that Scotland has its own distinct climate, one that can see all four seasons in a single day. We have had snow in April and sunburn in October. While it varies on when you visit and the season, keep in mind that this is not mainland Europe, so never think "I'll just pack my holiday clothes" - one day it could be bright blue skies, the next it could be blowing a hoolie (gale force winds) or dreich (wet and dismal).

So, in addition to your typical road trip travel attire, include the following items:
- Windproof lightweight jacket

- A warm fleece or jumper for cold days
- Durable footwear
- Jacket that is waterproof
- A hat made of wool
- Headlamp (more on that later)

If you're traveling in the fall or winter, you should take more layers (I recommend a thermal base), an extremely warm jacket, and a woolly cap.

2. EXTRA LARGE DUFFEL BAG

If you're driving about Scotland, you'll most likely be changing accommodations. So, when it comes to packing your goods, you'll want something lightweight and portable, preferably with a large aperture so you can see what's inside without having to empty it everything.

A huge duffel bag is ideal for containing all those layers yet being squishy enough to fit into the car.

3. EFFECTIVE WATERPROOFING

After all, this is Scotland, so be emotionally and physically prepared for rain! You're almost certain to require a waterproof jacket at some point, so don't let the weather ruin your plans. Waterproofs also serve as an excellent wind layer when the wind picks up.

The majority of Scotland's breathtakingly gorgeous sites to visit are best explored on foot; find hidden jewels along forest trails or untamed white sandy beaches nestled away along the coast.

So, in addition to comfortable driving shoes, bring waterproof walking shoes or sturdy boots that you don't mind getting dirty. Seriously, don't simply bring your white sneakers!

My favorite women's boots are the Meindl GTX Boots, which are both comfy and waterproof.

5. MIDGE RESISTANT

The dreadful midge. This small flying vampire has the power to spoil even the most beautiful treks, camps, hikes, or picnics. They tend to arrive in gangs when it's sunny, rainy, or wet (usually during the spring and summer months) and swarm on unsuspecting victims.

Midge repellent spray is required. One of the most popular is Smidge, which is deet-free and repels ticks hidden in long grass. And if you're going to be outside a lot, a midge net is not only practical but also fashionable.

If you are bitten, expect inflamed skin; I always bring antihistamines to relieve the itch.

6. RUCKSACK

You'll need a bag to carry your camera, waterproofs, a water bottle, layers, and midge spray. A backpack is important for any road trip, especially if you intend to go for walks.

My favorite sustainable rucksacks, depending on size, are:
- Craghoppers Rolltop 16L
- The North Face Daypack 22L
- Patagonia Arbor 25L

7. THERMOS FLASK

I'm the first to recommend that you make many stops along your trip to support the local economy by purchasing from local cafes and independent coffee shops. The freedom of a road journey, however, includes stopping for tea or coffee whenever you find a spot to appreciate the beautiful Highlands vistas.

If you're not sleeping in an Airbnb, I've always found that hotels will gladly fill your flask in the morning AND recommend a nearby café with tasty goodies to go. Win-win!

You require dependability, and the legendary Stanley flask is a timeless classic that will keep your drinks hot all day.

8. REFILLABLE WATER BOTTLE

There is just no excuse for using plastic water bottles these days.

Fill up from the tap every morning, whether you use a reusable container or an insulated metal water bottle - not to boast, but Scottish tap water is among of the cleanest and clearest in the world, and it tastes better than most bottled water.

9. COOL BAG + PICNIC EQUIPMENT

We almost never take a road trip without a cool bag.

We sometimes want to eat on the go, whether it's a picnic or a roadside lunch. So we stock up at a local store or get takeout from a nearby café and eat anytime we come across a breathtaking location. Which isn't difficult on a road trip through Scotland!

A cold bag like this one simply extends the life of perishable items like salads and sandwiches.

A waterproof picnic blanket is very useful for picnic days.
A nice picnic basket with all of your plates, utensils, and so forth, or a folding kitchen if you want to conserve room A sustainable spork
An environmentally friendly lunch box
Biodegradable garbage bags (Always take your trash home with you)

10. SNACKS

To be honest, having the correct food for any road trip is vital. Having goodies is one of the joys of road tripping, no matter where you go or how far you travel. And one of the simplest methods to cope with an irritated driver.

For sugary snacks, I like Haribo (the pack disappears quickly) and Deliciouslly Ella bars when I need something more substantial (and healthy). Popcorn, bananas, dried fruits and nuts, and crackers are also ideal healthy road trip snacks. Of course, a chocolate biscuit is always welcome.

11. OFFLINE GOOGLE MAPS

If you rent a car, GPS is almost certainly included, or you can lease a Sat-Nav.

However, if you want to plan your route ahead of time, pre-programming Google Maps is the only way to go. The beauty of Google Maps is that you can make it available offline, which means that the GPS tracker will continue to work even if you lose connectivity. This is a HUGE plus in Scotland's more remote areas, where 4G is frequently uncommon. You don't want to be driving aimlessly around the Highlands (which is difficult enough on single-track roads) when you might be cracking open a bottle in your Airbnb...

So, before you go on a road trip, ALWAYS make your map available offline. Things to bookmark in Google Maps:
- The best roads (not the fastest, but the most beautiful)
- Your place to stay
- Cafes and restaurants
- Attractions and sites that should not be missed
- Parking lots for hikes, beaches, and forest trails
- Service stations for gasoline

12. FUEL STOP LIST

If you live near one of Scotland's big cities, you won't have any trouble finding fuel. Going into the Highlands or the remote west coast peninsulas, on the other hand, is a very different scenario.

Once you've plotted your route, make sure you know where the gas stations are - as mentioned above, I recommend saving gas stations in

Google Maps. However, an old-fashioned list will suffice. If your road trip takes you somewhere exceptionally off-the-beaten-path, fill up before you begin.

13. A PHONE MOUNT

If you plan your route in Google Maps, bring a suction-mounted phone mount to keep your phone in place while driving. There will be no fidgeting with your phone while driving (oops, prohibited), relying on your passenger, or stopping every 5 minutes to check the map.

We use Quad Lock, but this one will suffice for £13.

14. BATTERY PACK OR CAR CHARGER

We rely so much on our phones these days. We save a lot of critical information on them: hotel confirmations, maps, cameras, music players, flashlights, weather forecasts, social media... If they run out of battery, it's a disaster.

Pack a charging wire and keep your phone battery charged while driving. This car charger plugs into the cigarette lighter and costs less than £10. It has saved my life numerous times, and I cannot suggest it highly enough!

Alternatively, go with a small and portable battery pack. These are useful for doubling up for other activities where you can't plug in, such as camping and trekking. There are other options available, depending on your budget and the amount of charge you require; this one will charge your phone 5 - 6 times for less than £20.

15. ROAD MAP

Do you enjoy looking at genuine maps? Me too! Something about a tactile map screams adventure. Or perhaps you've learned the hard way not to respond on digital maps and GPS...

Whatever your purpose, if you need a map, OS Road Maps will take you all over Scotland and are jam-packed with useful tourist information.

16. A GUIDE TO SCOTLAND

A guidebook, like having a proper map, has all the adventurous feelings. Yes, you can look stuff up online (if you have service), but there's nothing like flipping through a guidebook in the evening. My top Scotland guidebook recommendations for road trippers and landscape enthusiasts are:

Wild Guide Scotland is ideal for discovering outdoor activities.

Hidden Scotland is ideal for aspiring or experienced photographers who enjoy exploring natural areas.

Take the Slow Road: Scotland - Discover dozens of the best routes in Scotland, from Shetland to the Borders.

Alternatively, you can get these Scotland travel novels and more on Kindle Unlimited on your phone.

17. MONEY

Yes, I am old-school! However, if you travel north, you will likely come across little local shops that do not accept credit cards for small purchases. Or farms with honesty boxes offering fresh eggs and homegrown veggies - keep an eye out for these hidden gems on the side of the road.

Keep a cache of cash and change in your car just in case.

18. KIT OF FIRST AID

Because you'll be driving in isolated areas and help may be many miles away, it's a good idea to bring a small first aid kit with you.

19. HEADTORCH

This may appear to be an odd addition, but trust me when I say it comes in handy.

On a road trip to the Isle of Skye, Trev and I lingered a little too long at a local tavern drinking whisky. The community had no street lights, and our campsite was a two-kilometer hike in the dark. No issue, we reasoned, and pulled out our head lamps.

It's also necessary for camping and cabin stays where the facilities may be a long walk away in the dark. On the darkest of evenings, I use this headtorch, which is pleasant and brilliant.

20. A CAMERA
With scenery like this, you'll want to snap A LOT of shots!

Make sure to bring your camera or drone, as well as plenty of memory cards.

Alternatively, free up some space on your phone.

I'd also recommend bringing a tripod, which is ideal for photographing the entire group in front of the high mountains. This little Manfrotto travel tripod is strong, compact, and reasonably priced.

21. BINOCULARS
Okay, so these aren't completely necessary, but the Scottish Highlands and West Coast have so much to offer wildlife enthusiasts visiting Scotland.

You can expect to encounter eagles, seals, puffins, otters, pine martins, dolphins, and other wildlife in their natural habitat. Have binoculars like these in your glove box for the best chance of seeing these beautiful animals.

22. A ROAD TRIP PLAYLIST
I can't leave out some amazing music from my Scotland road trip needs!

A playlist of your favorite tunes is essential for any road trip. Are you looking for anything Scottish? The Proclaimers, Amy Macdonald, and Deacon Blue are all excellent choices.

Chapter 49: Essential Packing List for Scotland with Children

Making a list of things you intend to see and do with children in Scotland is the first step in determining what to pack for Scotland with children. Our three-week Scotland itinerary for families is jam-packed with ideas for the greatest things to do in Scotland with kids.

We knew we'd be spending a lot of time hiking with kids in Scotland, and even when we weren't trekking, we'd be outside. We needed to be prepared for the elements!

We try to pack as light as possible, which means that our outdoor gear is the most critical. In our Scotland packing list, you won't find anything to dress up for color matched Instagram photos. However, if you're searching for a Scotland summer packing list for active family, go no further!

While reading our Scotland packing list for July, keep the following in mind:

Our three-week itinerary in Scotland with children includes visits in Glasgow, Loch Lomond and the Trossachs National Park, Fort William, the Isle of Skye, and Edinburgh.

We spent the majority of our time outside walking and hiking, with very little time spent in towns or eating out.

Because our kids can now undertake long walks on their own, we didn't carry a backpack carrier or a soft structured toddler carrier like we do on most of our previous travels.

We had a variety of weather, but most days were gloomy with rain. The rain wasn't too awful most of the time, but there were a few times when it was so thick that we were only out for portion of the day.

We rented vacation home rentals with washing facilities, which allowed us to bring fewer clothing for everyone.

We're from Canada, so we're used to cooler weather; if you're from a warmer region, bring warmer clothes.

We were able to fit everything into two huge backpacks. We each brought a smaller backpack for our electronics, and the kids had their own backpacks for their books and toys.

We've attempted to provide photographs that depict the variety of weather we encountered during our visit; we hope you find this useful!

What to Wear in July in Scotland

The summer months in Scotland are the warmest, yet there is still plenty of rain. The afternoon highs will range from 15 to 18 degrees Celsius (59 to 64 degrees Fahrenheit). Unless there is a heat wave, which occurred when we were in Edinburgh with our children. That prompted us to dig out our shorts and go in search of ice cream.

We went from being bundled in the morning to abandoning our hoodies and rain jackets in the afternoon if the sun came out on any given day. As a result, layers are essential, and you should always be prepared with rain gear.

When the wind picks up, you'll be glad you layered up! We don't frequently wish for wind, but it makes for a lot nicer experience when it keeps the midges at bay.

Summer travel to Scotland with children

Here is our family packing list for Scotland, along with some commentary on what worked and didn't work for us.

Summer Packing List for Scotland - Parents 2 Pairs of Convertible Pants

These hiking pants make you look like a tourist, as has been mentioned a million times before. However, for hiking, especially when coping with rain and muck (or sunshine?), they are unrivaled.

They are simple to clean and dry quickly. They are ideal for hiking with children. To avoid looking like a tourist, I bought a black pair with few pockets.

Similar to what I have are these Marmot convertible pants and these Columbia convertible pants.

Here are some options for men's convertible pants.
Cropped Leggings with Shorts
My black skinny jeans are my favorite. They are comfy enough to wear on the airline and ideal for our city visits.

Cropped leggings are ideal for hiking on warmer days. They were also ideal for biking with children in Ireland.

The Foundation Layer
We each took a pair of wool thermal leggings to wear under our hiking pants if it got too cold. We didn't need them in the end.

Long-sleeved shirts and T-shirts
5-7 t-shirts On most days, a t-shirt and a sweatshirt sufficed.

1 tank top - I brought one tank top as well. I just wore it a few times. I could have easily left it behind.

2 long sleeve shirts - We wore a long sleeve tshirt under our hoodies and a rain jacket on the coldest days when it was windy and rainy.

Hoodie
This was the most important item in our backpacks. During our family trip to Scotland and Ireland, we all wore our hoodies virtually every day. I would

have been better off leaving my tank top and t-shirt at home and bringing a second hoodie.

Other Things
4-6 pairs of socks and pajamas

Packing List for Children in Scotland
6 pairs of socks + 1 merino wool pair
For the kids, we packed similarly. We did brought them thick wool socks to wear inside their rain boots. We knew they'd be jumping in puddles and complaining about their freezing feet, so the wool socks were a necessary. The Smartwool socks are pricey, but we believe it is worthwhile for each child to have a pair.

Long Sleeve Shirts and T-Shirts
We brought 3-5 t-shirts and two long-sleeve shirts for each child.

We didn't carry thermal base layers, but a warmer long sleeve shirt to wear under fleece hoodies was all they required on the colder days. They wore t-shirts under their hoodies otherwise.

3 Pant Pairs + 1 Convertible Pant Pair
We bought both kids a pair of zip off convertible pants (available in both girls and boys sizes) for the same reason we pack them. They dry quickly and allow you to start with pants on chilly mornings and switch to shorts later.

2 sets of shorts
This turned out to be two too many. During our trip to Scotland, our kids barely wore shorts. We could have gotten by with only the shorts from the zip off pants, but their shorts are little and don't take up much room either.

Hoodies
These fleece hoodies are similar to the ones our kids wore in Scotland, albeit theirs included a hood, which came in handy on very windy days.

We'd pack a wool cap or look for one with a hood, like this fleece jacket with a hood or this hoodie for boys.

Other Things
5-6 pairs of socks
1 set of pajamas
Outdoor Equipment for Scottish Families

Jackets for the rain
Everyone should have a rain jacket. Could you bring an umbrella instead? You could... but we don't advise it. Often, it will be windy as well, and an umbrella will not keep you dry. While an umbrella is good for a quick halt at a viewpoint, it is not the best solution for hiking.

What should a good rain jacket have?
A good rain jacket can be had for less than $100. Just make sure it has a hood (obvious, we know), is breathable, and has some form of liner for added warmth. Taped seams are also a wonderful way to keep dry.

Children's Rain Jackets
Our children use rain jackets from MEC (a Canadian retailer comparable to REI), but other possibilities include this Columbia rain jacket for boys and this Columbia rain jacket for girls.

Pants for the rain
We don't go overboard with our rain trousers. They'll do as long as they're watertight. We didn't wear them all the time. We didn't always bother if it was just a light rain. But we couldn't have survived without them on rainy days, so we kept them in the car just in case.

Hoodies
We stated it before, but it bears repeating. A thick fleece hoodie will come in handy in Scotland. They are ideal for chilly mornings, under rain jackets for added warmth, and when the wind blows.

Hiking Boots that are Waterproof
We rarely travel with our hiking boots because they take up so much room. A nice pair of waterproof hiking shoes is generally enough. I also had a pair of Columbia Women's Conspiracy III Titanium OutDry shoes that were suitable for city walking.

These Merrell Women's Siren 3 Waterproof Hiking Shoes are comparable to the ones I worn in Scotland.

Kids Waterproof Hiking Boots
This is our second pair of Keen waterproof hiking shoes for our kids. We've been quite pleased with them.

Though their "waterproofness" diminishes after all their puddle hopping, they still do a fantastic job of keeping their feet dry. They work better if we also wear rain pants that cover the top. Rain boots are preferable on rainy days, and we tend to hike less on those days anyhow.

Boots for the rain
The kids generally wore their waterproof hiking boots, but we also wore rain boots on rainy days. They were ideal for leaping in puddles and racing through the tall grass as we explored Fairy Glen. Unfortunately, the boots we were wearing are no longer available, but these appear to be folding rain boots.

Baseball Caps
Ball caps are appropriate for both rainy and sunny days. They keep the rain out of our eyes on rainy days.

Sandals To be honest, we could have saved room by leaving our Keen sandals at home. It was good to have a spare pair of shoes, but it took us three weeks to wear them in Edinburgh.

Small mitts or gloves

We brought little gloves for our children but did not use them in Scotland. We did use them more in Ireland, especially during rainy bike rides.

Bladders for Hydration
We bring our Platypus hydration bladders with us on each trip that involves a lot of hiking.

They simply fit into our backpacks and allow us to bring much more water than our reusable water bottles can. The drink tubes also make it easier for us and the kids to drink more water throughout the day.

Rain Covered Backpacks
For vacation, I recently purchased this Deuter Futura 26 L. Though I didn't have it with me on our vacation to Scotland (I traveled with a very comparable 26L bag), it's a fantastic backpack. I use it as a carry-on for the aircraft and then on a regular basis for hiking.

Water bottles that can be reused
Even when we travel with hydration packs, we always bring our reusable water bottles. For the youngsters, we use S'well bottles and the smaller S'ip by S'well bottles.

Travel Electronics Best Travel Camera
We brought our Canon Rebel DSLR with us when we arrived in Scotland. Though we liked the photos it took, it was cumbersome to travel with, especially for the type of travel we undertake.

Carrying it over your neck while hiking all day (plus carrying all your kids' gear on your back) might be exhausting. I can't tell you how many times I'd bend down to assist the kids with something, just to have them be hit in the head with it...

Unfortunately, our camera chose to die on us in Edinburgh. We did some study for a few days before sacrificing one of our days in Belfast with the kids to go to the camera store. We bought a Sony A6000 Mirrorless camera (with the additional 55-210 mm lens) and couldn't be happier. It could be the ideal travel camera!

It's light to carry while hiking (I nearly forget I have it), and instead of storing it in my bag when it rains, I can just tuck it into my rain jacket.

Don't forget to bring extra memory cards; you'll be snapping a LOT of photos in Scotland!

External hard drive
We always travel with a portable hard drive in addition to our camera, phones, and laptops. We couldn't bear the thought of losing all of our photos, so this provides us piece of mind.

Inflatable Airplane Cushion is one of our must-have items while flying with children.
On long-haul flights with children, we bring two Fly Tots. They take up a lot of space, but having children sleep on a long-haul journey is well worth it. When we arrive at our destination, we normally make room in our enormous backpacks, where they will remain until our return trip.

Headphones Mpow
This two-pack of headphones is ideal for parents who have more than one child. They are comfortable and even include a splitter so youngsters can share an iPad (ideal for lengthy vehicle rides on an Ireland road trip!)

Made in United States
Troutdale, OR
01/30/2024

17299507R00224